Calculations for Examination Physics

G. MILLER BSc MA CPhys MInstP ARCS
Charters School, Ascot

STANLEY THORNES (PUBLISHERS) LTD

First published in 1986 by
Stanley Thornes (Publishers) Ltd
Old Station Drive
Leckhampton
CHELTENHAM GL53 0DN

British Library Cataloguing in Publication Data

Miller, G.
    Calculations for examination physics.
    1. Mathematical physics — Examinations, questions, etc.
    I. Title
    530′.01′5   QC20.82
    ISBN 0–85950–212–0

Typeset in 10/12½ Times by KEYTEC, Bridport, Dorset.
Printed and bound in Great Britain at The Bath Press, Avon.

Contents

To A. E. H. Ward

Preface

Many students find that physics is one of the most enjoyable subjects that they study at school. They enjoy finding out how things work and why particular things happen. Doing experiments also gives many students a great deal of pleasure and sense of achievement. However there is one particular aspect of physics that causes a large number of physics students considerable difficulty — and that is doing numerical problems associated with the different topics.

The purpose of this book is — right from the start of a course leading to an examination at 16^+ — to help physics students to understand the use of physics equations and how to go about solving problems. A certain amount of background theory is included in each chapter, but it is assumed that the student will have access to one or more of the many theory textbooks already on the market. In addition, teachers will cover the theory in class and will, no doubt, help students to understand that theory. Students should check with their teacher or syllabus to find which material is inappropriate to their examination.

Every piece of theory in the book is followed by an example and a method by which it might be solved. In some cases a complete worked example is given, but usually students are expected to work out the answers by themselves, having been shown how to approach the problem. At the end of most chapters there is a selection of more straightforward numerical problems followed by questions from past examination papers. The past questions are, on the whole, included in their entirety to enable the student to see the full expectation of the public examination system. When available the appropriate mark allocation is given in brackets.

There is one brief chapter on revision technique and another on some of the mathematics used in physics problems. It is the author's intention that this book should be used to complement the work of the theory textbooks and the classroom teaching of the teachers, and that use of the book will enable students to achieve the best possible grades in all their physics examinations. It is also hoped that the students will acquire a more complete understanding of the subject.

G. Miller

Acknowledgements

The author is most grateful to the following Examination Boards for permission to print questions from recent examination papers. In a few cases, the wording of the questions has been changed slightly, for example, to ask students to plot results on a piece of graph paper, instead of on the question paper. The Boards are not responsible for the accuracy of the numerical answers.

The Associated Examining Board
University of Cambridge Schools Local Examinations Syndicate
Joint Matriculation Board
Southern Universities' Joint Board
Scottish Examination Board
South Western Examinations Board
Southern Regional Examinations Board
London Regional Examining Board
University of London School Examinations Council
Welsh Joint Education Committee
University of Oxford Delegacy of Local Examinations
Oxford and Cambridge Schools Examination Board

My thanks are also offered to those who have helped me during the preparation of the book, especially Mrs A. J. Smith, and D. M. Smith of Colfox School, Bridport.

Finally, I thank my family for their support and encouragement.

1. Some Useful Mathematics

In this introductory section we shall look at some of the mathematics necessary for solving physics problems. You can probably cope with addition, subtraction, multiplication and division — perhaps with the help of a calculator. Some additional knowledge is needed, though, for problem solving. This book should help you to learn how to use the mathematics. Then you will get better at doing calculations — and you should be able to get higher marks in examinations.

Rearranging formulae

One of the skills you will need is to rearrange a formula in order to work out an answer. You will probably have met the following type of question in a mathematics lesson.

Example If $y = 3x$, calculate values for y if x is:

a) 2   b) 30   c) 4000

Method: You find the y value by substituting the x values into the equation, e.g.

if $x = 2$, then
$$y = 3 \times 2$$
$$= 6$$

The larger numbers may cause a little difficulty if you forget the zeros, but you will probably find it straightforward.

Answers: a) 6   **b)** 90   **c)** 12 000

However, if you are given values for y and are asked to calculate x then difficulties sometimes arise.

Example If $y = 3x$, calculate values for x if y is:
a) 0.9   b) 12   c) 1800

Method: In this case you have to rearrange the formula, and cope with decimal quantities. You must move the 3 from one side of the equation to the other.

$$y = 3x$$

Divide both sides by 3:

$$\frac{y}{3} = \frac{3}{3}x$$

giving

$$\frac{y}{3} = x$$

or

$$x = \frac{y}{3}$$

values for y can then be substituted.

Answers: a) 0.3   **b)** 4.0   **c)** 600

In physics problems, different letters are used to represent different quantities. This may seem confusing, but if you understand the mathematics, all will be well!

The most straightforward formulae to rearrange are those which involve three terms — for example

$$V = I \times R$$

Potential difference = Current × Resistance

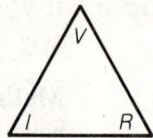

or

$$Q = I \times t$$

Electric charge = Current × Time

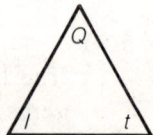

or

$$p = \frac{F}{A}$$

Pressure = $\left(\dfrac{\text{Force}}{\text{Area}}\right)$

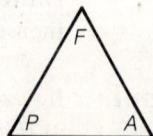

The little arrows show you which letter stands for which quantity. The triangles at the side will help you rearrange the equations. By placing a finger over the unknown quantity, the following equations are obtained.

$$I = \frac{V}{R}$$

or

$$R = \frac{V}{I}$$

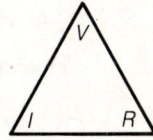

or

$$V = I \times R$$

You can create similar triangles for all equations involving three terms.

Example What are the triangles you would draw for the following formulae?

a) Density $= \dfrac{\text{Mass}}{\text{Volume}}$ b) Velocity = Frequency × Wavelength

c) Distance travelled = Velocity × Time

Method: Use the symbol letters (see p.316) and substitute for the words.

Answers: a) 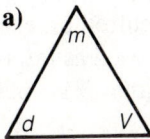 **b)** 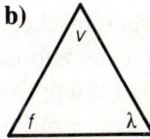 **c)** 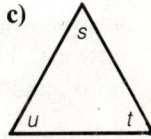

You can use these triangles to write down equations for the other terms in the triangle. You may find it easier to rearrange the formula first and before substituting numbers, or you may prefer to write in the numbers first and then rearrange the formula. Whatever you decide to do, remember that the units you use must be consistent — for example, when using the density formula, if the density is in g/cm^3, then the mass must be in g and the volume in cm^3; but if the density is in kg/m^3 then the mass must be in kg and the volume in m^3. You *cannot* and *must not* mix the units.

When you meet equations which contain more than three terms you cannot use the triangle approach. Instead you must use a slightly more mathematical approach.

Example Rearrange the formula:

$$H = m \times c \times \theta$$

Heat energy = Mass × Specific heat capacity × Temperature change to make the **a)** mass, **b)** specific heat capacity and **c)** temperature change, the subject of the formula.

Method: To make the mass the subject remove c and θ from one side of the equation and put them on the other side.

This can be done by dividing both sides by c and θ:

$$\frac{H}{c \times \theta} = \frac{m \times c \times \theta}{c \times \theta}$$

After cancelling on the right-hand side

$$\frac{H}{c \times \theta} = m$$

Answers: a) $m = \dfrac{H}{c \times \theta}$ **b)** $c = \dfrac{H}{m \times \theta}$ **c)** $\theta = \dfrac{H}{m \times c}$

You can then substitute the figures you are given. Alternatively you may find it easier to substitute the numbers first and then rearrange the equation.

Whatever you do you must write down all the stages of your calculation. This makes it easier for the person who reads your answer — either teacher, lecturer or examiner — to check your answers. This is the approach used as far as possible throughout this book, and it is the approach that is recommended to you.

The two hardest formulae which you may be asked to rearrange in an exam are both equations of motion (see p.130):

$$v^2 = u^2 + 2as \tag{1}$$

$$s = ut + \tfrac{1}{2}at^2 \tag{2}$$

where u = Initial velocity
v = Final velocity
a = Acceleration
s = Distance travelled
t = Time

Suppose in Equation [1] you were given values for v, u and s and asked to work out a. You must first rearrange the equation to have only that term involving a on one side of the equation, i.e.

$$v^2 - u^2 = 2as$$

You can then divide both sides by $2 \times s$ to make a the only term on one side of the equation; i.e.

$$\frac{v^2 - u^2}{2s} = \frac{2as}{2s}$$

Cancelling on the right-hand side gives

$$\frac{v^2 - u^2}{2s} = a$$

Suppose in the second equation you are asked to make a the subject of the equation. Again you must arrange for the term involving a to be on its own on one side of the equation:

$$s - ut = \tfrac{1}{2}at^2$$

and then remove $\tfrac{1}{2}t^2$ from the right-hand side by dividing both sides by t^2 and multiplying both sides by 2:

$$\frac{2}{t^2} \times (s - ut) = \tfrac{1}{2}at^2 \times \frac{2}{t^2}$$

Cancelling gives

$$\frac{2}{t^2}(s - ut) = a$$

It should be stated that you would be most unlikely to meet anything as complicated as this — you would not be asked to rearrange the Equation [2] to work out t — this is left until A-level.

Substitution into formulae

Nearly all the examples in this book involve substitution of numbers into formulae and so, apart from one simple example, we shall only look at two more difficult examples at this stage.

Example   The size of the current flowing in an electrical appliance is given by

$$\text{Current} = \frac{\text{Power}}{\text{Potential difference}}$$

or

$$I = \frac{P}{V}$$

Calculate:
a) the current if the power is 480 W and the potential difference is 240 V,
b) the power if the current is 5 A and the potential difference is 12 V,

c) the potential difference if the power is 2000 W and the current is 10 A.

Method: If you use the triangle approach your triangle will look like this:

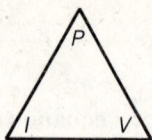

so that $\qquad P = I \times V$ or $I = \dfrac{P}{V}$ or $V = \dfrac{P}{I}$

Choose the formula which has the letter you require as the subject of the equation and substitute the numbers. Remember to include units in your answer.

Answers: a) 2 A   **b)** 60 W   **c)** 200 V

The calculations which tend to cause most difficulty are those which involve squaring a term or involving the square root of a term. Remember that you should only square the terms indicated or find the square root of the terms indicated.

Example The kinetic energy of a body is given by the formula:

$$\text{Kinetic energy} = \tfrac{1}{2} \times \text{Mass} \times (\text{Velocity})^2$$

or $\qquad\qquad\qquad \text{KE} = \tfrac{1}{2}mv^2$

Complete the following table:

	Kinetic energy (J)	Mass (kg)	Velocity (m/s)
a)	—	2	3
b)	200	—	5
c)	400	8	—

Method: Remember to square *only* the velocity term. If other terms were to be squared, the equation for kinetic energy would not be

$$\text{KE} = \tfrac{1}{2}mv^2$$

but $\qquad\qquad \text{KE} = \tfrac{1}{2}(mv)^2 \ or \ \text{KE} = (\tfrac{1}{2}mv)^2$

BOTH OF THE LOWER FORMULAE ARE WRONG!

Perhaps you would find a triangle approach more helpful:

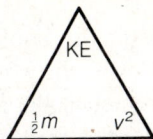

The third of the three problems in the example is the hardest because you must first calculate v^2 and then find the square root of this to obtain the velocity v.

Answers: a) 9 J   **b)** 16 kg   **c)** 10 m/s

Probably the most difficult formula you will meet is one of the equations of motion:

$$s = ut + \tfrac{1}{2}at^2$$

where s = distance travelled (m)
         u = initial velocity of body (m/s)
         t = time (s)
         a = acceleration (m/s²)

As you will discover later in Chapter 4, there are other equations of motion, and it is sometimes easier to use two of them rather than use this single equation. You may also find that the body starts from rest, i.e. $u = 0$ m/s, so that the equation becomes: $s = \tfrac{1}{2}at^2$.

However, you may like to have a go at the following example.

Example   A car is travelling at 4 m/s. If it accelerates at 2 m/s², calculate the distance travelled after:

a) 6 s   **b)** 3 s   **c)** 0.5 s

Method: First write down the quantities that you know:

u = 4 m/s
a = 2 m/s²
t = **a)** 6 s   **b)** 3 s   **c)** 0.5 s

Next write down the equation:

$$s = ut + \tfrac{1}{2}at^2$$

and substitute the quantities given:

$s = 4 \times t + \tfrac{1}{2} \times 2 \times t^2$ (t values have not been substituted)

Answers: a) 60 m   **b)** 21 m   **c)** 2.25 m

Did you get the answer to **c)** correct? Squaring numbers less than one is not as easy as squaring numbers greater than one.

Powers of ten

Most of the examples in this book are kept, deliberately, to relatively small numbers. However, the world of physics is filled with some very large and some extremely small numbers. For example, the speed of light is 300000000 m/s and the wavelength of red light is 0.0000007 m. There are different prefixes which can be used (see p.317) to simplify these, but in actual calculations you must be consistent with your units. One technique has been devised to write such large or small numbers in a shorter form.

Example The speed of light is written as 3.0×10^8 m/s and the red light wavelength becomes 7.0×10^{-7} m.

decimal point moves 8 places to the *left*
$$300000000. = 3.0 \times 10^8$$

decimal point moves 7 places to the *right*
$$0.0000007 = 7.0 \times 10^{-7}$$

The distance of the Earth from the Sun can be written as 1.496×10^{11} m, and the charge on the electron as 1.6×10^{-19} C. Try writing these out in longhand and you will appreciate the benefit of the shorthand or standard form.

Calculations involving such numbers are carried out as follows:

Example The speed of light is 3.0×10^8 m/s and the distance between the Sun and the Earth is 1.50×10^{11} m. Calculate the time taken for light from the Sun to reach the Earth.

Method: The formula to use is:

$$\text{Distance travelled} = \text{Speed} \times \text{Time}$$

or

$$\text{Time} = \frac{\text{Distance travelled}}{\text{Speed}}$$

$$= \frac{1.5 \times 10^{11}}{3.0 \times 10^8}$$

$$= \frac{1.5}{3.0} \times 10^{11} \times 10^{-8} \qquad \text{(dividing by } 10^8 \text{ is the same as multiplying by } 10^{-8})$$

Divide the numbers as they are, but the powers of ten are added or subtracted:

$$\text{Time} = 0.5 \times 10^3$$
$$= 5 \times 10^2$$
$$= 500 \text{ s}$$

Example The resistance R of a material is related to its resistivity ρ by the equation

$$R = \rho \times \frac{L}{A}$$

where L = length of sample and A = cross-sectional area of the sample.

If $\rho = 4.5 \times 10^{-7}\,\Omega.m$, $L = 20\,m$ and $A = 3 \times 10^{-6}\,m^2$ calculate the resistance of the sample.

Method: Write down the formula:

$$R = \rho \times \frac{L}{A}$$

and substitute the values given:

$$R = 4.5 \times 10^{-7} \times \frac{20}{3 \times 10^{-6}}$$

$$= \frac{4.5 \times 20}{3} \times 10^{-7} \times 10^{6} \quad \text{(dividing by } 10^{-6}$$
$$\text{is the same as}$$
$$= \frac{4.5 \times 20}{3} \times 10^{-1} \quad \text{multiplying}$$
$$\text{by } 10^{6})$$

$$= 30 \times 10^{-1}$$

$$= 3\,\Omega$$

Trigonometry

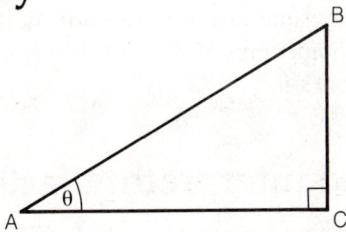

By definition:

$$\text{sine } \theta = \frac{BC}{AB} = \frac{\text{Length of side opposite the angle}}{\text{Length of hypotenuse of the triangle}}$$

$$\text{cosine } \theta = \frac{AC}{AB} = \frac{\text{Length of side adjacent to the angle}}{\text{Length of hypotenuse of the triangle}}$$

$$\text{tangent } \theta = \frac{BC}{AC} = \frac{\text{Length of side opposite the angle}}{\text{Length of side adjacent to the angle}}$$

These on their own are not often required in calculations. However, in problems to do with vectors you may have to use the above formulae, although scale diagrams can usually be drawn.

Example

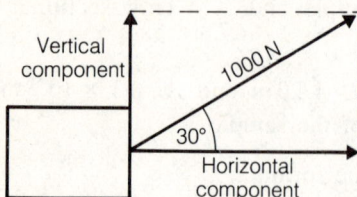

Calculate the horizontal and vertical components of the 1000 N force.

Method: The horizontal component is given by

$$\frac{\text{Horizontal component}}{1000} = \cos 30°$$

or $\quad$ Horizontal component $= 1000 \times \cos 30°$

$$= 866 \text{ N}$$

The vertical component is given by

$$\frac{\text{Vertical component}}{1000} = \sin 30°$$

or $\quad$ Vertical component $= 1000 \times \sin 30°$

$$= 500 \text{ N}$$

The 1000 N force is the *resultant* of the 500 N and the 866 N forces, i.e. it produces the same effect. Alternatively the 500 N and 866 N forces are called components of the 1000 N force. This is explained in more detail on pp.93–8.

Drawing graphs and interpreting facts from them

Note: This section on graphs may be a little difficult at this stage, and so you may want to come back to it when you are nearer to your main examination.

One of the main aims in doing a practical experiment is to produce results and to draw conclusions from them. In some experiments you will aim to obtain a single result — for example, when you want to find the specific heat capacity of a solid. In other experiments you may obtain a series of results. It may be helpful to draw a graph of your results if you are looking at how one quantity can be varied by varying a second quantity. The graph will probably help you to come to some conclusions about the experiment.

Example

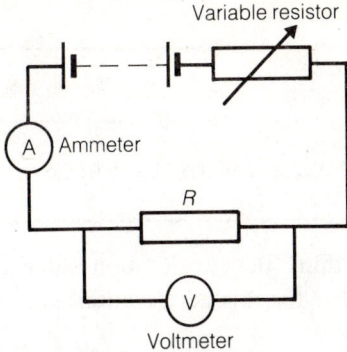

Variable resistor

A Ammeter

R

V

Voltmeter

In the circuit shown the current flowing through the resistor R was read on the ammeter. The corresponding potential difference across R was read on the voltmeter. By varying the variable resistor, several sets of values for current and potential difference were obtained:

Current (A)	0	0.5	1.0	1.5	2.0	2.5	3.0
Potential difference (V)	0	1.5	2.9	4.6	6.0	7.4	9.1

You may look at these results and come to the correct conclusion that, as the potential difference increases, so does the current: however, if you draw a graph you will come to the additional conclusion that these results produce a best straight line graph passing through the origin. A 'best straight line' means that not all of

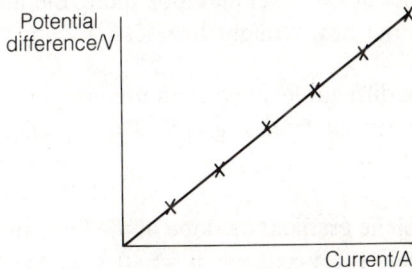

Potential difference/V

Current/A

the points necessarily lie on the line, but that the line takes the average path — it is in fact a way of using your eye and your own judgement to find an average. From mathematics lessons you may remember that such a graph tells you that:

Potential difference is proportional to current

which can also be written as:

Potential difference $\propto$ Current

Another advantage of drawing a graph is that it may enable you to pinpoint an error or errors in the results. You can then return to your experiment to check the point in question.

Example The following results were obtained using a ticker timer, trolley and various forces.

Applied force (N)	0	1	2	3	4	5	6	7	8	9	10
Acceleration of trolley (m/s²)	0	0.7	1.3	2.2	2.9	3.5	4.7	5.0	5.5	6.3	6.9

For which force do you think the acceleration value is incorrect? What is a more likely value for this acceleration?

Method: With experience, you may be able to look at the table of results and pinpoint the error. However, if you draw a graph, the incorrect point will lie well off the best straight line.

Answer: The acceleration for the 6 N force is incorrect and should lie between 4.1 and 4.3 m/s².

Did you notice again that the 'best straight line' did not pass through all the points? In practice there should be an equal spread of points either side of the line. Alternatively, if you imagine lying all the points along a knife edge, the best straight line would be the line along which the graph would balance. Another way is to hold the graph paper at eye level and look along the line — this may help you to decide the best straight line.

At a more difficult level you can use your mathematics knowledge to make predictions from a graph. The equation for a straight line is:

$$y = mx + c$$

where m is the gradient or slope of the line, and c is the point at which the line cuts the y-axis when $x = 0$ (i.e. the y-intercept).

Example Find the gradient and y-intercept for the following equations:
a) $y = 3x + 4$ b) $y = 6x$ c) $2y = 7x + 2$

Method: First write the equation in the form

$$y = mx + c$$

In part c) you have to divide throughout by 2. Then match up the number in front of the x term — this will give the gradient m. The number on its own, the y-intercept, gives the value for c.

Answers:

	Gradient, m	y-intercept, c
a)	3	4
b)	6	0
c)	3.5 (or $\frac{7}{2}$)	1

Note: The y-intercept can be found by putting $x = 0$ into the equation, and the x-intercept can be found by setting $y = 0$.

Example   The potential difference V across an unknown resistor R is related to the current I flowing through the resistor by the equation: $V = I \times R$

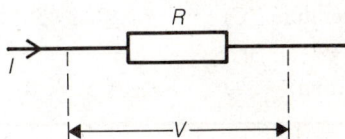

State one graph that could be plotted to prove this equation and how you could find a value for the resistance of the resistor.

Method: Match up the equation given with the equation for a straight line:

$$V = I \times R + 0$$
$$y = m \times x + c$$

The two variables are V and I, and so a graph of $y = V$ against $x = I$ should be a straight line through the origin (because $c = 0$), and have a gradient of R.

What was the value for R in the first example in this section?

Answer: The gradient of that graph was 3 V/A or 3 Ω.

Example   The second graph that you plotted related the force F to the acceleration a. The equation which applies to this is:

$$F = m \times a$$

where m = mass of the trolley.

Again comparing this equation with the equation for a straight line gives:

$$F = m \times a + 0$$

$$y = m \times x + c$$

or a graph of $y = F$ against $x = a$ should be a straight line with a gradient equal to the mass m of the trolley, and should pass through the origin, because $c = 0$.

What was the mass of the trolley in the second graph? You should find a value for the mass of 1.43 kg.

Here is an example which involves an intercept. It is adapted from an O-level exam question.

Example   A 180 watt heater and a thermometer were immersed in 0.5 kg of water in a copper calorimeter. The following readings were obtained:

Temperature (°C)	30	36	40	45	49	54	57
Time (min)	3	4	5	6	7	8	9

Plot a graph of temperature against time starting at time $t = 0$ and use your graph to find:

a) room temperature, and
b) the specific heat capacity of water.

[London (part)]

Method: You would probably not find it difficult to plot the graph, and you would realize that when the heater is first switched on, i.e. at time $t = 0$, then the water and calorimeter would be at room temperature. Having drawn the best straight line graph, the point at which the best straight line cuts the temperature (y) axis will give you a value for room temperature.

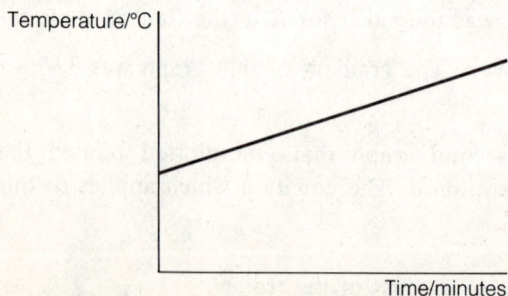

However, this fact also emerges when we look at the theory:

Electrical energy supplied $=$ Heat energy gained by water (and calorimeter) $+$ (Heat energy lost to surrounds)

Neither of these bracketed terms
is included in the calculation

or

Power × Time in seconds = Mass × Specific heat capacity of water × Temperature rise

$$P \times t = m \times c \times (\theta_t - \theta)$$

where θ_t = temperature after time t
θ = room temperature (or starting temperature)

Rearranging this equation gives:

$$(\theta_t - \theta) = \frac{P \times t}{m \times c}$$

or

$$\theta_t = \left[\frac{P}{m \times c}\right] \times t + \theta$$

$$y = a \times x + c$$

i.e. the c value (y-intercept) is θ (the room temperature) and a (the gradient) is $\frac{P}{m \times c}$.

Note: a has been used for the gradient to avoid confusion because mass m is included in the equation.

You can calculate the gradient, but remember that the time must be in seconds (i.e. minutes × 60). The specific heat capacity can then be calculated by rearranging the formula for the gradient to give

$$c = \frac{P}{m \times \text{Gradient}}$$

Answers: a) 16–18°C (depending on your 'best' line)
b) 4800 J/kg °C or 4800 J/kg K.

This value is greater than the accepted value of 4200 J/kg K for water. Can you see why this might be? Look at the theory of the problem and decide what was ignored in the calculation.

The previous graph was not difficult to draw, but the theory is rather complicated. The following problems are not easy either, but persevere because the graph is a very useful way of drawing conclusions on many physics practical exercises. Three separate examples will be considered because each has its own particular point of interest.

Example   In an experiment to find g, the acceleration due to gravity, a steel ball bearing was dropped through a vertical height s and the time t taken to fall this distance was measured electrically. A series of results for s and t was obtained by varying the height s.

s (m)	0.4	0.5	0.6	0.7	0.8	0.9	1.0
t (s)	0.28	0.32	0.34	0.37	0.40	0.42	0.45

Plot a graph of s on the y-axis against t^2 on the x-axis, and hence find a value for g, the acceleration due to gravity.

Method: The equation of motion which applies to this calculation is

$$s = ut + \tfrac{1}{2}at^2$$

where s = distance
$\quad\quad u$ = initial velocity
$\quad\quad a = g$ = acceleration
$\quad\quad t$ = time

The ball starts from rest and so $u = 0$. The equation therefore becomes

$$s = \tfrac{1}{2}gt^2 \quad\quad\quad \text{because } a = g$$

Compare this with the equation for a straight line:

$$s = \underbrace{\tfrac{1}{2} \times g}_{} \times t^2 + 0$$
$$y = m \times x + \quad c$$

A graph of $y = s$ against $x = t^2$ should be a straight line of gradient $\tfrac{1}{2}g$ passing through the origin ($c = 0$).

Draw up a new table of s and t^2 before plotting the graph. Remember to start both axes at 0. Having calculated the gradient of the graph equate this to $\tfrac{1}{2}g$.

i.e. gradient $\quad\quad\quad\quad\quad = \tfrac{1}{2} \times g$

or $\quad\quad\quad\quad\quad\quad\quad g = 2 \times$ gradient

Answer: $g = 10 \text{ m/s}^2$

Example The periodic time T (i.e. the time for one complete oscillation) of a pendulum is given by

$$T = 2\pi\sqrt{\frac{l}{g}}$$

where l = length of pendulum
and g = acceleration due to gravity.

The following values for T and l were obtained during an experiment to test the formula:

T (s)		0.63	0.90	1.10	1.27	1.43	1.55	1.68	1.80
l (m)		0.1	0.2	0.3	0.4	0.5	0.6	0.7	0.8

Plot a suitable graph to show that the formula is a possible relationship between T and l, and use the graph to obtain a value for g.

Method: Do *not* be put off by an apparently complicated formula. Several graphs might be plotted but perhaps the two most obvious are obtained as follows:

Graph 1 Rewrite the formula to give

$$T = \frac{2\pi}{\sqrt{g}} \times \sqrt{l}$$

and compare with the straight line equation

$$T = \left[\frac{2\pi}{\sqrt{g}}\right] \times \sqrt{l} + 0$$

$$y = m \times x + c$$

so that a graph of T on the y-axis against $\sqrt{l}$ on the x-axis will be a straight line through the origin (because $c = 0$) with a gradient of $2\pi/\sqrt{g}$. If the graph is a straight line through the origin, then the original equation is a possible relationship. Note that both axes must start at 0. A value for g can be calculated from

$$\text{gradient} = \frac{2\pi}{\sqrt{g}}$$

or

$$\sqrt{g} = \frac{2\pi}{\text{gradient}}$$

Squaring both sides gives

$$g = \frac{4\pi^2}{(\text{gradient})^2}$$

Graph 2 Square both sides of the equation to remove the square root sign:

$$T = 2\pi\sqrt{\frac{l}{g}}$$

becomes

$$T^2 = 4\pi^2\frac{l}{g}$$

Compare with the equation for a straight line:

$$T^2 = \left[\frac{4\pi^2}{g}\right] \times l + 0$$

$$y = m \times x + c$$

The graph to plot is therefore T^2 on the y-axis against l on the x-axis. The graph will pass through the origin ($c = 0$) and have a gradient $4\pi^2/g$. Again, if the graph is a straight line, then the formula is a possible relationship. A value for g can be calculated by rearranging the equation for the gradient, i.e.

$$\text{gradient} = \frac{4\pi^2}{g}$$

or

$$g = \frac{4\pi^2}{\text{gradient}}$$

Answers: The equations *are* valid, and the value for g is 9.8 m/s².

Can you think of any other graphs which might be plotted?

Example   The velocity of sound v is related to its frequency f and its wavelength λ by the formula $v = f \times \lambda$. In an experiment, the following values for frequency and wavelength were obtained:

Frequency (Hz)	200	250	300	350	400	450	500
Wavelength (m)	1.65	1.32	1.10	0.94	0.83	0.73	0.66

Plot a suitable graph to show that the formula is valid and calculate a value for the velocity of sound.

Method: A value for the velocity of sound v could be obtained by working out v for each set of results and then taking an average. However, rewriting the equation and comparing it with the equation for a straight line leads to a suitable graph:

$$\lambda = v \times \frac{1}{f} + 0$$
$$y = m \times x + c$$

A graph of wavelength (λ) on the y-axis against 1/frequency on the x-axis will be a straight line passing through the origin ($c = 0$). The gradient of the graph is equal to the velocity of sound.

Answer: Velocity of sound = 330 m/s

Can you see other graphs which might be plotted? Mathematically, the relationship is that

Wavelength $\propto$ 1/Frequency

or

Wavelength is inversely proportional to frequency.

Throughout the book an attempt has been made to include as many graphs as possible.

Questions

These questions do not need calculators.

1. If $y = 5x$, calculate values for y if x is:
    a) 0.5   b) 2   c) 900

2. If $y = 7x$, calculate values for x if y is:
    a) 0.7   b) 49   c) 630

3. If $y = \frac{1}{2}x^2$, calculate values for y if x is:
    a) 0.4   b) 2   c) 350

4. If $y = 3x^2$, calculate values for x if y is:
    a) 27   b) 300   c) 507

5. If $F = 2a$, calculate values for F if a is:
    a) 0.2   b) 4   c) 10

6. If $V = 10I$, calculate values for I if V is:
    a) 0.5   b) 6   c) 20

7. If $s = 5t^2$, calculate values for s if t is:
    a) 0.3   b) 4   c) 10

8. If $v^2 = 20s$, calculate values for s if v is:
    a) 5   b) 10   c) 12

9. Either by drawing a formula triangle or by rearranging the equation write down separate equations in which each of the letters is the subject of the equation.

    a) $a = \dfrac{v}{t}$ b) $H = m \times L$ c) $C = \dfrac{Q}{V}$

10. Rearrange the equation: $R = \rho \times \dfrac{L}{A}$ to make:

    a) ρ b) L c) A
    the subject of the equation.

11. Rearrange the equation: $a = \dfrac{\lambda \times D}{s}$ to make:

    a) λ b) D c) s
    the subject of the equation.

12. Calculate:
    a) $(3 \times 10^2) \times (2 \times 10^5)$ b) $(4 \times 10^3) \times (5 \times 10^8)$
    c) $(6 \times 10^4) \times (7 \times 10^{10})$

13. Calculate:
    a) $\dfrac{(4 \times 10^7)}{(2 \times 10^2)}$ b) $\dfrac{(5 \times 10^{10})}{(2 \times 10^8)}$ c) $\dfrac{(9 \times 10^4)}{(3 \times 10^4)}$

14. Calculate:
    a) $(2 \times 10^{-2}) \times (3 \times 10^{-4})$ b) $(4 \times 10^{-3}) \times (5 \times 10^{-5})$
    c) $(1.5 \times 10^{-6}) \times (2 \times 10^{-2})$

15. Calculate:
    a) $\dfrac{(2 \times 10^{-3})}{(4 \times 10^{-5})}$ b) $\dfrac{(8 \times 10^{-2})}{(4 \times 10^{-1})}$ c) $\dfrac{(6 \times 10^{-11})}{(3 \times 10^{-2})}$

16. Calculate:
    a) $(4 \times 10^{-7}) \times (3 \times 10^5)$ b) $(2 \times 10^3) \times (3 \times 10^{-8})$
    c) $\dfrac{(8 \times 10^{-6})}{(2 \times 10^{-4})}$ d) $\dfrac{(6 \times 10^{-4})}{(2 \times 10^{-8})}$

You will need a calculator or book of tables for the following questions.

17. What are the sines of the following angles:
   a) 20°   b) 35°   c) 58°   d) 82°?

18. What are the angles which have the following sines:
   a) 0.5000   b) 0.7071   c) 0.8660   d) 0.9848?

19. What are the cosines of the following angles:
   a) 25°   b) 40°   c) 55°   d) 70°?

20. What are the angles which have the following cosines:
   a) 0.8660   b) 0.6428   c) 0.5000   d) 0.1736?

21. What are the tangents of the following angles:
   a) 10°   b) 30°   c) 45°   d) 60°?

22. What angles have the following tangents:
   a) 0.2679   b) 0.4663   c) 1.192   d) 2.747?

23.

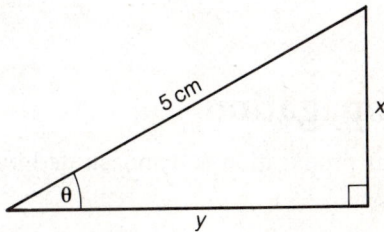

Calculate values for x and y if the angle θ is:
   a) 30°   b) 45°   c) 60°   d) 75°

24. Write down the gradient and y-intercept for the following equations:
   a) $y = 2x + 5$ b) $y = 0.5x + 3$
   c) $2y = 4x + 3$ d) $3y = x + 7$

2. Light

Light is a form of energy given out by luminous objects such as the Sun, a star, a lamp, a candle flame or a fluorescent screen. Most objects are not luminous and can only be seen if they reflect light. There are two models used by scientists for the way in which light travels — the wave model and the particle model. The wave model is discussed in Chapter 8, while in this chapter we use the particle model. In the particle model rays of light travel in straight lines (sometimes called the rectilinear propagation of light). The two ways in which a ray can change direction are by

a) reflection — when the ray bounces off a surface, or

b) refraction — when the ray goes from one transparent material to another, e.g. air to glass.

Rectilinear propagation

Rectilinear propagation is demonstrated by the pinhole camera.

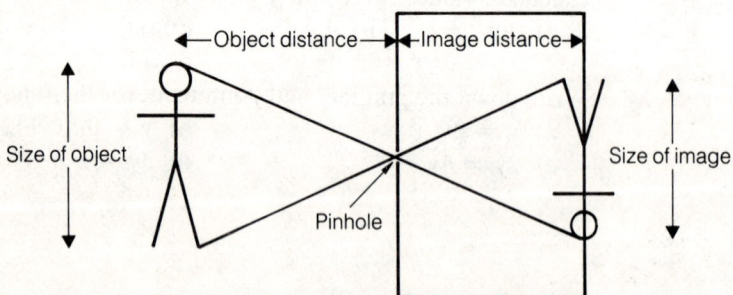

$$\text{Magnification} = \frac{\text{Size of image}}{\text{Size of object}} = \frac{\text{Image distance}}{\text{Object distance}}$$

Example 1 What would be the magnification produced by a pinhole camera of length 20 cm if an illuminated object is placed:

a) 60 cm from it   **b)** 20 cm from it   **c)** 10 cm from it?

Method: Using the formula

$$\text{Magnification} = \frac{\text{Image distance}}{\text{Object distance}}$$

and the fact that the image distance is the distance between the image and the pinhole, i.e. the length of the pinhole camera (see the diagram), then

$$\text{Magnification} = \frac{20 \text{ cm}}{\text{Object distance}}$$

Answers: a) 0.33   **b)** 1.0   **c)** 2.0

Example 2 What would be the size of the image produced by a pinhole camera of length 15 cm when an illuminated object of size 10 cm is placed at the following distances from the pinhole?
a) 30 cm   **b)** 20 cm   **c)** 10 cm

Method: The formula in example 1 is developed to include

$$\text{Magnification} = \frac{\text{Size of image}}{\text{Size of object}} = \frac{\text{Image distance}}{\text{Object distance}}$$

and since the object is 10 cm tall this becomes

$$\text{Magnification} = \frac{\text{Size of image}}{10} = \frac{\text{Image distance}}{\text{Object distance}}$$

The image distance is equal to the length of the camera, which is 15 cm, so that this equation becomes

$$\frac{\text{Size of image}}{10} = \frac{15}{\text{Object distance}}$$

or $$\text{Size of image} = \frac{10 \times 15}{\text{Object distance}}$$

Answers: a) 5.0 cm   **b)** 7.5 cm   **c)** 15.0 cm

Reflection of light by mirrors

There are three main types of mirrors:

Type of mirror	Representation in diagrams
1. Plane (flat)	
2. Concave (converging)	
3. Convex (diverging)	

The two types of curved mirror are sections of large spherical surfaces — you can imagine what would be obtained if you used a very sharp knife and cut a slice from a table tennis ball. The centre of the sphere is called the centre of curvature and for a concave mirror the following points can be labelled.

Concave mirror

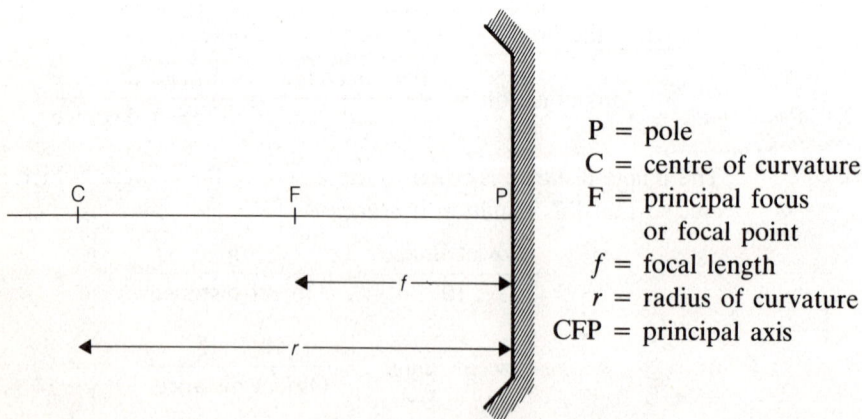

P = pole
C = centre of curvature
F = principal focus
    or focal point
f = focal length
r = radius of curvature
CFP = principal axis

$$\text{Focal length} = \frac{\text{Radius of curvature}}{2}$$

Example Calculate the focal length of a concave mirror if its radius of curvature is:

a) 50 cm   **b)** 40 cm   **c)** 10 cm

Method: You will remember that

$$\text{Focal length} = \frac{\text{Radius of curvature}}{2}$$

Answers: a) 25 cm   **b)** 20 cm   **c)** 5 cm

Ray diagram solutions to concave mirror problems

In this type of question you may be told the *object distance* and *image distance* from the mirror and asked to find the *focal length* of the mirror and the *magnification* produced by the mirror. Alternatively, you may be told any two of these quantities and asked to find the other two. There are two ways in which you can do this:

a) using a ray diagram, or
b) by calculation.

We shall look at the calculation method on p.46 but here we use ray diagrams.

When drawing a ray diagram the diagram is drawn to scale and three rays may be drawn:

1) A ray parallel to the principal axis will be reflected through the principal focus.

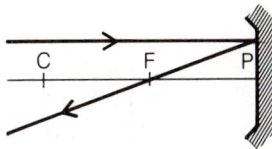

2) A ray through the principal focus will be reflected parallel to the principal axis.

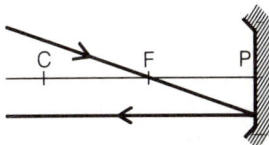

3) A ray passing through the centre of curvature will be reflected back along the same path.

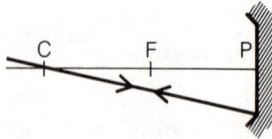

(There is a fourth ray which can be drawn, but it is rarely used in ray diagrams. Such a ray is incident at the pole and is reflected such that the reflected ray makes the same angle with the principal axis as the incident ray.)

Combining all three rays into one diagram:

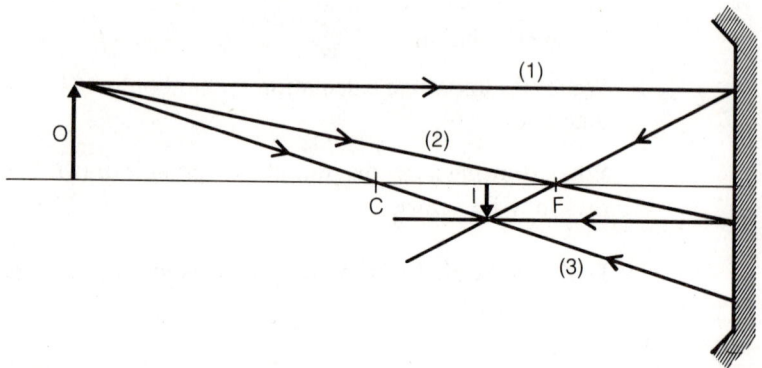

In practice, you will find that only two of these rays need to be drawn. You will also find it easier if you draw your ray diagrams on graph paper. Remember that rays of light from the object will travel in every possible direction (so that an observer will see the object from anywhere in the room). The three rays we have used are chosen because they behave in special ways.

Example   Draw separate diagrams for each of the three objects **a**, **b** and **c**, drawing at least two rays each time. From your diagrams find the image distance from the mirror.

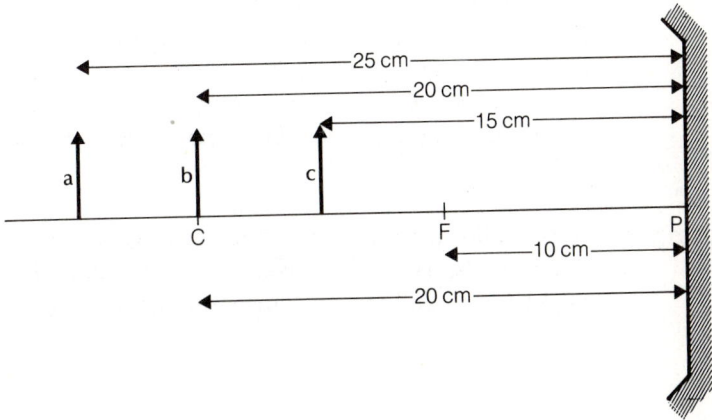

Method: Draw a rapid sketch first in order to find the approximate image position and size. This will help you to decide on a suitable scale before you draw your accurate ray diagrams. Using graph paper draw the principal axis and mark on the focal point, centre of curvature and object position. (You will probably find that your diagram is improved by turning the graph paper so that the longer edge is horizontal.) Because the object size is not stated you should choose a convenient value so that either the object or the image is as large as possible. The easiest rays to draw from the top of the object are:

1. The ray parallel to the principal axis which is reflected through the focal point, and
2. The ray through the focal point which is reflected parallel to the principal axis.

These two rays come from the top of the object and so where they cross again, *after reflection at the mirror*, is the top of the image. Assuming no distortion, the bottom of the image lies on the principal axis and so you can draw the image by drawing a vertical line from the crossing point to the principal axis. The image distance is equal to the distance between the image and the mirror, but remember that your diagram is drawn to scale.

Note: The image in all three of these examples is upside-down (inverted).

Answers: a) 16.7 cm   **b)** 20.0 cm   **c)** 30.0 cm
Your answers should lie within 1 cm of these values.

As with the pinhole camera, you may be asked to find the size of the image produced by the concave mirror for a particular object. Because the ray diagrams are to scale, you have to measure the size of the image and compare it with the size of your scale object. The scale used for object distance, image distance and focal length need not be, and is usually not, the same as the scale used for object and image sizes.

Example   In the following diagram, an object which is 20 cm tall is placed at different distances from a concave mirror. In each case find the size of the image and the magnification of the image.

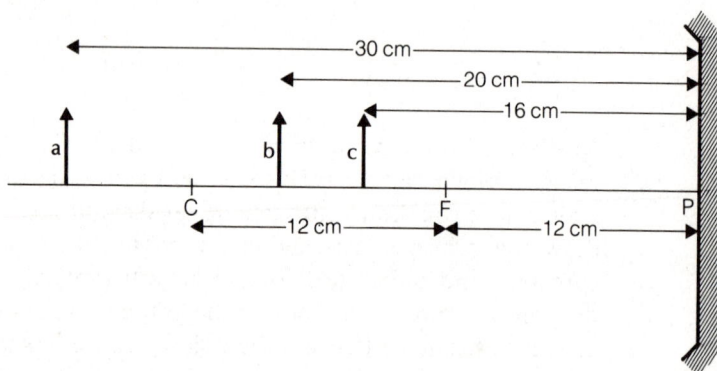

Method: As in the previous example, draw a quick sketch before deciding on the best scale. Remember, too, that the vertical scale does not have to be the same as the horizontal scale (you may care to do this example with several different sets of scales to check that this is true).

Again, the easiest rays to draw are:

1. The ray parallel to the principal axis which is reflected through the focal point, and

2. The ray through the focal point which is reflected parallel to the principal axis.

Having drawn these rays, you will be able to find the image position. The size of the image can be found by measurement and the magnification can be calculated using the formula

$$\text{Magnification} = \frac{\text{Size of image}}{\text{Size of object}}$$

Answers:

	a	b	c
Size of image (cm)	13.3	30.0	60.0
Magnification	0.7	1.5	3.0

Your image sizes may differ by 1 cm either way and so your magnification values may not be exactly the same as those given.

Note: The image has a definite size and can be measured in centimetres or metres but the magnification is a comparison of sizes and is a number only.

Concave mirror as a magnifying mirror

In the examples above the images were formed where the rays of light crossed. Because of this they are called *real* images and can be seen on a screen. The images were also upside-down (inverted). This is not always the case.

You may also find that it is more complicated to draw the ray diagram for the magnifying mirror and so you must take care. The object is placed inside the focal point, e.g.

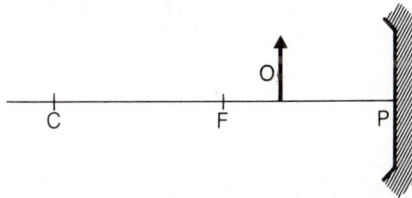

In practice, you would draw the following two rays on the same diagram. They are only drawn separately here to make it clear what is happening.

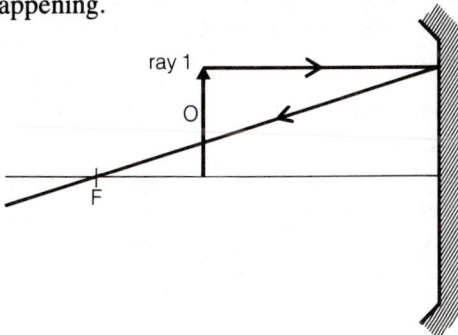

A ray parallel to the principal axis is reflected through the focal point.

ray 2

A ray through the focal point is reflected parallel to the principal axis.

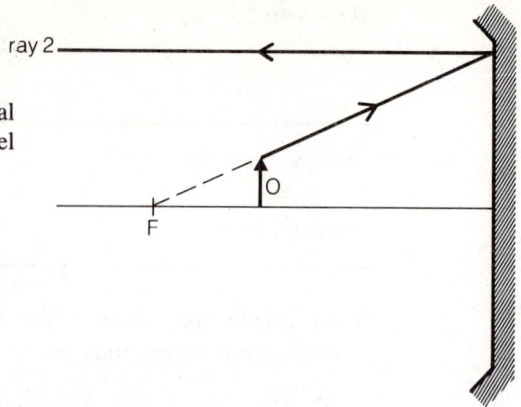

O

F

Note: In this case the ray is travelling as if it had passed through the focal point *before* it passed through the top of the object.

Combining the two separate diagrams into one diagram gives:

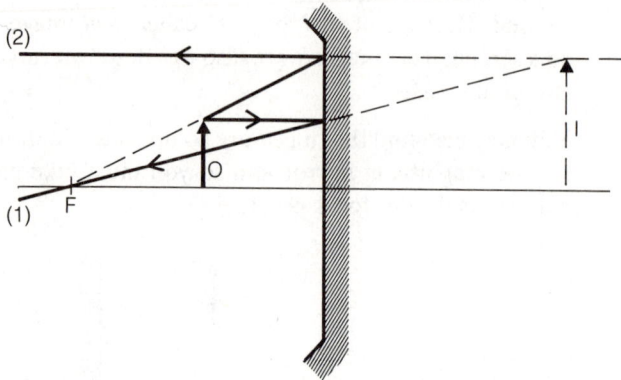

(2)

O

(1)   F

I

It is seen that the two reflected rays marked (1) and (2) will not meet but will get further apart. Although the rays will never meet, the fact that they are getting further apart means that they must have *started* at a point. This can be shown by producing the reflected rays back behind the mirror. The point where they cross is the top of the image, as shown.

Because the rays cannot actually travel behind the mirror they are normally drawn with dotted lines, as is the image because it only *appears* to exist behind the mirror. It is called a *virtual* image. When the object is placed inside the focal point the image is *always* magnified. Can you see anything else about the image that is different from the previous examples when the objects were outside the focal point?

Example   Find the image position, image size and magnification when a 10 cm tall object is placed in front of a concave mirror of focal length 16 cm in the positions shown:

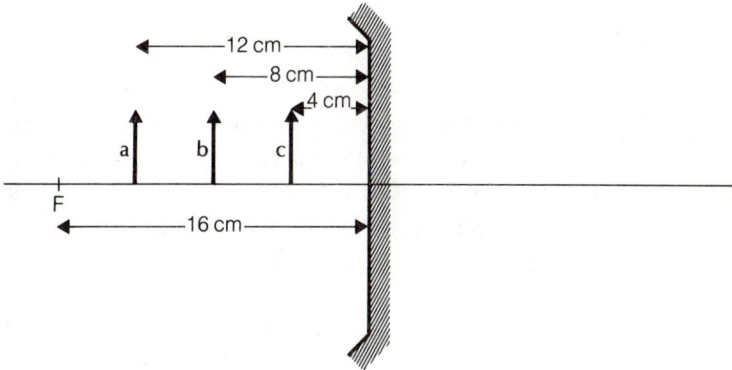

Method: After drawing a quick sketch and having decided upon scales draw your ray diagram on graph paper, making sure that you have left plenty of space *behind* the mirror. Since the image is always the same way up as the object, (sometimes called upright or erect), your principal axis can be at the bottom of the graph paper. The two rays to draw are:

1. A ray parallel to the principal axis which will pass through the focal point after reflection.

2. A ray which passes through the focal point *and* the top of the object will be reflected parallel to the principal axis.

Answers:

	a	b	c
Image position behind mirror (cm)	48.0	16.0	5.3
Image size (cm)	40.0	20.0	13.3
Magnification	4.0	2.0	1.3

Ray diagram solutions to convex mirror problems

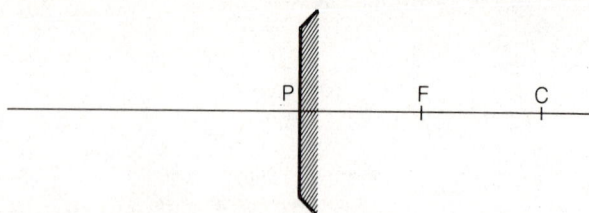

The difference between a concave and a convex mirror is that the focal point and centre of curvature of a convex mirror lie behind the mirror. The rays of light used in ray diagrams behave as follows:

1. A ray of light parallel to the principal axis is reflected *as if it had come from* the focal point:

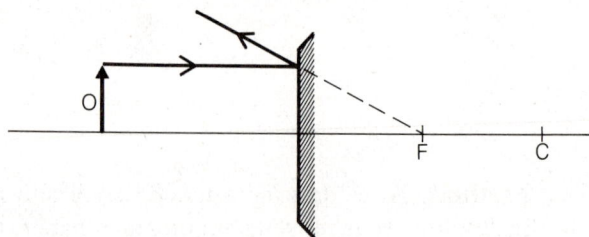

2. A ray of light directed at the focal point is reflected parallel to the principal axis:

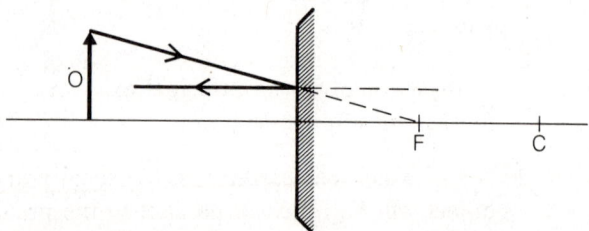

3. A ray of light directed at the centre of curvature will be reflected back along the same path:

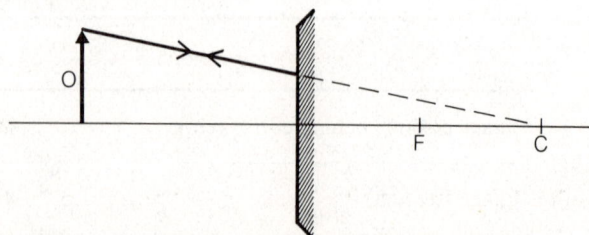

Note: The dotted lines show that the rays of light do not actually go behind the mirror, but only appear to do so.

Combining all three rays into one diagram gives:

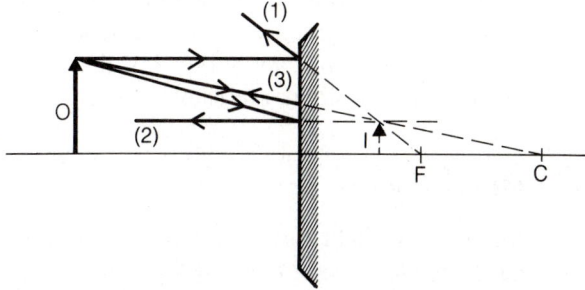

Example An object 40 cm tall is placed in different positions in front of a convex mirror of focal length 30 cm. Draw ray diagrams for each of the positions and find the image position, size of image and magnification in each case.

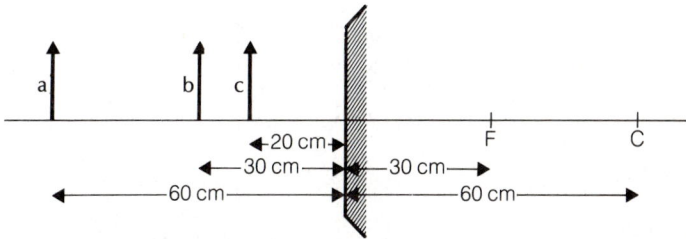

Method: After drawing a quick sketch, decide on a scale which allows maximum use of your graph paper. Any two of the three rays can be drawn. The point where they cross behind the mirror is the top of the image. Draw a vertical line onto the principal axis and you have the image. You can then find the image distance from the mirror and the image size by measuring and using your scale. The magnification is given by

$$\text{Magnification} = \frac{\text{Size of image}}{\text{Size of object}}$$

Answers:

	a	b	c
Image distance behind mirror (cm)	20.0	15.0	12.0
Size of image (cm)	13.3	20.0	24.0
Magnification	0.3	0.5	0.6

Have you seen that the image produced by a convex mirror is always smaller than the object and always lies between the mirror and the focal point? Can you see anything else about the image? This means that you need only learn *one* ray diagram for a convex mirror, because all the others are similar to it.

Refraction of light

When rays of light travel from one transparent material to another, e.g. air to glass, water to air, they may change direction. This is called refraction.

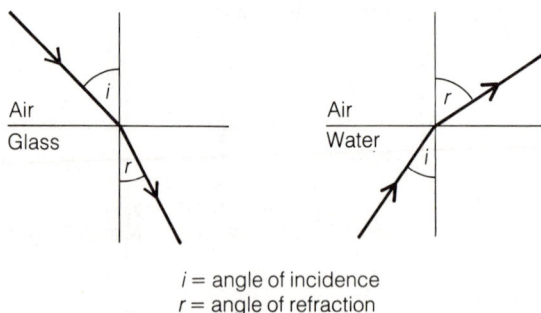

i = angle of incidence
r = angle of refraction

There is a relationship between the angles of incidence and refraction. It is

$$\frac{\text{sine(angle of incidence)}}{\text{sine(angle of refraction)}} = \text{Constant value}$$

The constant value is fixed for two materials. For air to glass the constant value is 3/2 or 1.5; for water to air it is 3/4 or 0.75. If the rays travel in the opposite direction, the constant value is turned upside down. For glass to air, the constant value is 2/3 or 0.67 and for air to water is 4/3 or 1.33. The constant value is called the refractive index. The general formula becomes

$$\frac{\sin i}{\sin r} = \text{Refractive index} = n$$

Example   Calculate the angle θ in each of the following diagrams (refractive index from air to glass = 3/2, or 1.5, air to water = 4/3, or 1.33):

a)

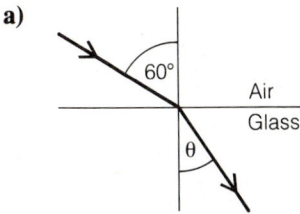

b)

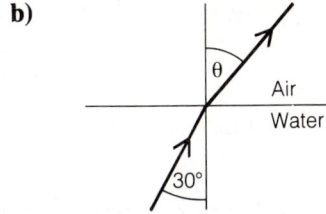

c)

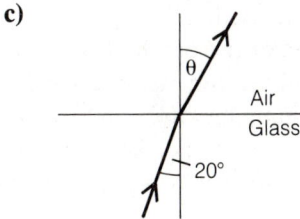

d)

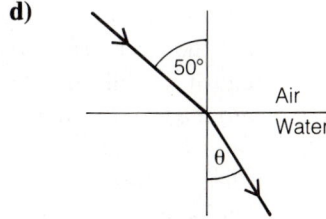

Method: Write down the general formula and fill in the values given. The formula should then be rearranged to make the unknown quantity the subject of the equation.

Note: In each of these examples make sure that the refractive index is in the right direction e.g. air to glass is 3/2, but glass to air is 2/3.

Answers: a) 35°   **b)** 42°   **c)** 31°   **d)** 35°

Example   It is slightly harder when you have to do some geometry during your calculation. In the following calculations find the angle θ:

a)

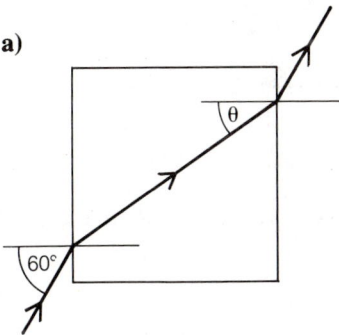

b)

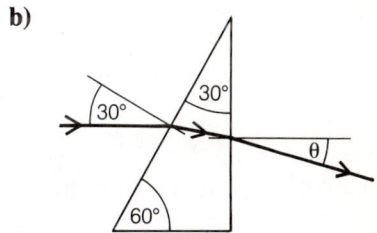

c)

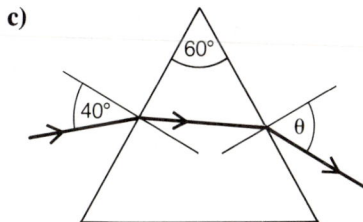

Method: Do the calculation a step at a time, checking at all times whether the ray is going from air to glass (refractive index 3/2) or from glass to air (refractive index 2/3).

Answers: a) 35°   **b)** 16°   **c)** 59°

Real and apparent depth

One interesting effect of the refraction from glass or water into air, is that the thickness of the glass or the depth of the water appears less than it actually is. The next time you visit the swimming pool look into the water — if you then jump into the water you will find that the water is deeper than it appeared to be. When the light leaves the water or glass at right angles to the surface, the real and apparent depths are related by the equation:

$$\frac{\text{Real depth}}{\text{Apparent depth}} = \text{Refractive index}$$

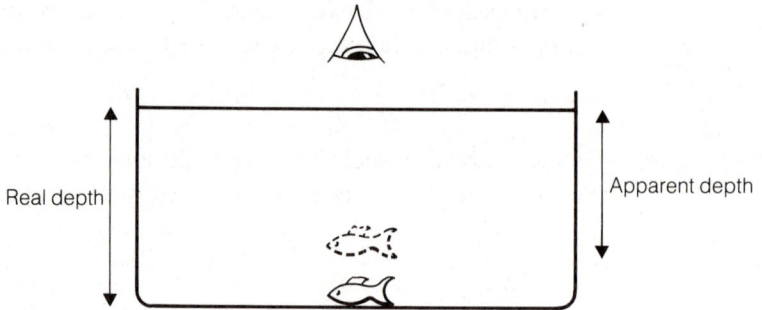

Example   The refractive index of water is 1.33. Calculate the apparent depth of a river if the real depth is:

a) 3 m   **b)** 4.5 m   **c)** 7 m

Method: The equation must be rearranged to make the apparent depth the subject of the equation. This gives

$$\text{Apparent depth} = \frac{\text{Real depth}}{\text{Refractive index}}$$

$$= \frac{\text{Real depth}}{1.33}$$

Answers: a) 2.25 m   **b)** 3.38 m   **c)** 5.25 m

Critical angle and total internal reflection

You have already seen that if a ray of light is travelling from glass into air or from water into air (indeed from any optically dense to optically less dense material) it is refracted away from the perpendicular to the surface.

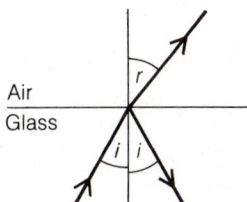

There will also be some reflection of the ray back into the glass.

As the angle *i* gets bigger, a stage is reached when angle *r* becomes 90°. The angle of incidence is then called the *critical angle*.

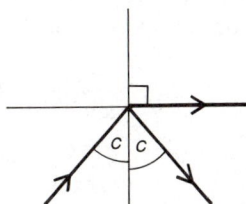

When the angle of incidence is bigger than the critical angle, the ray of light cannot be refracted out of the glass because it is physically impossible for the angle of refraction to be any bigger than 90°. As a result *all* of the light is reflected back into the glass. This is called *total internal reflection*. It is of considerable practical importance — for example in periscopes, prism binoculars and cat's-eyes on the road. The value for the critical angle can be calculated using the general formula

$$\frac{\sin i}{\sin r} = \text{Refractive index}$$

Example Calculate the critical angle for light travelling to air from:
a) glass, of refractive index 1.4
b) water, of refractive index 1.33
c) perspex, of refractive index 1.5
d) diamond, of refractive index 2.4

Method: The refractive index is normally given from air into the material and so for the light travelling from the material into air the refractive index is given by the reciprocal of the given value. For example in part a), the refractive index from air to glass is 1.4 and so the refractive index from glass to air is 1/1.4.

The critical angle can be calculated using the formula

$$\frac{\sin i}{\sin r} = \text{Refractive index}$$

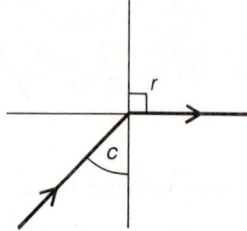

and making the angle of incidence i equal to the critical angle c, and the angle of refraction r as 90°, giving the equation

$$\frac{\sin c}{\sin 90} = \text{Refractive index}$$

$$\frac{\sin c}{1.0000} = \frac{1}{1.4}$$

$$\text{therefore} \quad \sin c = \frac{1}{1.4} = 0.7142$$

This is the sine of the critical angle and, by using sine tables or a calculator, the critical angle can be found.

Answers: a) 45.6°   **b)** 48.8°   **c)** 41.8°   **d)** 24.6°

Example   Calculate the refractive index of the material if the critical angle is:
a) 50°   **b)** 45°   **c)** 40°   **d)** 35°

Method: The critical angle is equal to the angle of incidence when the angle of refraction is 90°. Substituting in

$$\frac{\sin i}{\sin r} = \text{Refractive index}$$

gives

$$\frac{\sin c}{\sin 90°} = \text{Refractive index}$$

The refractive index you have calculated is for light travelling from the material to air. Usually the refractive index is given for the light travelling from air to the material, and so you must find the reciprocal of your calculated refractive index.

Answers: a) 1.31 (0.77)   **b)** 1.41 (0.71)   **c)** 1.56 (0.64)
d) 1.74 (0.57)
(Both values are given, with the material to air value in the bracket.)

Refraction of light by lenses

There are two main types of lens:

Type of lens	Representation in diagrams
1. Convex (converging)	or
2. Concave (diverging)	or

The following points can be labelled for a convex lens:

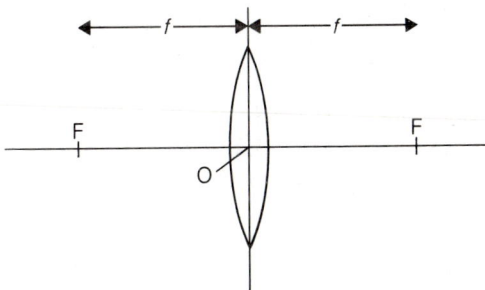

FOF = principal axis
O = optical centre
F = principal focus or focal point
f = focal length

Ray diagram solutions to convex lens problems

As for mirrors, you may be told the *object distance* and *image distance* from the lens and asked to find the *focal length* of the lens and the *magnification* produced by the lens. Or you may be told any two of these quantities and asked to find the other two. There are two ways in which you can do this:

a) using a ray diagram, or
b) by calculation.

We shall look at the calculation method on p.46 but here we use ray diagrams.

When drawing a ray diagram, the diagram is drawn to scale and three rays can be drawn:

1. A ray parallel to the principal axis will be refracted through the principal focus.

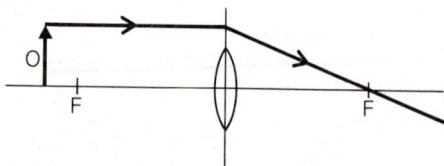

2. A ray through the principal focus will be refracted parallel to the principal axis.

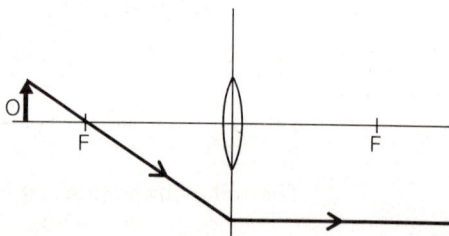

3. A ray through the optical centre emerges undeviated.

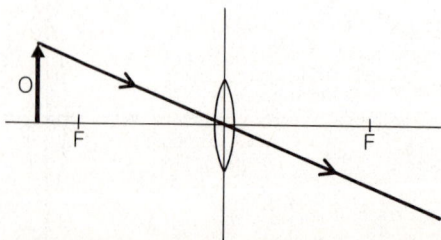

Combining all three gives:

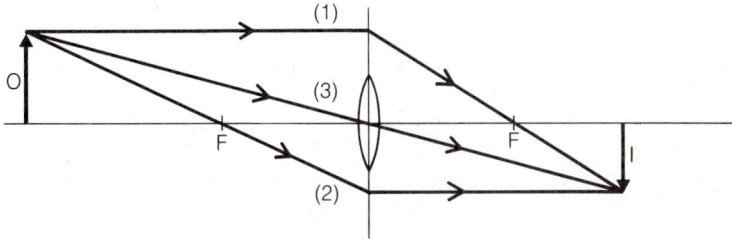

In practice you will find that only two of these rays need to be drawn. The problems are made easier if you use graph paper.

Example   Draw separate diagrams for each of the three objects **a**, **b** and **c**, drawing at least two rays each time. From your diagrams find the image distance from the lens.

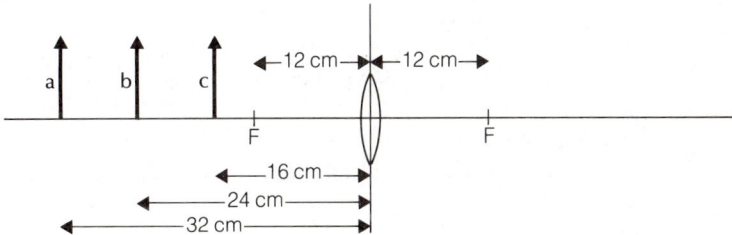

Method: Draw a rapid sketch to find the approximate image position and size. A suitable scale for your accurate diagram can then be chosen. Using graph paper draw the principal axis and mark on the *two* focal points, optical centre and object position. (You will probably find that your diagram is improved by turning the graph paper so that the longer edge is horizontal.)

Because the object size is not stated, choose a convenient value so that either the object or image is as large as possible.

Choose any two of the three rays and draw them from the top of the object. Where they cross again is the top of the image. Assuming no distortion, the bottom of the image lies on the principal axis. Using your scale you can work out the distance of the image from the lens.

Answers: a) 19.2 cm   **b)** 24 cm   **c)** 48 cm

Example Draw separate diagrams for each of the three objects **a**, **b** and **c**, all 20 cm tall, drawing at least two rays each time. From your diagram find the size of the image and its magnification.

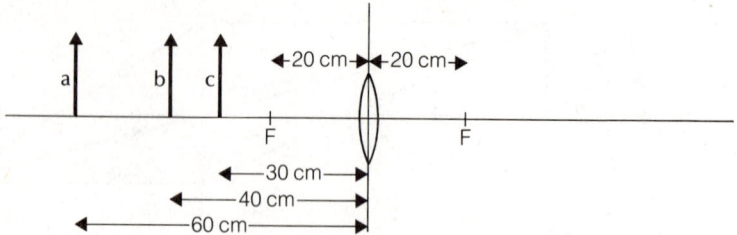

Method: Draw a rapid sketch diagram to find the approximate image position and size. Decide on a suitable scale, but remember that the vertical scale need not be the same as the horizontal scale. On graph paper, draw the principal axis and mark on the *two* focal points, optical centre and object position.

Choose any two of the three rays and draw them from the top of the object. Where they cross is the top of the image. The bottom of the image lies on the principal axis directly above. Using your vertical scale work out the size of the image and calculate the magnification using the formula:

$$\text{Magnification} = \frac{\text{Size of image}}{\text{Size of object}}$$

Answers:

	Image position (cm)	Size of image (cm)	Magnification
a)	60	40	2
b)	40	20	1
c)	30	10	0.5

Convex lens as a magnifying glass/simple microscope

In the above examples the images were formed where the rays of light crossed. The images were also upside-down. There is, however, a special case when the image is the same way up as the object. This happens when the object is placed inside the focal length. (Do you remember a similar situation with the concave mirror?) Rays 1 and 2 are seen to move further apart after passing through the lens. To the eye (see the diagram) the rays appear to come from a point on the same side of the lens as the object.

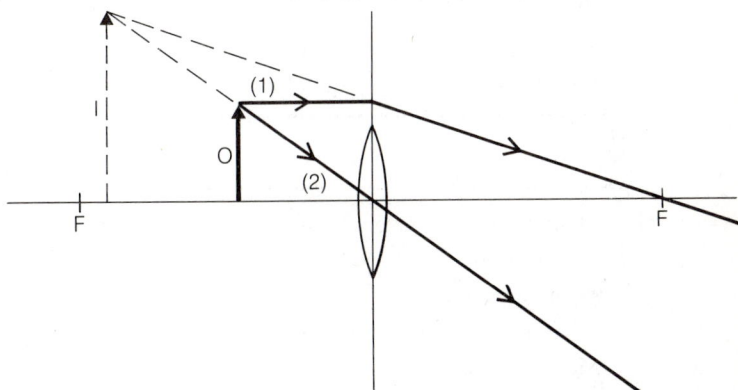

The diagram shows that the image is both magnified and the same way up as the object.

Because the image only appears to exist it is called a *virtual* image, unlike the previous convex lens problems when the rays actually crossed to produce a *real* image.

Example Find the image position, image size and magnification when a 20 cm tall object is placed at the marked distances from a convex lens of focal length 10 cm.

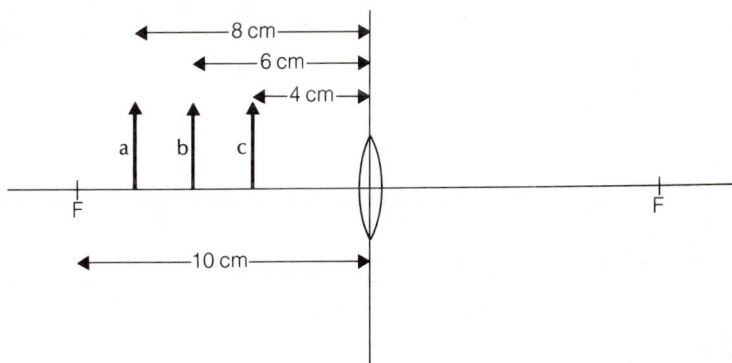

Method: After drawing a quick sketch and having decided on your scale, draw your ray diagram on graph paper. Make sure that you have left plenty of space on the same side of the lens as the object. Because the object and image are the same way up as the object you can draw the principal axis at the bottom of the graph paper. The two rays to draw are:

1. A ray parallel to the principal axis which will pass through the focal point after refraction.

2. A ray through the optical centre will continue in a straight line (it will be undeviated).

Draw the rays back until they cross to give the top of the image.

Answers:

	a	b	c
Image position from lens (cm)	40	15	6.7
Image size (cm)	100	50	33.3
Magnification	5	2.5	1.7

Ray diagram solutions to concave lens problems

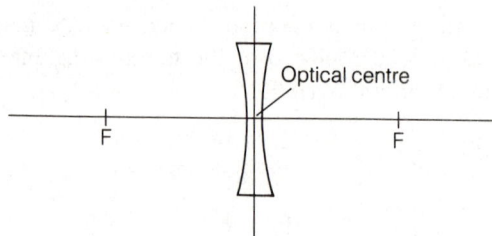

The rays of light used in ray diagrams with concave lenses are:

1. A ray of light parallel to the principal axis is refracted *as if it had come from* a focal point.

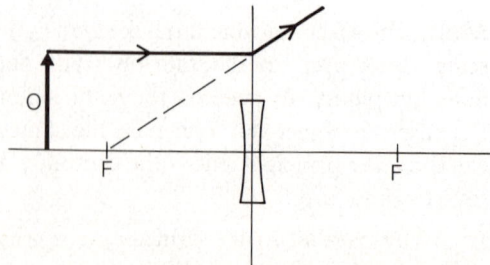

2. A ray of light directed at a focal point is refracted parallel to the principal axis.

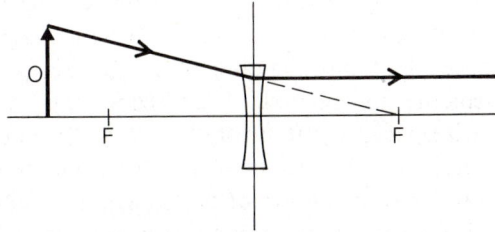

3. A ray of light directed at the optical centre passes through the lens undeviated.

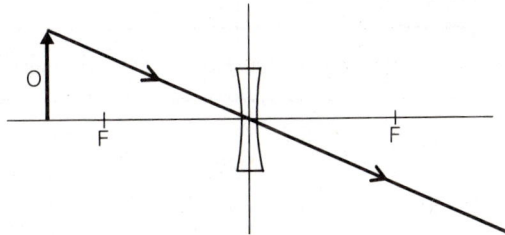

Note: The dotted lines show that the rays of light do not actually pass along those paths, but only appear to do so.

Combining all three rays into one diagram gives:

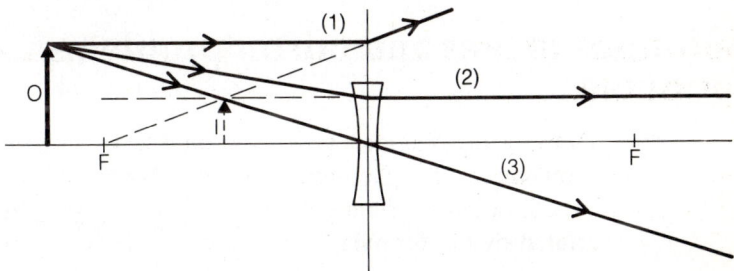

Example Draw separate ray diagrams for each of the three objects **a**, **b** and **c**, all 40 cm tall, drawing at least two rays each time. From your diagram find the image position and its size.

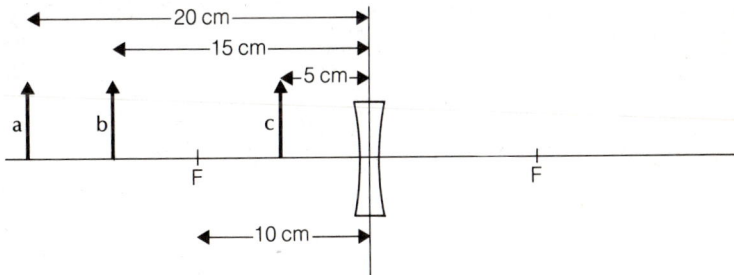

Method: With concave lenses, the image is always between the object and the lens. It is also always the same way up as the object, and so you can draw the principal axis at the bottom of your graph paper and you can draw the object as large as possible. Draw a ray from the top of the object through the optical centre — this ray will emerge undeviated. The second ray should be parallel to the principal axis. After refraction this will appear to have come from the focal point F on *the same side* of the lens as the object. Where the two rays cross is the top of the image. The bottom of the image will lie directly below the top. Remember that the image only appears to exist and is therefore a virtual image.

Answers:

	Image position (cm)	Size of image (cm)
a)	6.7	13.3
b)	6	16
c)	3.3	26.7

Solutions to lens and mirror problems using formulae

Drawing ray diagrams is not the only way in which you can solve problems involving lenses and mirrors. More advanced theory shows that the object distance u, image distance v and focal length f are related by the formula

$$\frac{1}{f} = \frac{1}{u} + \frac{1}{v}$$

e.g.

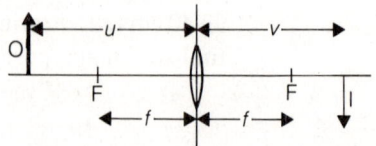

or

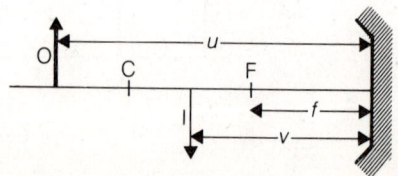

The magnification m is given by

$$m = \frac{\text{Size of image}}{\text{Size of object}} = \frac{v}{u}$$

These two formulae can be used for both lens and mirror problems. This approach is sometimes called the 'real is positive' approach. (Later work will show that this could be rewritten as the 'virtual is negative' approach.)

Note: These calculations apply to both convex lenses and concave mirrors although only one is stated in each example to avoid confusion.

Example   Find the focal length of the convex lens if
a)   object distance = 90 cm, image distance = 30 cm
b)   object distance = 40 cm, image distance = 40 cm
c)   object distance = 20 cm, image distance = 60 cm

Method: Use the formula

$$\frac{1}{f} = \frac{1}{u} + \frac{1}{v}$$

where u is the object distance from the lens and v is the image distance from the lens.

The equation can be rearranged to give

$$\frac{1}{f} = \frac{v + u}{u \times v} = \frac{v}{u \times v} + \frac{u}{u \times v}$$

Having substituted for u and v, we find a value for $1/f$ and this must be inverted to obtain f:

a) $\dfrac{1}{f} = \dfrac{1}{90} + \dfrac{1}{30}$

$= \dfrac{30 + 90}{90 \times 30}$

$= \dfrac{\cancel{120}^{4}}{90 \times \cancel{30}_{1}}$ (dividing top and bottom by 30)

$= \dfrac{4}{90}$

$= \dfrac{2}{45}$

$\therefore f = \dfrac{45}{2} = 22.5\text{ cm}$

Answers: b) 20 cm   **c)** 15 cm

Example   Calculate the focal length of the concave mirror and the magnification produced for the following values of object and image distances from the mirror if

	Object distance (cm)	Image distance (cm)
a)	36	18
b)	12	60
c)	30	60

Method: The focal length is calculated in the same way as in the first Example, using the formula

$$\frac{1}{f} = \frac{1}{u} + \frac{1}{v}$$

The magnification is calculated using the formula

$$m = \frac{v}{u}$$

Answers:

	Focal length (cm)	Magnification
a)	12	0.5
b)	10	5
c)	20	2

Example   A harder calculation is to find the focal length when given the magnification and either the object or image distance.
a) Magnification = 4.0, object distance = 20 cm
b) Magnification = 0.3, object distance = 90 cm
c) Magnification = 2.0, image distance = 50 cm

Method: First use the formula $m = v/u$ to calculate either the object or image distance, whichever is not known. Having done that calculate the focal length using the formula

$$\frac{1}{f} = \frac{1}{u} + \frac{1}{v}$$

Answers:
a) Image distance = 80 cm, focal length = 16 cm
b) Image distance = 30 cm, focal length = 22.5 cm
c) Object distance = 25 cm, focal length = 16.7 cm

Virtual images

It has already been stated that lens and mirror problems may be solved using formulae. If, however, you include images which do not actually exist, but only appear to exist (i.e. virtual images), then the problems become slightly more difficult. In equations, the distance of a virtual image from a lens or mirror is written as a negative quantity. Similarly, if a calculation gives a negative value for an image distance you can conclude that the image must be virtual. However, when calculating the magnification ignore the minus sign, since the magnification only tells you by how much the image is bigger (or smaller) than the object.

To produce a virtual image, you will remember from the section on ray diagrams, that either you use:

a) a convex lens or concave mirror and place the object inside the focal length, or
b) a concave lens or convex mirror with the object at any distance.

We look first at convex lenses and concave mirrors.

Example   Using a concave mirror of focal length 20 cm, calculate the image distance from the mirror if the object is placed at the following distances from it:

a) 15 cm   b) 10 cm   c) 5 cm

Method: Since the object is real its distance from the mirror is given a *positive* value when substituted in

$$\frac{1}{f} = \frac{1}{u} + \frac{1}{v}$$

All three of the calculations will produce *negative* values for v, showing that the image is virtual.

Answers: a) −60 cm   **b)** −20 cm   **c)** −6.7 cm

Example Using a convex lens of focal length 15 cm, calculate the image distance from the lens and the magnification produced, if the object is placed at the following distances from it:
a) 12 cm   b) 9 cm   c) 5 cm

Method: Again the object is real and so its distance from the lens has a positive value when substituted in

$$\frac{1}{f} = \frac{1}{u} + \frac{1}{v}$$

Having calculated a value for the image distance v it will be found to have a negative value. This means that the image is virtual. This negative sign can then be ignored when calculating the magnification using

$$m = \frac{v}{u}$$

Answers:

	Image distance (cm)	Magnification
a)	−60	5.0
b)	−22.5	2.5
c)	−7.5	1.5

When concave lenses and convex mirrors are examined things become more complicated because both concave lenses and convex mirrors spread light out *as if it* came from the focal point. For this reason the focal lengths of both are given negative values in calculations.

Example Calculate the image distance from a concave lens of focal length 10 cm when an object is placed at the following distances from it:

a) 30 cm   b) 20 cm   c) 5 cm

Method: The focal length value is given a negative sign when substituted into

$$\frac{1}{f} = \frac{1}{u} + \frac{1}{v}$$

Since the object actually exists, its distance from the lens is given a positive sign.

Answers: a) −7.5 cm   **b)** −6.7 cm   **c)** −3.3 cm

A similar calculation would apply for a convex mirror. Similarly, when calculating the magnification, any negative signs are ignored and the equation $m = v/u$ is applied.

Example Calculate the position and the magnification of the image produced when an object is placed at the following distances from a convex mirror of focal length 20 cm:

a) 60 cm   **b)** 30 cm   **c)** 10 cm

Method: The focal length value is given a negative value when substituted into

$$\frac{1}{f} = \frac{1}{u} + \frac{1}{v}$$

Having obtained a negative value for the image distance from the mirror, you can conclude that the image is virtual. This negative sign is ignored when the magnification is calculated using

$$m = \frac{v}{u}$$

Answers:

	Image distance (cm)	Magnification
a)	−15	0.25
b)	−12	0.40
c)	−6.7	0.67

Questions

1. A girl stands 1.5 m away from a plane vertical mirror. How far
   a) behind the mirror is her image?
   b) is her image from her?

2.

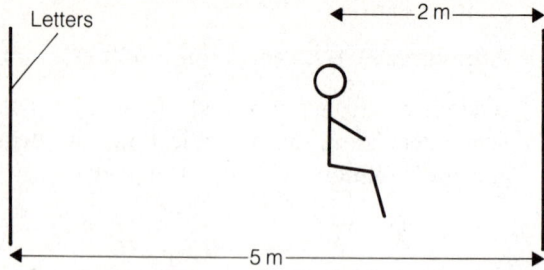

A man has his eyes tested at the optician's. How far from his eyes will the image in the mirror be?

3.

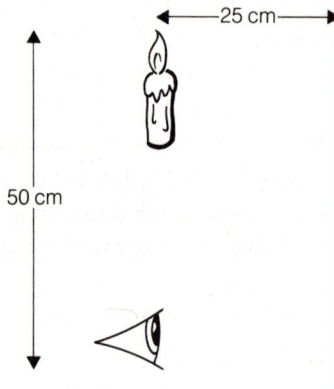

Copy the diagram and draw on it two rays from the top of the candle flame, which will reach the eye after reflection at the mirror. Produce these reflected rays back in order to find the position of the image in the mirror. How far behind the mirror is the image?

4.   Copy and complete the following table:

i	$\sin i$	r	$\sin r$	Refractive index
30°	—	20°	—	—
—	—	40°	—	1.33
70°	—	—	—	1.45

5.   Copy out and complete the following tables:

a)

u (cm)	$\dfrac{1}{u}$ $\left(\dfrac{1}{cm}\right)$	v (cm)	$\dfrac{1}{v}$ $\left(\dfrac{1}{cm}\right)$	$\dfrac{1}{f} = \dfrac{1}{u} + \dfrac{1}{v}$ $\left(\dfrac{1}{cm}\right)$	f (cm)
20	—	30	—	—	—
—	—	60	—	—	20
45	—	—	—	—	15

b)

u (cm)	v (cm)	f (cm)
20	30	—
—	60	20
45	—	15

6.   a)

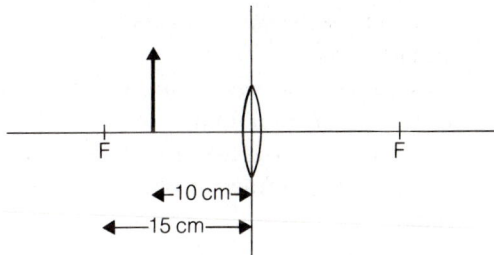

Draw a ray diagram using three rays to find the image position. What are the properties of the image?

b)

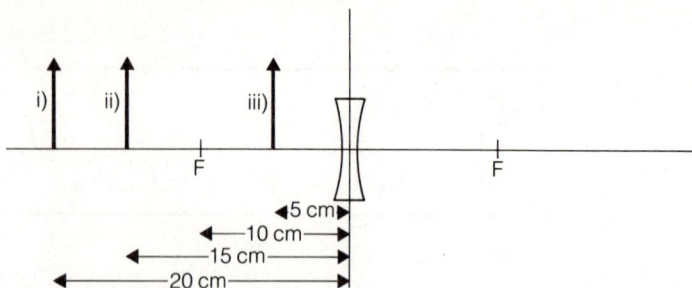

Draw separate diagrams for each of the three objects, drawing three rays each time. What are the similarities between the three images?

7. The following results were obtained in an experiment to find the refractive index of glass. Copy out and complete the table:

i		10°	20°	30°	40°	50°	60°	70°
sin i								
r		7°	13°	19°	25°	31°	35°	39°
sin r								
Refractive index = $\dfrac{\sin i}{\sin r}$								

a) What is the average value for the refractive index of glass?
b) Using the same results, draw a graph of sin i on the y-axis against sin r on the x-axis. Calculate the slope (gradient) of the best straight line.
    How does this value compare with the average value for the refractive index obtained in part a)?
c) What feature(s) of the original experiment might explain why the values of the refractive index obtained in part a) are not all the same?

8. Given the following information, draw ray diagrams in order to find the image position. In each case state the properties of the image, e.g. real or virtual, upright or inverted, magnified or diminished or same size:

a) Concave mirror, $f = 15$ cm, $u = 20$ cm, object 10 cm tall
b) Concave mirror, $f = 15$ cm, $u = 30$ cm, object 10 cm tall
c) Concave mirror, $f = 15$ cm, $u = 40$ cm, object 20 cm tall
d) Concave mirror, $f = 15$ cm, $u = 50$ cm, object 20 cm tall
e) Concave mirror, $f = 15$ cm, $u = 60$ cm, object 30 cm tall
f) Convex lens, $f = 20$ cm, $u = 30$ cm, object 10 cm tall
g) Convex lens, $f = 20$ cm, $u = 40$ cm, object 10 cm tall
h) Convex lens, $f = 20$ cm, $u = 50$ cm, object 20 cm tall
i) Convex lens, $f = 20$ cm, $u = 60$ cm, object 20 cm tall
j) Can you see any similarity between f) and i)?
k) Concave mirror, $f = 15$ cm, $u = 10$ cm, object 10 cm tall
l) Suggest two possible uses of the arrangement in k)
m) Convex lens, $f = 20$ cm, $u = 15$ cm, object 20 cm tall
n) Suggest two people who might use the arrangement in m).

9. Repeat Question 8 (except parts j), l) and n)) using formulae.

10. a) An object 10 cm high is placed 15 cm from a convex lens of focal length 10 cm. Draw a ray diagram to find the position and magnification of the image produced.
    b) On the *same* piece of paper, redraw part a) but make the object 20 cm high (perhaps this diagram could be drawn using a coloured pencil). What is the position and magnification of this image?
    c) Does the image size in parts a) and b) make any difference to the position and/or magnification of the image?

11. In the following questions find, by ray diagram, a value for the focal length of the convex lens (choose your own object size):
    a) $u = 60$ cm, $v = 15$ cm
    b) $u = 30$ cm, $v = 15$ cm
    c) $u = 13$ cm, $v = 24$ cm

12. Repeat Question 11 using formulae.

13. In the following questions, find by ray diagram the focal length of the concave mirror. (Choose your own suitable object size.)
    a) $u = 90$ cm, $v = 30$ cm
    b) $u = 40$ cm, $v = 40$ cm
    c) $u = 20$ cm, $v = 60$ cm

14. Repeat Question 13 using formulae.

15. The following results were obtained during an experiment to find the focal length of a concave mirror:

u (cm)	v (cm)	$\dfrac{1}{u}$ $\left(\dfrac{1}{cm}\right)$	$\dfrac{1}{v}$ $\left(\dfrac{1}{cm}\right)$	$\dfrac{1}{f} = \dfrac{1}{u} + \dfrac{1}{v}$ $\left(\dfrac{1}{cm}\right)$	f (cm)
80	23	—	—	—	—
60	26	—	—	—	—
40	33	—	—	—	—
30	45	—	—	—	—
20	180	—	—	—	—

Copy out and complete the table and hence find an average value for f.

16. The following results were obtained in an experiment to check the formula,

$$\text{Magnification} = \frac{\text{Size of image}}{\text{Size of object}} = \frac{\text{Image distance}}{\text{Object distance}}$$

Complete the table and decide whether the formula is valid.

u (cm)	v (cm)	Size of object (cm)	Size of image (cm)	$\dfrac{\text{Size of image}}{\text{Size of object}}$	$\dfrac{v}{u}$
18	80	2.0	8.9	—	—
20	60	2.0	6.0	—	—
24	40	2.0	3.3	—	—
30	30	2.0	2.0	—	—
60	20	2.0	0.7	—	—

17. The following results were obtained in an experiment to find the focal length of a convex lens:

u (cm)	$\dfrac{1}{u}$ $\left(\frac{1}{cm}\right)$	v (cm)	$\dfrac{1}{v}$ $\left(\frac{1}{cm}\right)$
25	—	100	—
30	—	60	—
35	—	47	—
40	—	40	—
45	—	36	—
50	—	33	—
60	—	30	—

a) Copy and complete the table. The focal length could be found in the same way as in Question 15. However, there is also a graphical method. Plot a graph of $1/u$ on the y-axis against $1/v$ on the x-axis, starting both axes at 0 and taking them up to $0.05\frac{1}{cm}$. Draw the best straight line through the points. The points at which the line crosses the two axes should have the same value, and this equals $1/f$. Find the two values and hence obtain a value for f.

b) Can you work out the theory behind the graph?

Past examination questions

1. a) In an experiment to determine the refractive index of a glass block, several values for the angles of incidence, i, and refraction, r, were obtained and listed in the following table.

Angle of incidence, i	9°	20°	30°	46°	62°
Angle of refraction, r	6°	15°	21°	30°	40°
Sin i					
Sin r					

(i) Copy the table on graph paper and complete by inserting values for sin i and sin r in the table. Use these results to plot a straight-line graph on the graph paper. [8]

(ii) Calculate the refractive index for the glass block. [3]

b)

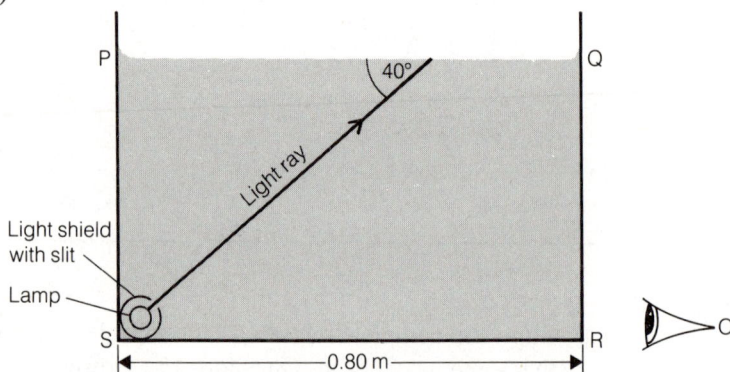

The diagram shows a side view of a water-filled aquarium PQRS. An electric lamp, surrounded by a shield with a narrow slit, is immersed in one corner of the aquarium at S. The light ray from the slit shines on the water surface PQ at an angle of 40° as shown.

(i) If the refractive index of water is 1.33, calculate the critical angle for a ray travelling from water to air. [3]

(ii) Draw a diagram of the light ray shown above meeting the water surface PQ, and show its path after meeting the surface. Calculate the angle that this new path makes with PQ and label the angle. [3]

(iii) The shield surrounding the lamp is turned slightly so that when an observer O looks perpendicularly at the side QR the lamp is directly visible. Calculate how far the image of the lamp appears to be from QR. [3]

[London]

2. Describe, with the aid of a ray diagram, how you would measure the focal length of a converging lens. [5]

   Draw a further diagram to show how such a lens is used as the eyepiece in a telescope or microscope. [5]

   An illuminated object is set up 2 m from a white screen. Where should a converging lens be placed in order to give a clear image, four times the height of the object, on the screen? What focal length lens is necessary? [5]

   [SUJB]

3. a) Give a ray diagram to show the action of a simple magnifying glass. Name the type of lens used and state fully the nature of the image. [6]

   A screen is placed 80 cm from an object. A lens is used to produce on the screen an image which is three times the height of the object. What is the distance between the object and the lens? What is the focal length of the lens? [6]

   b) Explain, with diagrams, how a human eye can produce clear images for objects at different distances. [4]

   With the aid of a diagram explain the use of a diverging lens in correcting a named eye defect. [4]

   [London]

4. a) Draw a labelled diagram to show the subsequent path of a narrow beam of light which is incident in air at about 45° on one face of a rectangular glass block. Use your diagram to explain the meaning of the term 'refractive index'. [5]

   If the refractive index for glass is 1.50, calculate the speed of light in glass. (Speed of light in air $= 3.0 \times 10^8$ m s^{-1}.) Calculate also the critical angle for a glass/air interface and draw a diagram to show the meaning of this angle. [6]

   b) Show how a suitable glass prism may be used to deviate a ray of light through 90°. Why is this method preferable to using a plane glass mirror for the same purpose? [4]

   [SUJB]

5. a) Describe and explain how a right-angled isosceles prism may be used to deviate a parallel beam of light through 90°. Refer briefly to a practical application of this. [8]

   b) An object 2 cm tall is placed on the axis of a spherical converging (concave) mirror at a distance of 5 cm from the mirror, which has a radius of curvature of 20 cm. Draw a clear ray diagram, showing how the image is formed and by scale drawing, or otherwise, find the position and height of this image. [7]

   [SUJB]

6. To a person under water, looking upwards, all objects above and outside the water appear to be within a certain cone of vision. Explain this, using a clear diagram. If the refractive index of water is 1.33, calculate the vertical angle of the cone.   [5]

[SUJB]

7. a)

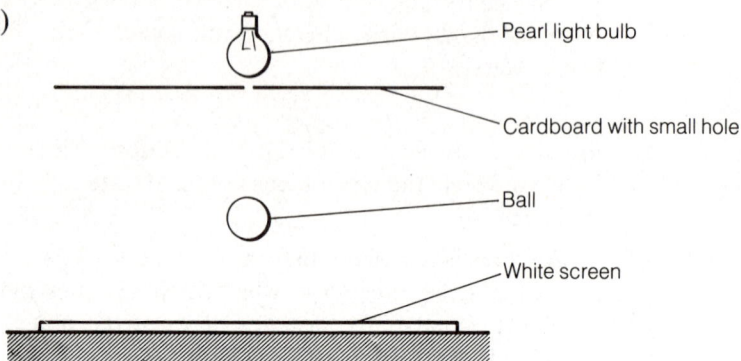

Pearl light bulb

Cardboard with small hole

Ball

White screen

Using the information in the diagram
(i)   sketch what you would see on the screen,
(ii) sketch what you would see on the screen if the cardboard were removed.   [6]

b)

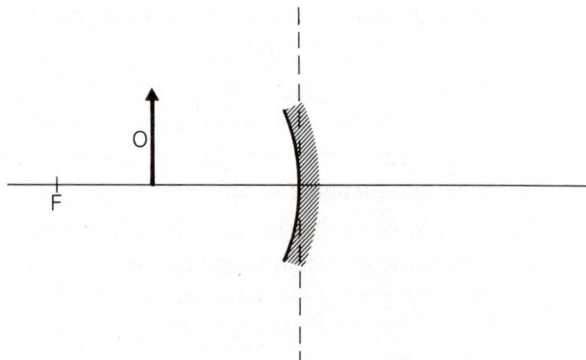

The diagram shows an object O placed in front of a converging (concave) mirror. F is the principal focus.
(i)   Copy the diagram on to your paper. On your diagram draw two rays from the top of the object to locate the top of the image. Draw the image.
(ii) Name a practical use of the converging mirror when used as shown in the diagram.   [6]

c) An object, 20 mm tall, is placed 300 mm from a diverging (concave) lens of focal length 150 mm.

(i) Make a sketch of the ray diagram showing the location of the image.

(ii) The object is now moved 100 mm nearer the lens. Find by calculation, or by scale drawing on graph paper, the position and magnification of the image. State whether the image is real or virtual. [10]

d) Draw a labelled diagram to show the construction of a single lens camera and explain how the camera can be adjusted for varying conditions of distance of object and light intensity. [9]

[AEB]

8.

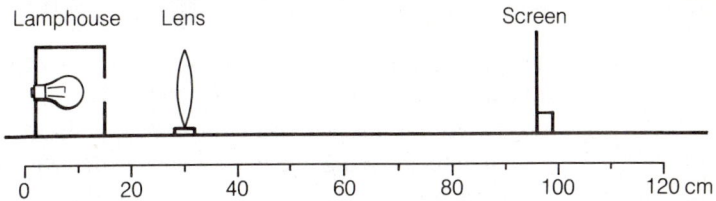

A lamphouse containing a filament lamp was fixed on a bench in front of a convex lens as in the diagram. A white screen was adjusted until a sharp image of the filament was obtained. The positions of the lamp, lens and screen on the bench were noted in the table of results below. The lens and screen were moved and a second set of readings obtained.

Position of filament (cm)	Position of lens (cm)	Position of screen (cm)	Object distance (cm)	Image distance (cm)	Magnification
8.0	30.0	96.0			
8.0	71.0	92.0			

(i) Copy and complete the table of results. Compare the sizes of the two images obtained. [6]

(ii) Using the first set of readings above determine a value for the focal length of the lens. [5]

(iii) Explain why it was impossible to adjust the screen to obtain an image when the lens was placed at the 20-cm position on the bench. How can an image of the filament be seen with the lens in this position? Briefly describe the appearance of the image seen. [6]

[London (part)]

9.   It is required to project the image of a slide 5 cm square on to a screen, so that the picture observed is 50 cm square. The slide is 11 m from the screen. What type of lens is needed, where is it placed and what is its focal length? Illustrate the image formation by means of a ray diagram. [9]

[SUJB (part)]

10. a)

Plane mirror

The diagram shows a letter L on a horizontal piece of paper on which a plane mirror is placed vertically.
(i)   Copy the diagram on your paper, and draw suitable rays to locate the image of the corner of the letter L nearest to the mirror.
(ii) On your diagram draw the image of the letter L. [5]

b) Draw diagrams to show how a 45°–90°–45° glass prism can turn a narrow beam of light through
(i)   90°
(ii) 180°. [3]
On both your diagrams show the paths of the beams of light in the glass.

c) You are given two 45°–90°–45° glass prisms and a cardboard tube of rectangular cross-section.
(i)   Show, by diagram, how you would mount the prisms in the tube so that you could see objects behind you.
(ii) Draw two rays of light from an object, to show how you would see the image of the object.
(iii) State what is wrong with the system.
(iv) State how you would correct it. [8]

d) An object is placed on the axis of a converging (concave) mirror of focal length 200 mm. The image produced is inverted and has a magnification of 1.5. By calculation or by scale drawing on graph paper determine the position of the object. [5]

[AEB 1982]

11. a) Explain, with the aid of ray diagrams, how (i) a converging lens and (ii) a concave mirror can form a virtual image of a suitably placed object. On each diagram show clearly the position of each principal focus. [4, 4]

b) A camera has a single lens of focal length 100 mm which focuses light from an object on to a light-sensitive film. The position of the lens relative to the film is adjustable.
   (i)   What is the separation of the lens and film when a distant scene is to be photographed? [2]
   (ii) Explain, without detailed calculation, how the separation of the lens and film should be changed if an object 2 m from the camera is to be photographed. [3]
   (iii) When taking a photograph, care is taken that too much light does not enter the camera. How is the amount of light which enters the camera controlled? [4]

c) In a pinhole camera the screen is 0.20 m from the pinhole. An object of length 3.0 m is at a distance of 12 m from the pinhole. Calculate the length of the image on the screen. (Neglect the size of the pinhole.) [3]

[Oxford and Cambridge]

12. Describe an experiment you would perform to determine the refractive index of glass. [4]

Explain what is meant by *critical angle* and *total internal reflection* and calculate the refractive index of a transparent substance which has a critical angle of 43.38°. [6]

With suitable diagrams, explain
Either, (a) how an optical fibre works,
Or ,   (b) how a prism periscope is constructed. [4]

[WJEC]

13. A convex lens of focal length 6 cm is held 4 cm from a newspaper which has print 0.5 cm high. By calculation or scale drawing, determine the size and nature of the image produced. [8]

Draw a diagram showing how *two* suitable lenses can be used to produce a compound microscope. Indicate on your diagram
(i)   the focal points of the lenses,
(ii) the position of the object,
(iii) the position and nature of the final image. [8]

[WJEC]

14. An object 240 mm in front of a converging lens gives a real image 400 mm from the lens on the opposite side.
a) Draw a suitable scale diagram to show how the image is formed and hence find the focal length of the lens. [6, 2]

b) The object, 240 mm from the lens, is moved gradually further away. What happens to
   (i) the size of the image,
   (ii) the position of the image? [4]

c) How far from the lens would an object have to be to give an image the same size as itself? Show on a diagram how the image is formed. [4]

d) (i) A lens of identical shape is made of glass of a higher refractive index. Explain how its focal length would differ from the first lens. [2]
   (ii) Explain how a lens made from the glass of higher refractive index would need to differ in shape to have the same focal length as the first lens. [2]

[Oxford]

15.

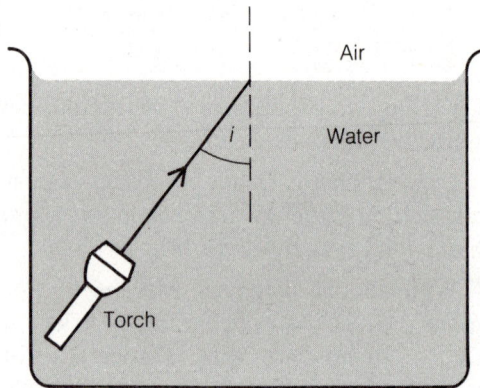

a) The diagram above shows a torch being held under water in such a way that a ray of light is produced which can strike the surface of the water at different angles i. Calculate a value for the critical angle; the refractive index of water is 4/3. [3]

Draw sketches to show what will happen to the ray of light after it has struck the water–air boundary when i is about 20° and when i is about 60°. Account for the different behaviour of the ray in the two cases. [3]

Why in one case has the resulting ray coloured edges whereas in the other case it has not? [4]

b) In an experiment to determine the refractive index of water a black line is painted on the bottom of a tall glass container which is then partially filled with water. On looking vertically down into the water the black line appears to be closer than it really is. Explain, with the help of a ray diagram, why this is so. [4]

The following results were obtained in such an experiment.

Real depth/cm	8.1	12.0	16.0	20.0
Apparent depth/cm	5.9	9.1	12.0	15.1

Plot a graph of real depth (y-axis) against apparent depth (x-axis) and hence determine a value for the refractive index of water.

[6]

[London]

3. Machines and Mechanics

We use machines in everyday life with the main purpose of making our lives easier. You may like to write down a list of machines. This list will probably include such things as cars and washing machines. However, these are complex pieces of machinery and you will meet much simpler machines in calculations, some of which will go to make up the more complex machines.

In this section we will look at several simple machines, some of which it may seem odd to call machines. However, if you ask yourself 'Does it make life easier?' then you will probably see that it is a machine. The machines we shall look at are levers, pulleys, inclined planes and gears. In all of these an effort force is applied to move a load force.

There are several formulae which apply to all machines:

Mechanical advantage

1. $$\text{Mechanical advantage (MA)} = \frac{\text{Load}}{\text{Effort}}$$

Example Complete the following table:

	Mechanical advantage (no units)	Load (N)	Effort (N)
a)	–	200	50
b)	6.0	120	–
c)	0.5	–	40

Method: Use the formula MA = Load/effort and substitute the values given.

Answers: a) 4 **b)** 20 N **c)** 20 N

Can you see why mechanical advantage has no units?

Velocity ratio

2. Velocity ratio (VR) = $\dfrac{\text{Distance moved by the effort force}}{\substack{\text{Distance moved by the load force in} \\ \text{the same time.}}}$

Example If a machine has a velocity ratio of 2.5, what distance will be moved by the load force if the effort force moves:

a) 20 cm   **b)** 4 m   **c)** 6.20 m?

Method: Using the formula

$$VR = \frac{\text{Distance moved by effort}}{\text{Distance moved by load (in the same time)}}$$

(*Note*: Some of the words in the original definition have been removed because they are usually taken for granted.)

You must rearrange the formula to make the distance moved by the load the subject of the equation. This gives

$$\text{Distance moved by load} = \frac{\text{Distance moved by effort}}{VR}$$

$$= \frac{\text{Distance moved by effort}}{2.5}$$

Answers: a) 8 cm   **b)** 1.6 m   **c)** 2.48 m

Efficiency

3. a) Efficiency = $\dfrac{\text{Useful work done by a machine}}{\text{Total work put into machine}} \times 100\%$

(The idea of 'useful work' implies some 'useless work'. This is usually work done by the machine in overcoming friction and in moving certain parts of the machine, e.g. in a pulley system work must be done to move the lower pulley system.)

The efficiency can also be written as:

b)   Efficiency = $\dfrac{\text{Mechanical advantage}}{\text{Velocity ratio}} \times 100\%$

Example   Complete the following table:

	Efficiency (no units)	Useful work out (J)	Total work in (J)	MA (no units)	VR (no units)
a)	25%	—	100	2	—
b)	70%	14	—	—	10
c)	85%	—	50	17	—

Method: You must approach this problem a stage at a time. Remember that the two formulae for efficiency are:

$$\text{Efficiency} = \frac{\text{Useful work out}}{\text{Total work in}} \times 100\%$$

and

$$\text{Efficiency} = \frac{\text{MA}}{\text{VR}} \times 100\%$$

Each problem is divided into two parts, separated by the vertical line. Substitute the figures given into the appropriate formula.

Answers: a) 25 J, 8   **b)** 20 J, 7   **c)** 42.5 J, 20

Work

In the previous section on efficiency, the idea of work was used. In physics, work is done when one form of energy is converted to another. Like energy, work is measured in joules. It is defined by the equation:

Work done = Force × Distance moved (in the direction of the force.)

Example   Calculate the work done when a horizontal force of 4 N moves an object a horizontal distance of

a) 2 m   b) 5 m   c) 100 m.

Method: Use the formula:

Work done = Force × Distance moved

Because both the force and the distance moved are horizontal, they are both in the same direction. Substituting in the formula gives:

Work done = 4 × Distance moved

Answers: a) 8 J   **b)** 20 J   **c)** 400 J

The idea of work can also be applied when an object is moved upwards. In this case the object is given potential energy.

Example   How much work is done when a mass of

a) 2 kg   **b)** 6 kg   **c)** 100 kg

is lifted on to a shelf 2 m high?

Method: The lifting force must be at least the same size as the weight of the mass. Weight is calculated using the formula:

$$\text{Weight} = \text{Mass} \times \text{Acceleration due to gravity}$$
$$= \text{Mass} \times 10$$
$$\therefore \text{Work done} = \text{Force} \times \text{Vertical distance moved}$$
$$= \text{Weight} \times \text{Vertical distance}$$
$$= (\text{Mass} \times 10) \times 2$$
$$= \text{Mass} \times 20$$

Answers: a) 40 J   **b)** 120 J   **c)** 2000 J

In both these examples, the force and the distance moved were both in the same direction. We shall now consider a situation when this is not so.

Example   A tractor pulls a log along the ground. The towing chain makes an angle of 30° with the horizontal. Calculate the work done if the log moves a distance of 20 m along the ground and the force applied is:

a) 200 N   **b)** 500 N   **c)** 1000 N

Method: It is helpful to draw a simple diagram:

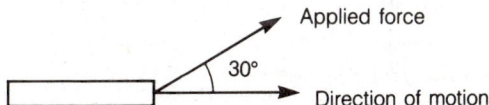

You may like to read the section on resolution (p.93) to help you understand this, but the formula for work done is developed to become:

$$\text{Work done} = \text{Force} \times \cos 30° \times \text{Distance moved}$$
$$= \text{Force} \times \cos 30° \times 20$$
$$= \text{Force} \times 0.8660 \times 20$$
$$= \text{Force} \times 17.32$$

Answers: a) 3464 J   **b)** 8660 J   **c)** 17 320 J

It is unlikely that you will meet anything as difficult as this in an examination.

Power

This is the rate at which one form of energy is converted to another form and is given by the equation:

$$\text{Power} = \frac{\text{Work done}}{\text{Time taken}}$$

Power is measured in joules/second or watts.

Electrical power is discussed on p.189 but in the following example we shall look at the conversion of the chemical energy in a student's body into potential energy.

Example A student has a weight of 600 N. Calculate the power of the student if he runs up a flight of stairs of vertical height 4 m in:

a) 10 s   **b)** 15 s   **c)** 25 s

Method: Using the formula:

$$\text{Power} = \frac{\text{Work done}}{\text{Time taken}}$$

and using the formula for work done we get:

$$\text{Power} = \frac{\text{Force} \times \text{Distance moved}}{\text{Time taken}}$$

$$= \frac{600 \times 4}{\text{Time taken}}$$

$$= \frac{2\,400}{\text{Time taken}}$$

Answers: a) 240 W   **b)** 160 W   **c)** 96 W

How powerful are you?

We can now look at problems on the individual machines.

Levers

These are the only machines which approach 100% efficiency, because the only friction is at the pivot or fulcrum. The only useless load to be moved is the weight of the lever itself, and this can often be very small compared to the load or effort. There are three main ways in which effort, load and fulcrum can be arranged.

1. With the fulcrum between the effort and the load (1st order).

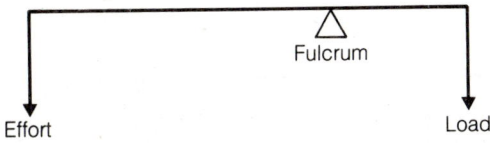

Fulcrum

Effort

Load

Example: A teaspoon to lift the lid off a tin.

2. With the load between the fulcrum and the effort (2nd order).

Effort

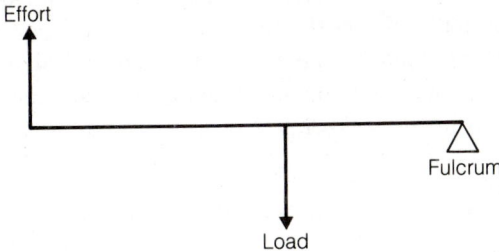

Fulcrum

Load

Example: A wheelbarrow with the fulcrum being the front wheel axle, the load being the barrow and its contents, and the effort being provided by you!

3. With the effort between the fulcrum and the load (3rd order).

Effort

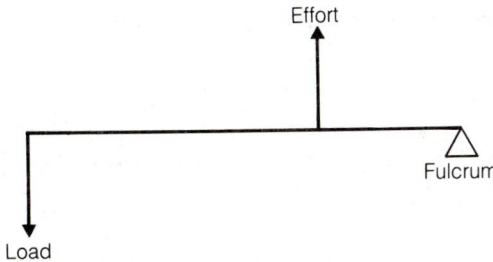

Fulcrum

Load

Example: A forearm lifting a heavy weight — the fulcrum is the elbow, the effort is supplied by the muscle in your upper arm and the load is the heavy weight.

Example What is the effort E required to lift the load using the following levers?

a)

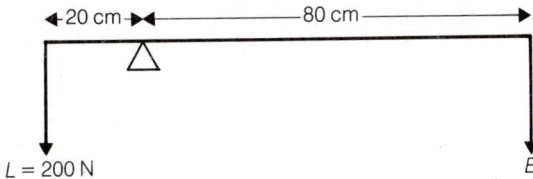

20 cm

80 cm

$L = 200$ N

E

b)

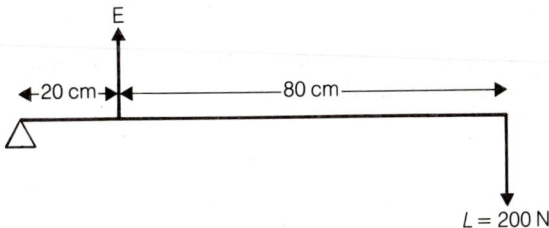

E

20 cm

80 cm

$L = 200$ N

c)

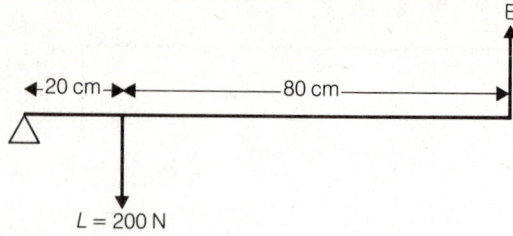

$L = 200\,N$

Method: With lever systems, unless you are told otherwise, the efficiency is 100%. From the formula relating efficiency to MA and VR you will see that this means that the mechanical advantage must equal the velocity ratio. In the levers shown you can work out the velocity ratio in the following way:

$$VR = \frac{\text{Distance moved by effort}}{\text{Distance moved by load in the same time}}$$

To work out both of these distances look at the position of the fulcrum and imagine, or sketch, what happens when the lever moves.

For example, in the first question

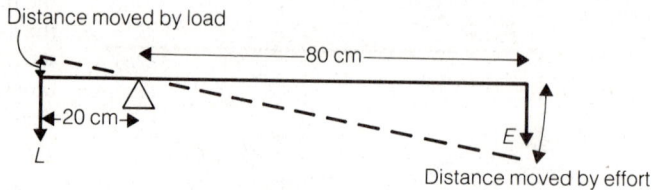

By proportions you should see that

$$\frac{\text{Distance moved by effort}}{80\,\text{cm}} = \frac{\text{Distance moved by load}}{20\,\text{cm}}$$

or

$$VR = \frac{\text{Distance moved by effort}}{\text{Distance moved by load}} = \frac{80\,\text{cm}}{20\,\text{cm}} = 4$$

Having calculated the velocity ratio, and assuming 100% efficiency, you then know that

$$VR = MA$$

Since

$$MA = \frac{\text{Load}}{\text{Effort}}$$

Rearrangement gives:

$$\text{Effort} = \frac{\text{Load}}{\text{MA}}$$

Note: In parts **b)** and **c)** make sure that you work out the effort and load distances *from the fulcrum*.

Answers: a) 50 N   **b)** 1000 N   **c)** 40 N

You may realize that these problems can also be solved using the principle of moments (see p.90).

Pulley systems

You will probably have seen pulleys on cranes, in engine hoists in a garage, and on yachts to vary the positions of the sails. The major disadvantage of pulleys is friction, but by oiling them regularly this can be reduced. Pulley systems are usually made up of two separate sets of pulleys, one set attached to a fixed point and the other attached to the object which is to be moved. Each pulley system will consist of one or more separate pulleys side by side, but in order to show the whole arrangement as clearly as possible the individual pulleys are usually shown below each other and of different sizes. For example:

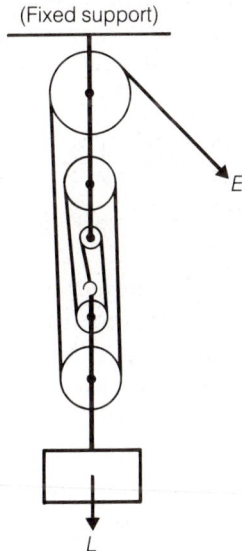

(Fixed support)

E

L

Note: If there is an odd number of pulleys in the whole system the extra pulley is on the fixed pulley unit.

In a pulley system like the one shown, the mechanical advantage is given by

$$MA = \frac{Load}{Effort}$$

where the effort is that force which will *just* lift the load at a constant velocity.

The velocity ratio is given by

$$VR = \frac{Distance\ moved\ by\ effort}{Distance\ moved\ by\ load\ in\ the\ same\ time}$$

In the diagram, suppose the load rises a vertical distance of 1 cm. This will happen if each of the vertical ropes (five in all) is shortened by 1 cm, and so the effort must pull off 5 cm of rope. Thus the velocity ratio of this system is given by

$$VR = \frac{5\ cm}{1\ cm} = 5$$

On all occasions the velocity ratio of a pulley system is equal to the total number of pulleys on the upper and lower system. (Do not be confused by an extra pulley placed out to one side. This is usually only included to make sure that the effort does not get tangled in the strings.) The efficiency of a pulley system is given by the formula:

$$Efficiency = \frac{MA}{VR} \times 100\%$$

The efficiency of a pulley system increases as the load gets bigger. The total load is made up of the actual load being lifted *plus* the weight of the lower pulley system, since the lower pulley system also moves with the load.

For relatively small loads the weight of the lower pulley system may form a significant part of the total load. As the load gets bigger, the weight of the lower pulley system forms a smaller and smaller part of the total load. This may sound odd but it can be explained using actual values. For example, suppose the lower pulley system has a weight of 1 N. Then for a measured load of 1 N, the total load being lifted will be 2 N (weight of lower pulley system + measured load). Thus the lower pulley system contributes 50% of the total load. However, if the measured load is 49 N, the total load being lifted will be 50 N (weight of lower pulley system + measured load) with the lower pulley system now contributing only 2% ($\frac{1}{50} \times 100$) of the total load.

Example   A student carried out an experiment with a pulley system of VR 5. The following results were obtained:

	Load (N)	Effort (N)	MA (no units)	VR (no units)	Efficiency
	0	0	0	5	0
a)	1.00	0.71	—	5	—
b)	2.00	0.91	—	5	—
c)	3.00	1.13	—	5	—
d)	4.00	1.36	—	5	—
e)	5.00	1.61	—	5	—
f)	6.00	1.88	—	5	—

Work out the mechanical advantage and efficiency of the pulley system for each load.

Method: The mechanical advantage can be calculated using

$$MA = \frac{Load}{Effort}$$

Having done this you can then work out the efficiency using

$$Efficiency = \frac{MA}{VR} \times 100\%$$

and substituting the velocity ratio value gives

$$Efficiency = \frac{MA}{5} \times 100\%$$

$$= 20 \times MA$$

Answers: a) 1.41, 28.2%
b) 2.20, 44.0%
c) 2.65, 53.0%
d) 2.94, 58.8%
e) 3.11, 62.2%
f) 3.19, 63.8%

You may like to plot a graph of y = efficiency against x = load, and estimate the maximum efficiency of the pulley system.

Can you suggest an approximate value for the weight of the lower pulley system?

Inclined planes

The inclined plane is not an obvious machine, but it makes it easier to move an object to a higher or lower position. You will probably have seen a workman running a wheelbarrow up a plank before emptying it into a skip, or someone pushing a supermarket trolley up a ramp. But a flight of stairs and a winding mountain road are also inclined planes. The mechanical advantage of an inclined plane is given by

$$MA = \frac{Load}{Effort}$$

Similarly, the velocity ratio of the inclined plane is given by

$$VR = \frac{Distance\ moved\ by\ effort}{Distance\ moved\ by\ load\ in\ the\ same\ time}$$

In order to work out these distances it is worth looking at the inclined plane as it would appear to someone out in space:

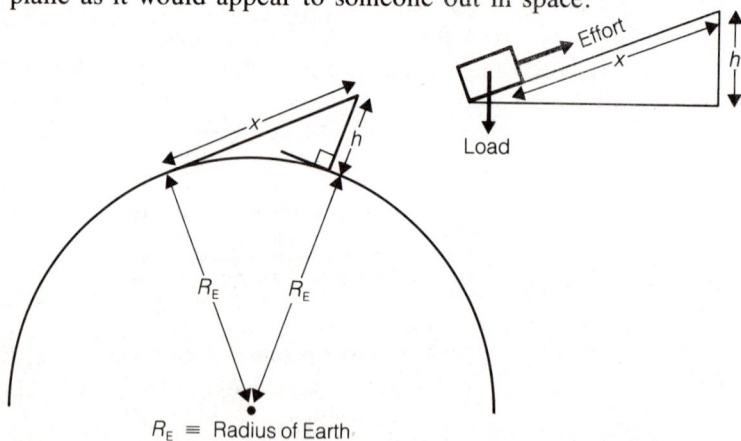

$R_E \equiv$ Radius of Earth

The distance moved by the effort force is x. In the same time the load will have moved a distance h farther away from the centre of the Earth. The velocity ratio can then be written:

$$VR = \frac{Length\ of\ inclined\ plane}{Vertical\ height\ of\ inclined\ plane}$$

$$= \frac{x}{h}$$

Example   An inclined plane is 12 m long. Calculate the velocity ratio of the plane if the vertical height is

a) 2 m   **b)** 3 m   **c)** 6 m

Method: Use the fact that the velocity ratio of an inclined plane is given by

$$VR = \frac{\text{Length of inclined plane}}{\text{Vertical height of inclined plane}}$$

$$= \frac{12}{h}$$

Answers: a) 6   **b)** 4   **c)** 2

Can you see how the thread on a screw is a sort of inclined plane?

Gears

Gears are used in many different types of more complicated machinery. You may have met them on a bicycle or in a car.

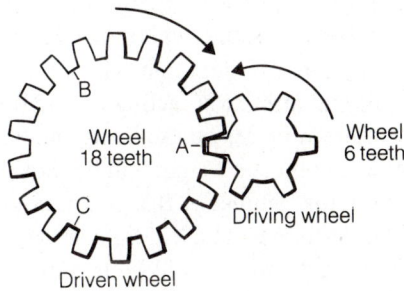

Driven wheel — Wheel B 18 teeth, C

Wheel A 6 teeth — Driving wheel

In the diagram, when the driving wheel turns once, the wheel being driven will make one-third of a revolution, i.e.

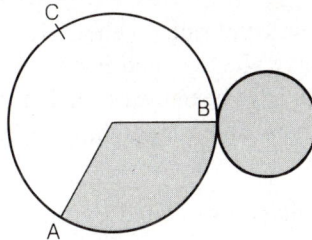

The driving wheel to which the effort has been applied has to turn three times to make the large driven wheel (connected to the load) turn once. The velocity ratio is given by:

$$VR = \frac{\text{Number of teeth on driven wheel}}{\text{Number of teeth on driving wheel}}$$

In this case the VR of the system is

$$VR = \frac{18}{6} = 3$$

Example Calculate the velocity ratio of a gear system when the driving wheel has 8 teeth, and the number of teeth on the wheel being driven is

a) 16   **b)** 12   **c)** 4

Method: Substitute the appropriate values into the formula

$$VR = \frac{\text{Number of teeth on driven wheel}}{\text{Number of teeth on driving wheel}}$$

Answers: a) 2.0   **b)** 1.5   **c)** 0.5

Mass and weight

Any object must have mass. This depends on the amount of matter it contains. In stable substances the number of protons, neutrons and electrons in the object is unlikely to change, and so the mass of the object will be the same wherever the object is taken. Mass is measured in grams or kilograms. The weight is the force of gravity, or the gravitational attraction, acting on the object. Because this varies between different places on the Earth, an object's weight will vary — for example an object's weight will be more at the North Pole than it is at the Equator. Similarly, the gravitational attraction force on the surface of the Moon will be less than anywhere on the Earth's surface and so the object's weight will be less on the Moon than it is on the Earth (about $\frac{1}{6}$ of its weight on Earth in fact). Being a force, weight is measured in newtons, although you may also meet gf and kgf (grams force and kilograms force respectively).

This may seem confusing — after all, you use a weighing machine to find how heavy you are, and it gives your weight in kilograms! The weight should have been measured in newtons, but the interchange of the words mass and weight has traditionally become part of the language we use.

Weight and mass are related by the formula:

$$\text{Weight} = \text{Mass} \times \text{Acceleration due to gravity}$$

or $W = m \times g$

Example Find the weight of a 4 kg mass when it is on a planet where the acceleration due to gravity is

a) $10 \, \text{m/s}^2$ **b)** $5 \, \text{m/s}^2$ **c)** $2 \, \text{m/s}^2$

Method: Using

$$W = m \times g$$

substitute the value for the mass

$$W = 4 \times g$$

and then use the different values for the acceleration due to gravity.

Answers: a) 40 N   **b)** 20 N   **c)** 8 N

The acceleration due to gravity on the Earth is usually taken to be $10 \, \text{m/s}^2$ but look at the front of an examination paper to be sure. This means that a mass of 1 kg will have a weight of 10 N.

Volume

The space occupied by anything is called its volume and can be measured in cm^3 or m^3. It is relatively easy to work out the volume of regularly shaped objects, but harder for bodies of irregular shape.

Irregularly shaped solids: You may be asked to find the volume of objects such as stones, clamp bosses or a quantity of lead shot. The easiest way to do this is to use a measuring cylinder of suitable size containing liquid, usually water, up to a given mark. The solid whose volume you wish to find should then be lowered *carefully* into the measuring cylinder until it is totally submerged.

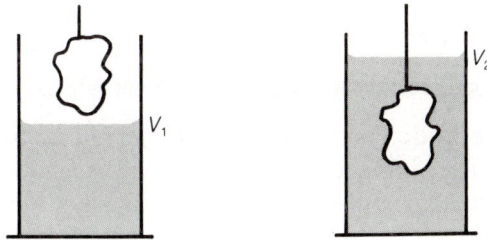

The volume of liquid displaced ($V_2 - V_1$) is equal to the volume of the solid.

Example   The level of water in a measuring cylinder is on the $50 \, \text{cm}^3$ mark. Calculate the volume of a solid which, when totally submerged, produces a new reading of

a) $75 \, \text{cm}^3$ **b)** $100 \, \text{cm}^3$ **c)** $200 \, \text{cm}^3$

Method: The volume of the solid is given by the difference in the two readings, i.e. $(V_2 - V_1)$

Answers: a) 25 cm³   **b)** 50 cm³   **c)** 150 cm³

This approach assumes that the body sinks and does not float. Can you think how you might find the volume of an object that floats? One way is to attach a dense object of known volume to the object whose volume you want to find. This will pull the object which previously floated below the liquid level.

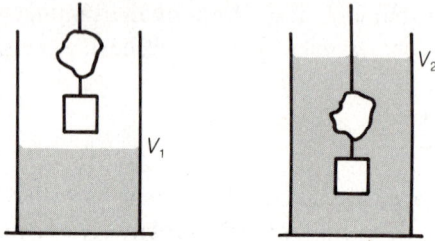

The difference in the two liquid levels $(V_2 - V_1)$ is then equal to the volume of the two objects. If you know the volume of the dense object, you can find the volume of the object which previously floated.

Example   An object which floats in water has a dense object of volume 12 cm³ attached to it. When the two objects are carefully lowered into the water the liquid level rises from 40 cm³ to:

a) 70 cm³   **b)** 85 cm³   **c)** 100 cm³.

Calculate the volume of the object which previously floated.

Method: First work out the volume of the two objects. This is equal to the difference in the two liquid levels. Having worked out this volume, you then subtract the volume of the dense object. This will give you the volume of the solid which previously floated.

Answers: a) 18 cm³   **b)** 33 cm³   **c)** 48 cm³

An alternative method of measuring the volume of an irregularly shaped object is to use the displacement can discussed in the section on Archimedes' Principle (see p.85). The volume of liquid flowing out of the spout is equal to the volume of the irregularly shaped object.

Liquids: A liquid will take up the shape of the container into which it is poured. If you choose a container such as a measuring cylinder which has graduations marked on it, you can work out the volume of the liquid.

Gases: Similarly, gases take up the volume of their container, so if you know the volume of the container you also know the volume of the gas. If the container has an irregular shape, for example a test tube, you can find its volume by pouring water into it and then pouring the water into a measuring cylinder. The volume of the water will be equal to the volume of the container.

Density

In order to calculate the density of any material use the formula

$$\text{Density} = \frac{\text{Mass}}{\text{Volume}}$$

The mass can be found using a balance, or set of scales, and the volume can be worked out using one of the ways outlined in the previous section.

Example Complete the following table:

	Material	Mass (kg)	Volume (m³)	Density (kg/m³)
a)	Iron	16 000	2	—
b)	Petrol	4 000	5	—
c)	Air	78	60	—

Method: In each case use

$$\text{Density} = \frac{\text{Mass}}{\text{Volume}}$$

Answers: a) 8000 kg/m³   **b)** 800 kg/m³   **c)** 1.3 kg/m³

Slightly more difficult are problems where you must rearrange the equation to calculate the mass or the volume.

Example   Complete the following table:

Material	Mass (kg)	Volume (m³)	Density (kg/m³)
a) Water	—	8	1000
b) Aluminium	5400	—	2700
c) Mercury	—	0.002	13 600

Method: Again use

$$\text{Density} = \frac{\text{Mass}}{\text{Volume}}$$

but this time rearrange the formula to make either the mass or the volume the subject of the equation. You may find the use of a triangle helpful (see p.2):

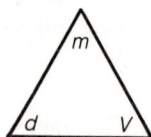

where d = density, m = mass and V = volume.
So that

$$\text{Density} = \frac{\text{Mass}}{\text{Volume}}, \quad \text{Volume} = \frac{\text{Mass}}{\text{Density}}, \quad \text{Mass} = \frac{\text{Density}}{\text{Volume}}$$

Answers: a) 8000 kg   **b)** 2 m³   **c)** 2.72 kg

Relative density

If you make, or help to make, wine or beer you may have heard relative density referred to as *specific gravity*. Both mean exactly the same thing although relative density is the usual term in physics. It tells you how dense a substance is relative to water and can be measured using a piece of equipment called a hydrometer. This device floats upright to different depths depending on the density of the liquid in which it is placed. There are several formulae used to work out relative density, but all are based on the formula

$$\text{Relative density} = \frac{\text{Density of substance}}{\text{Density of water}}$$

Example You are given the densities of several different materials. Work out their relative densities. (The density of water is 1 g/cm^3.)

Material	Density (g/cm^3)	Relative density (no units)
a) Methylated spirit	0.8	—
b) Copper	8.9	—
c) Mercury	13.6	—

Method: Substitute the values you are given in to

$$\text{Relative density} = \frac{\text{Density of substance}}{\text{Density of water}}$$

Answers: a) 0.8   **b)** 8.9   **c)** 13.6

Note: The relative density has no units and is just a number.

Pressure

Pressure is defined by the equation:

$$\text{Pressure} = \frac{\text{Force}}{\text{Area}}$$

Example A brick has a mass of 2 kg and has dimensions of 30 cm × 12 cm × 10 cm. Calculate the pressure that it exerts when placed on
a) face A   **b)** face B   **c)** face C

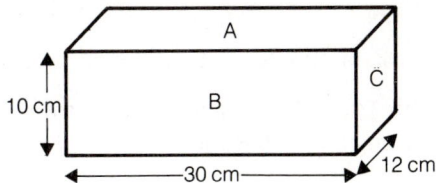

Method: The force exerted by the 2 kg brick is the weight of the brick. The weight is given by $W = m \times g$ (see p.78). The weight of the 2 kg brick is therefore 20 N. You can then use

$$\text{Pressure} = \frac{\text{Force}}{\text{Area}}$$

$$= \frac{20 \text{ N}}{\text{Area}}$$

To calculate the area of one face use the formula for the area of a rectangle, which is

$$\text{Area} = \text{Length} \times \text{Breadth}$$

Calculate the area in cm^2, so that the units of pressure become N/cm^2.

Answers: a) 0.056 N/cm^2 **b)** 0.067 N/cm^2 **c)** 0.17 N/cm^2

Was the greatest pressure exerted when the force acted over the smallest area?

When calculating pressure in fluids (liquids and gases), another formula to use is

$$\text{Pressure} = d \times g \times h$$

where d = density of substance
  g = acceleration due to gravity
  h = vertical height above point at which pressure is being calculated.

Example If the acceleration due to gravity is 10 m/s^2 and the density of water is 1000 kg/m^3, calculate the pressure due to the water at depths of

a) 5 m   **b)** 20 m   **c)** 30 m

Method: Use

$$p = d \times g \times h$$

and substitute the values given:

$$p = 1000 \times 10 \times h$$
$$= 10\,000 \times h$$

The units are N/m^2 or Pascals. The answers are given in kPa (Pa $\times$ 10^3).

Answers: a) 50 kPa   **b)** 200 kPa   **c)** 300 kPA

From this you will see that the pressure in the water increases with depth. Remember that the total pressure at any depth is given by

Total pressure = Atmospheric pressure + Water pressure

because atmospheric pressure presses on the water surface.

Example A mercury barometer can be used to measure air or atmospheric pressure. If the density of mercury is 13 600 kg/m^3, calculate the height of the mercury column if the atmospheric pressure is:

a) 100 kPa   **b)** 103 kPa   **c)** 105 kPa

Method: Again use

$$p = d \times g \times h$$

Rearrange to make h the subject of the equation, i.e.

$$h = \frac{p}{d \times g}$$

Substituting the values of d and g gives

$$h = \frac{p}{13\,600 \times 10}$$

Remember to convert kPa into Pa by multiplying by 1000.

Answers: a) 0.74 m   **b)** 0.76 m   **c)** 0.77 m

Archimedes' Principle and the Law of Flotation

Archimedes' principle: If you go for a swim, you will know that the water supports your body and indeed makes you appear to weigh less. This would be the case in any liquid because, when you displace some liquid, the liquid exerts an upthrust. This is also true of gases, but because your body would displace a much smaller weight of gas, the upthrust is much less.

There are three possible situations for the body shown:

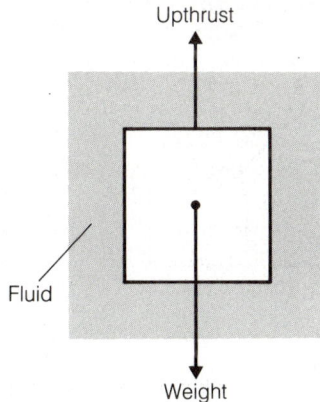

1. If its weight is greater than the upthrust of the fluid then it will sink, e.g. a stone in water.
2. If the upthrust is greater than the body's weight then the body will rise, e.g. a helium-filled balloon in air.
3. If the weight is exactly balanced by the upthrust then the body will float, e.g. a ship in sea water.

Archimedes' Principle tells us that when a body is either partly or totally immersed in a fluid it will experience an upthrust equal to the weight of fluid displaced.

Example A body weighs 50 N in air. Calculate its apparent weight in a fluid which provides an upthrust of:

a) 10 N   **b)** 15 N   **c)** 40 N

Method: The expression to use is

$$\text{Apparent weight} = \text{Weight in air} - \text{Upthrust}$$

In theory, the weight of a body in air is only its apparent weight because the displaced air will exert an upthrust but typically this is so small compared to the weight of the body that it can be ignored.

Answers: a) 40 N   **b)** 35 N   **c)** 10 N

You should remember that the upthrust is also equal to the weight of fluid displaced. Since the body is presumed not to change shape when placed in all three fluids, which of the fluids do you think is densest?

Archimedes' Principle can be tested by experiment.

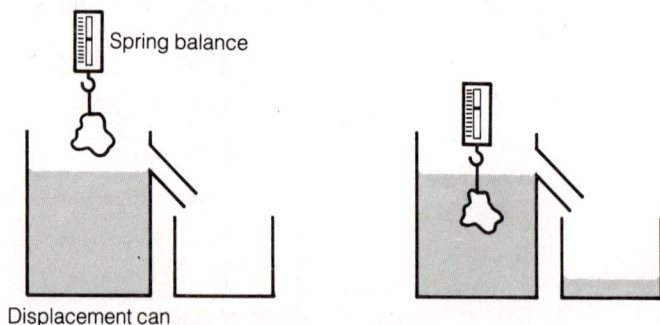

Spring balance

Displacement can

An object, which does not float in the liquid, is weighed in air on a spring balance. The liquid level in the displacement can (sometimes called the eureka can) is made level with the spout. The object is then carefully lowered into the liquid, and the liquid displaced by the object is collected in the previously weighed beaker. The weight of water displaced can be found and the apparent weight of the object can be read on the spring balance.

Example   If the following results were obtained for several different objects, show that Archimedes' Principle is true:

Weight of object in air (N)	Apparent weight of object in liquid (N)	Weight of empty beaker (N)	Weight of beaker plus liquid (N)
2.5	2.0	1.1	1.6
1.8	1.5	1.1	1.4
4.2	3.6	1.1	1.7
3.7	3.3	1.1	1.5
5.0	4.2	1.1	1.9

Method: Archimedes' Principle tells us that the upthrust is equal to the weight of fluid displaced. In this case the weight of fluid displaced is the difference in weight between the beaker containing liquid and the empty beaker. The upthrust is the apparent loss of weight, or the difference between the weight of the object in air and its apparent weight in the liquid. Copy and complete the following table:

Apparent loss of weight (N)	Weight of liquid displaced (N)

If Archimedes' Principle is true, then:

Apparent loss of weight = Weight of liquid displaced

Is this so?

Archimedes' Principle can also be used to work out other things like relative density. You will remember that

$$\text{Relative density} = \frac{\text{Density of substance}}{\text{Density of water}}$$

which can be rewritten as

$$\text{Relative density} = \frac{\text{Mass of substance/Volume of substance}}{\text{Mass of water/Volume of water}}$$

or

$$\text{Relative density} = \frac{\text{Weight of substance/Volume of substance}}{\text{Weight of water/Volume of water}}$$

(Because Weight = Mass × Acceleration due to gravity.)

If the object is totally submerged in water, then the object will displace a volume of water equal to the volume of the object. The equation can then be written as

$$\text{Relative density} = \frac{\text{Weight of substance}}{\text{Weight of water}}$$

since the volume of substance is equal to the volume of water.

Remember that the weight of water displaced is equal to the Archimedes' upthrust, or apparent loss of weight of object, and so the equation becomes

$$\text{Relative density} = \frac{\text{Weight of substance}}{\text{Apparent loss of weight of substance}}$$

Example When an object is hung from a spring balance, the balance reads 10 N. When it is totally submerged in water, the balance reads:

a) 8 N   **b)** 5 N   **c)** 2 N

Calculate the relative density of the object.

Method: Use

$$\text{Relative density} = \frac{\text{Weight of substance}}{\text{Apparent loss of weight of substance}}$$

$$= \frac{\text{Weight of substance}}{\text{Weight of substance} - \text{Weight of substance in water}}$$

Answers: a) 5.00   **b)** 2.00   **c)** 1.25

The law of flotation: This is really a special case of Archimedes' Principle and is the situation in which the weight of the body is exactly balanced by the upthrust from the fluid. A possible way of stating the law is to say that, if a body is to float, it must displace its own weight of the fluid in which it is floating.

What you should remember is that, if the body is floating in a liquid, the body is likely to float with a certain amount of itself above the fluid.

Example
A flat-bottomed barge has a base area of $24\,m^2$, and weight of $15\,000\,N$. Calculate the depth to which the barge will sink in fresh water of density $1000\,kg/m^3$ when it carries:

a) no cargo   **b)** cargo of weight $5000\,N$ **c)** cargo of weight $7500\,N$

Method: When it floats, the barge, with or without cargo, must displace its own weight of water.

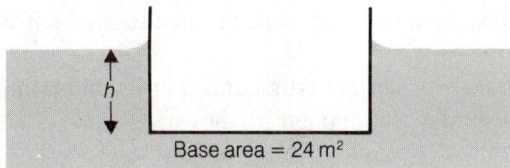

Base area = 24 m²

Thus

Weight of barge + Weight of cargo = Weight of water displaced

The weight of water displaced is given by

$$W = \text{Mass} \times \text{Acceleration due to gravity}$$

$$= m \times g$$

$$= \text{Density} \times \text{Volume} \times g \quad \left(\text{since } d = \frac{m}{V}\right)$$

$$= d \times V \times g$$

$$= d \times A \times h \times g \qquad (\text{since } V = A \times h)$$

Substituting gives

$$W = 1000 \times 24 \times h \times 10$$
$$= 240\,000 \times h$$

Then following the law of flotation equate the weight of water displaced to the weight of barge and cargo, i.e.

$$\text{Weight of barge and cargo} = 240\,000 \times h$$

or
$$h = \frac{\text{Weight of barge and cargo}}{240\,000}$$

Answers: a) 0.063 m or 6.3 cm **b)** 0.083 m or 8.3 cm
c) 0.094 m or 9.4 cm

Moments and the centre of gravity (or centre of mass)

Moments: You will have been aware since you were very small that it takes at least two people to make a seesaw work. You will also know that the plank must rest on a pivot (also called a *fulcrum*). Usually the plank is balanced on the pivot (see the later section on centre of gravity). Any force which is applied to the plank will have a moment, or turning effect, about the pivot. This moment is given by the expression

Moment = Force × Perpendicular distance from the pivot

and, for the plank to balance, the moment on one side of the pivot must be equal and opposite to the moment on the other side.

Example   A metre ruler is first balanced at its mid-point. It then has forces of 20 N and y N applied as shown:

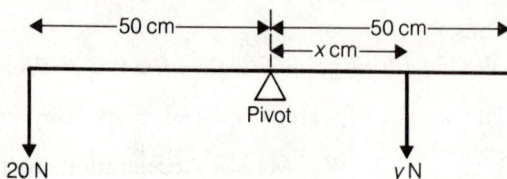

The metre ruler is in equilibrium and so the moments of the 20 N and y N forces are equal and opposite. Calculate the value for y if x is:

a) 20 cm   **b)** 30 cm   **c)** 40 cm

Method: The 20 N force creates an anticlockwise moment trying to turn the ruler in an anticlockwise direction. This moment is given by

Anticlockwise moment = Force × Perpendicular distance from pivot
$$= 20\,\text{N} \times 50\,\text{cm}$$
$$= 1000\,\text{N cm}$$

This is balanced by the clockwise moment given by the y N force and is given by

Clockwise moment = Force × Perpendicular distance from pivot
$$= y\,\text{N} \times x\,\text{cm}$$
$$= y \times x\,\text{N cm}$$

In equilibrium

$$\text{Anticlockwise moment} = \text{Clockwise moment}$$

$$1000\,\text{N cm} = y \times x\,\text{N cm}$$

or

$$y = \frac{1000}{x}\,\text{N}$$

Answers: a) 50 N   **b)** 33.3 N   **c)** 25 N

A slightly more complicated situation arises when there is more than one force on either or both sides of the pivot.

Example

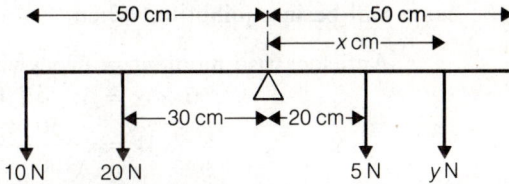

Again the ruler is in equilibrium under the action of the four forces. What is the value for y if x is:

a) 30 cm   **b)** 40 cm   **c)** 50 cm?

Method: In equilibrium:

Sum of anticlockwise moments = Sum of clockwise moments

or

$$10 \times 50 + 20 \times 30 = 5 \times 20 + y \times x$$
$$500 + 600 = 100 + y \times x$$
$$1100 = 100 + y \times x$$
$$1000 = y \times x$$

or

$$y = \frac{1000}{x}$$

Answers: a) 33.3 N   **b)** 25 N   **c)** 20 N

Note: the reaction force at the pivot is equal to the sum of the forces acting downwards, i.e. $(35 + y)\,\text{N}$.

Example A uniform beam is balanced as shown in the diagram by a force of 50 N. Calculate the weight of the beam if x is:

a) 10 cm   **b)** 25 cm   **c)** 40 cm

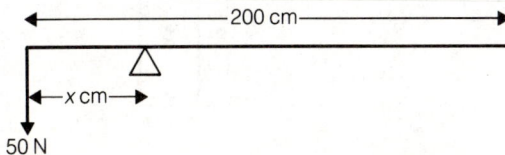

Method: As you will see in the next section, all of the weight of an object is assumed to act at a single point. In the case of a *uniform* beam this point will be at the half-way mark. The diagram can then be redrawn as

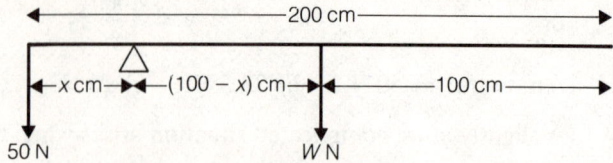

You will see that the distance of W from the pivot is $(100 - x)$ cm. The beam will be in equilibrium when

$$\text{Anticlockwise moment} = \text{Clockwise moment}$$
$$50 \times x = W \times (100 - x)$$

or
$$W = \frac{50 \times x}{(100 - x)}$$

Answers: a) 5.6 N   **b)** 16.7 N   **c)** 33.3 N

Centre of gravity or centre of mass: This is defined as the point in a body at which all of its weight or mass appears to act. This means that when the body is balanced at this point, the sum of the clockwise moments acting on the body is equal to the sum of the anticlockwise moments:

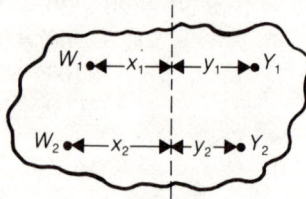

i.e. $W_1 x_1 + W_2 x_2 + \ldots = Y_1 y_1 + Y_2 y_2 + \ldots$

Example Calculate the angle through which the object in the following diagram can be tilted before it will topple if h is:

a) 1 m   **b)** 2 m   **c)** 4 m

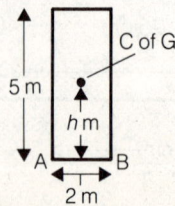

Method: The object will topple when the centre of gravity is directly over the pivot point, i.e. when the C of G is directly over A or B. You must calculate the angle through which the object must turn before this situation arises. A sketch diagram will aid the solution.

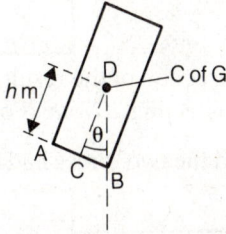

The object must turn through the angle θ which is given by

$$\tan \theta = \frac{BC}{DC} = \frac{1}{h}$$

and so you can calculate θ.

Answers: a) 45.0°   **b)** 26.6°   **c)** 14.0°

How does the position of the centre of gravity affect the stability of the object?

Vectors, scalars, resultants and resolution

Vectors and scalars: At first sight this seems to be one of the most difficult topics in the physics course — but it can be mastered! What you must accept is that a vector quantity has both a size (magnitude) and a direction. This distinguishes it from a scalar quantity, which has size only. For example, if you live in Manchester and you are told to get on your bicycle and travel at 10 km/hour you could, in time, find yourself in Glasgow, Liverpool, Newcastle, Cardiff or Birmingham, amongst many other places. This is because you have only been told the *size* of the speed at which you should travel. If you had been told the *direction* in which you were to travel you would have known exactly where to go. You would, in fact, have been given a *velocity*.

Speed is a scalar quantity, having size only; velocity is a vector quantity having size and direction. Other examples of scalar quantities are mass, temperature, energy and frequency. Other vector quantities include acceleration, force and momentum.

Resultants: Consider an object on which two forces are acting in opposite directions as shown.

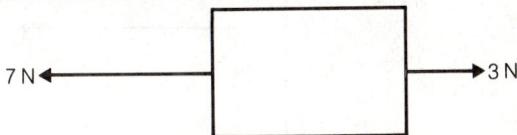

The resultant is the single force which would have the same effect as the two separate forces, i.e.

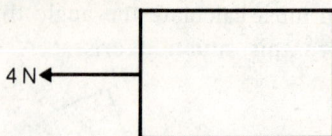

4 N ←

Note that the direction of the resultant is to the left — the direction in which the 7 N is acting. (*Note*: Force is a *vector*.)

Suppose instead the two forces had been acting in the same direction:

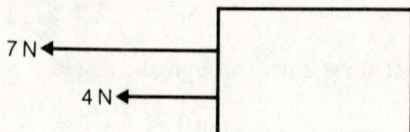

7 N ←

4 N ←

The resultant force which would produce the same effect is:

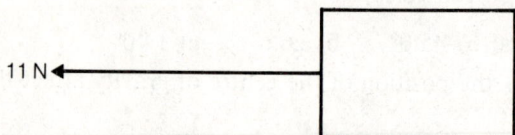

11 N ←

with the resultant force acting in the same direction as the two forces.

The situation becomes more complicated if the forces do not act in the same or opposite directions.

There are two ways in which to approach such problems. One is by drawing scale diagrams and the other is by using trigonometry. We shall consider the scale diagram first — it is the easier of the two methods.

1. Scale diagram method:

Any vector can be represented by a line, the length of which is proportional to the magnitude (or size) of the quantity and the direction of which is shown by the direction of the line. For example, the lines AB and CD represent vectors of the same size (they are the same length) but with different directions: in fact there is a 90° difference in direction. (The arrows show the direction in which the vectors act.)

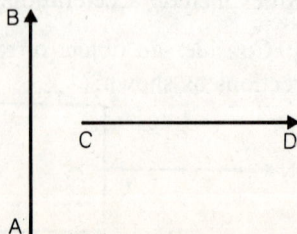

B ↑

C ──────────→ D

A

This fact can then be used to find the resultants of two or more vectors.

Example   Find the resultant of an 8 N and a 6 N force, when the angle between the two forces is

a) 60°   **b)** 90°   **c)** 120°

Method: First draw a line proportional in length to one of the forces — say an 8 cm line to represent the 8 N force. A protractor is then used to measure the appropriate angle on one end of the line. A 6 cm line can then be drawn to represent the 6 N force:

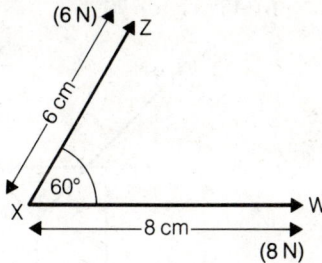

Complete the parallelogram of which these two forces form two sides:

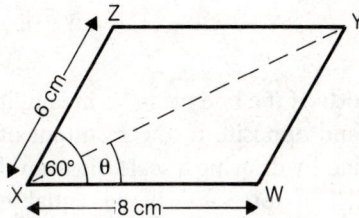

The diagonal XY will be equal in length and in the same direction as the resultant of the 6 N and the 8 N forces. By measuring the length of XY and remembering the scale that you used, in this case 1 cm = 1 N, you can work out the size of the resultant force. The angle θ can be measured using a protractor, so that you can then state the direction of the resultant force relative to the 8 N force (or alternatively the angle between the resultant and the 6 N force can be stated).

Answers:
a) 12.2 N at an angle of 28° to the 8 N force
b) 10 N at an angle of 41° to the 8 N force
c) 7.2 N at an angle of 51° to the 8 N force

Your answer should be within 0.5 N of these values and within 2° of the angle.

Remember that this resultant force is the single force that will produce exactly the same effect as the 6 N and 8 N acting together. The direction in which it acts is most important and must be stated.

You may meet a problem in which a body is in equilibrium under the effect of three or more forces, i.e. the forces all balance out and the body remains stationary.

Example   A force F keeps a body in equilibrium when acted upon by a 5 N and a 7 N force as shown. What is the size of the force F when the angle θ is:

a) 20°   **b)** 45°   **c)** 70°?

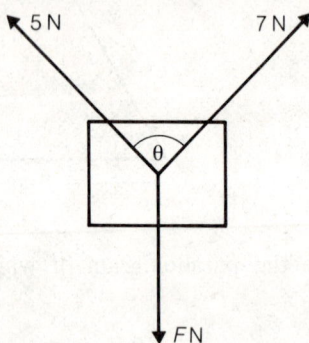

Method: If the body is to be in equilibrium then the force F must be equal and opposite to the resultant of the 5 N and 7 N forces. You must find by drawing a scale diagram the resultant of the 5 N and 7 N forces. The force F will be equal in magnitude but opposite in direction to this resultant.

Answers:
a) 11.8 N at an angle of 168° to the 5 N force
b) 11.1 N at an angle of 154° to the 5 N force
c) 9.9 N at an angle of 138° to the 5 N force

2. Mathematical method:

The mathematical approach is harder and you will probably find problems not involving at least one right angle too difficult unless your mathematics ability is very good. In any case you are most unlikely to meet problems which are too complicated in your examinations.

Example

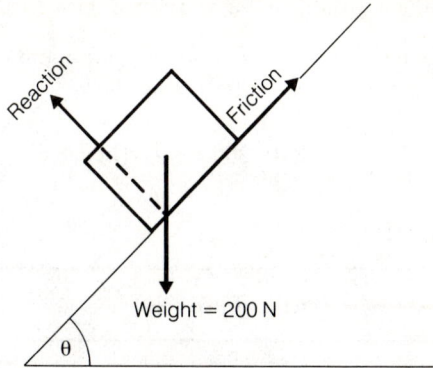

Weight = 200 N

The diagram shows a block of weight 200 N at rest on a slope which makes an angle θ with the horizontal. All the forces acting on the block are shown. Calculate the friction and reaction forces if the angle θ is:

a) 20°   **b)** 30°   **c)** 50°

Method: You could draw a scale diagram and remember that the weight must be equal in magnitude but opposite in direction to the resultant of the friction and reaction forces. However, you can also approach the problem mathematically. To do this it is helpful to redraw the diagram and add some extra information.

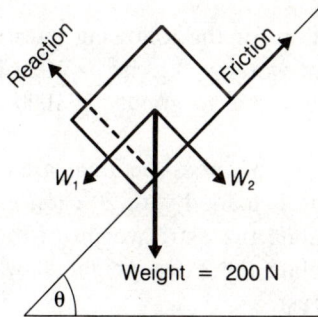

Weight = 200 N

The forces which are parallel to the plane must balance.

∴ Friction force = Resolved component of weight down the plane (W_1)

$$F = 200 \sin\theta \quad \text{because} \quad \frac{W_1}{200} = \sin\theta$$

The forces that are perpendicular to the plane must balance or else the block would move at right angles to the plane.

$\therefore$ Reaction force = Resolved component of weight at right angles to the plane (W_2)

$$R = 200\cos\theta \quad \left(\text{because } \frac{W_2}{200} = \cos\theta\right)$$

Answers:

	Friction force (N)	Reaction force (N)
a)	68.4	188
b)	100	173
c)	153	129

Why not try the problem by drawing a scale diagram? You should expect an accuracy of $\pm 5\,\text{N}$ when you use the scale diagram approach.

Questions

Information for the following questions:
density of water = $1\,\text{g/cm}^3$ = $1000\,\text{kg/m}^3$;
acceleration due to gravity = $1000\,\text{cm/s}^2$ = $10\,\text{m/s}^2$.

1. A car ferry of cross-sectional area = $500\,\text{m}^2$ in the region of the water line is loaded with 20 cars, each of mass $1000\,\text{kg}$.
    a) Calculate the extra weight of the cars.
    b) Calculate the extra weight of water displaced, i.e. Archimedes upthrust.
    c) Calculate the volume of water displaced.
    d) Hence calculate the extra depth to which the car ferry sinks.

2. A cube of oak ($15\,\text{cm} \times 15\,\text{cm} \times 15\,\text{cm}$) floats in water so that $10\,\text{cm}$ is beneath the surface. The density of water is $1\,\text{g/cm}^3$
    a) State the law of flotation.
    b) Calculate the volume of the water displaced (this is easier if you draw a diagram).

c) Calculate the mass (and hence the weight) of the water displaced.

d) Calculate the weight of the cube (and hence its mass).

e) Calculate the density of the oak.

3. A block of wood, volume 30 cm^3 and density of 0.4 g/cm^3 floats on water.
    a) Calculate the mass and hence the weight of wood.
    b) State the law of flotation.
    c) Using the fact that the density of water $= 1$ g/cm^3, calculate the volume of the water displaced.
    d) Hence calculate the volume of wood immersed.

4. A stone of mass 100 g was lowered into water and displaced 60 cm^3 of water (density $= 1$ g/cm^3).
    a) Calculate the volume of stone.
    b) Calculate the mass (and hence the weight) of the water displaced.
    c) State Archimedes' Principle.
    d) Calculate the Archimedes upthrust on the stone.
    e) Calculate the apparent weight of stone in water.
    f) What is the density of the stone?

5. A balloon and its basket weigh 5000 N. If the balloon is of volume 2000 m^3 and contains helium, and the whole system is suspended in the atmosphere, held by a steel cable, calculate the tension in the cable. (Density of air $= 1.3$ kg/m^3, density of helium $= 0.20$ kg/m^3.)
    Suggested approach:
    a) Calculate the mass (and hence the weight) of the helium in the balloon.
    b) Hence calculate the total weight of system.
    c) Calculate the weight of air displaced.
    d) Calculate the Archimedes upthrust.
    e) You will appreciate from the diagram that

$$\frac{\text{Archimedes}}{\text{upthrust}} = \frac{\text{Tension in}}{\text{cable}} + \frac{\text{Weight of}}{\text{system}}$$

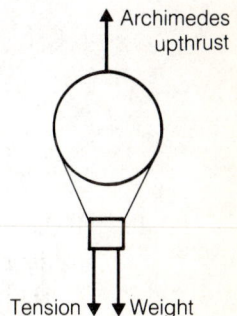

and so you can calculate the tension in the cable.

6. Draw a diagram of a single string pulley system with a velocity ratio of 5 (the upper pulley block will have three pulleys).

   For a given load, describe how you would determine the mechanical advantage of the system.

   How would you check that the velocity ratio was 5?

   Give two practical applications of pulleys.

7. The following results were obtained for a pulley system:

Load (N)	0	50	100	150	200	250	300
Efficiency (%)	0	15	30	40	45	47	48

   Plot these results on a graph of y = efficiency against x = load.

   Estimate the maximum efficiency of the system.

   Explain in detail the shape of the curve.

8. A person has a weight of 700 N and the total area of both his feet is 400 cm². Calculate the pressure he exerts when:
   a) standing on the ground;
   b) walking (one foot leaves the ground).
   c) Estimate the area of your body and then calculate the pressure if the person (with the same body area as you) were lying on the ground.

9. Calculate the pressure exerted on the ground by the box, the weight of which is 1200 N, when it is placed on the faces A, B and C.

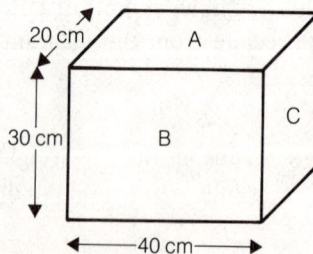

10. If the density of air is 1.29 kg/m³, calculate the mass of air in a room of dimensions:
    a) 3 m × 4 m × 2 m   b) 3 m × 10 m × 3 m
    c) 20 m × 30 m × 4 m
    In each case suggest a room that might fit these dimensions.

11.

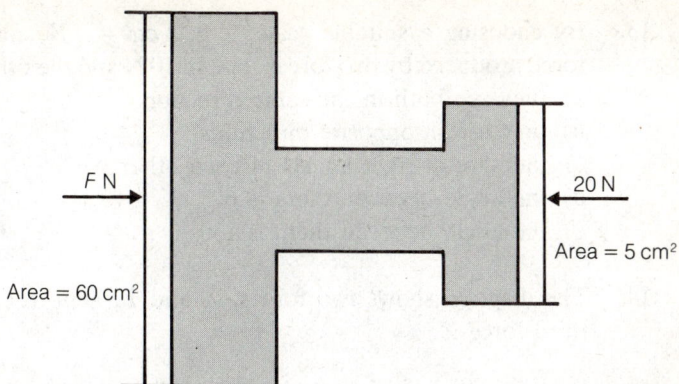

a) Calculate the pressure exerted by the force of 20 N on the 5 cm^2 face.
b) Knowing that pressure is transmitted equally through the fluid, calculate the force F exerted on the 60 cm^2 face.

12. The following results were obtained in an experiment to investigate how the length of a spring varied with the load hung from it.

Total length of spring (cm)	Load on spring (N)
3.5	10
4.5	20
5.9	34
6.7	42
8.1	56
9.5	70
10.4	79

a) What is the original length of the spring?
b) What is the weight of a stone giving an extension of 7.2 cm?
c) What extension will be produced by a load of 50 N?

13. By choosing a suitable scale, e.g. 1 cm = 1 N, find the resultant force produced by two forces, one of 10 N and the other of 7 N when:
   a) they are both in the same direction.
   b) they are in opposite directions
   c) they are at right angles to each other
   d) the angle between them is 60°
   e) the angle between them is 130°.

14. The diagram shows two forces, X and Y, kept in equilibrium by a third force Z.

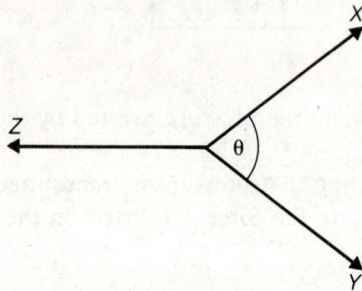

Find the value of Z and its direction relative to the force X, if the values of X, Y and θ are:

	X (N)	Y (N)	θ
a)	6	9	40°
b)	9	12	90°
c)	10	10	60°
d)	14	20	30°

15.

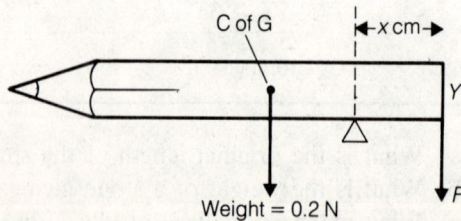

Weight = 0.2 N

A pencil has a weight of 0.2 N. It is balanced by placing it on a pivot and suspending a weight F from the end of the pencil. Calculate the distance of the centre of gravity of the pencil from Y if the values for F and x are:

	F (N)	x (cm)
a)	0.1	4
b)	0.2	3
c)	0.4	2
d)	0.5	1

16. Two boys carry a cricket holdall as shown:

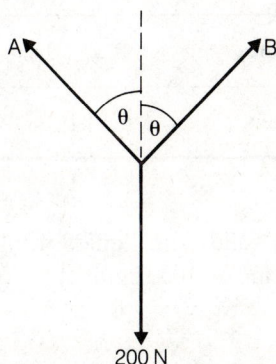

200 N

Determine the effort exerted by each boy if θ is:
    a) 20°   b) 30°   c) 40°

17. Calculate the density of:

a) aluminium in the shape of a cube of side 2 cm and mass 22 g
b) stainless steel in the shape of a block 3 cm × 4 cm × 10 cm, of mass 960 g
c) brass in the shape of a sphere of radius 2 cm and mass 860 g
d) water in an aquarium 20 cm × 25 cm × 30 cm and mass 15 kg.

18.   Complete the following table, remembering to include units:

Substance	Mass	Volume	Density
a) Gold	0.5 g	0.026 cm³	—
b) Zinc	—	4 cm³	7.14 g/cm³
c) Graphite	4 g	—	2.30 g/cm³
d) Concrete	1000 kg	0.42 m³	—
e) Rubber	7.3 g	8 cm³	—
f) Oak	—	0.036 m³	650 kg/m³
g) Alcohol	790 g	1000 cm³	—
h) Turpentine	—	250 cm³	0.87 g/cm³
i) Methane	—	200 m³	0.71 kg/m³
j) Nitrogen	625 kg	500 m³	—

Which of the solids and liquids would float on water? (Density of water = 1 g/cm³ or 1000 kg.m³.)

19.   Calculate the pressure exerted by the water at the following depths below the surface of the ocean:

a) 2 m   b) 30 m   c) 400 m

(Density of water is assumed uniform and equal to 1025 kg/m³, acceleration due to gravity = 10 m/s².)

What else would you have to know to find the *total* pressure at these depths?

How do a) fish, b) submarines manage to withstand the pressure at considerable depths?

20. Complete the following table for different machines:

Machine	Load (N)	Effort (N)	Mechanical advantage (no units)	Effort distance (m)	Load distance (m)	Velocity ratio (no units)	Efficiency (no units)
a) Lever	40	10	—	0.08	0.02	—	—
b) Pulley	—	10	3	1.0	0.25	—	—
c) Inclined plane	100	—	4	5.0	1.0	—	—
d) Pulley	24	4	—	—	0.5	—	60%
e) Inclined plane	500	—	2	2.5	1.0	—	—

Past examination questions

1. A, B and C are three identical blocks of wood measuring 2 cm × 5 cm × 10 cm. Each stands on a different face.

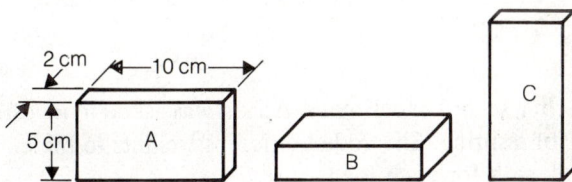

a) What is the area (in cm²) on which
   (i)   A rests?
   (ii) B rests?
   (iii) C rests?

b) (i)   Which block exerts the greatest pressure on the surface?
   (ii) Explain your answer.
   (iii) If each block weighs 1 newton, calculate the greatest pressure. [SWEB]

2. a)

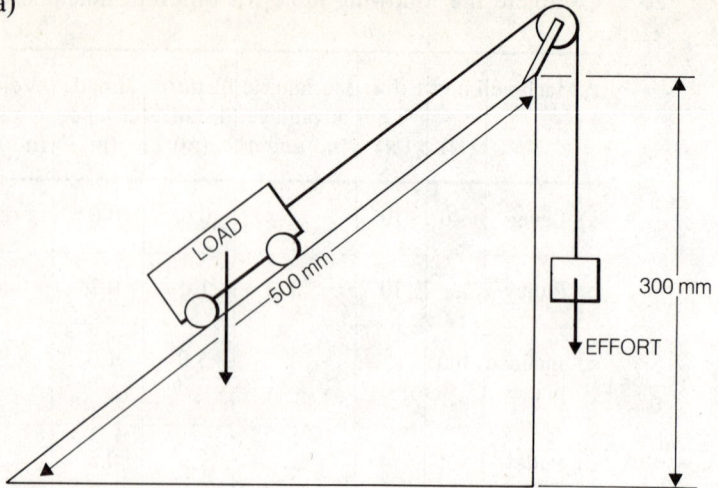

(i)   Give the equation used to work out *velocity ratio*.

(ii) Calculate the velocity ratio of the inclined plane shown in the diagram. Show your working. Give your answer in its simplest form.

(iii) The velocity ratio of a *bicycle* is *less* than 1. What is unusual about this?

b) (i)   Draw a diagram, showing a pulley system with a velocity ratio of 3. Label the load and effort.

(ii) In the above pulley system, what would be the *mechanical advantage* if the machine's efficiency was 50 per cent?

(iii) What would be the *efficiency* if the mechanical advantage was 2?

[SWEB (part)]

3. In a school experiment, Alison was asked to investigate the stretching of a spring. She added different weights to the end and measured its length for each load.

Her results are given in the table below:

Weight (newtons)	1	2	3	4	5	6	7	8	9
Length (centimetres)	3.6	4.6	4.8	5.6	6.6	6.8	7.6	8.2	9.2

She then plotted the graph shown.

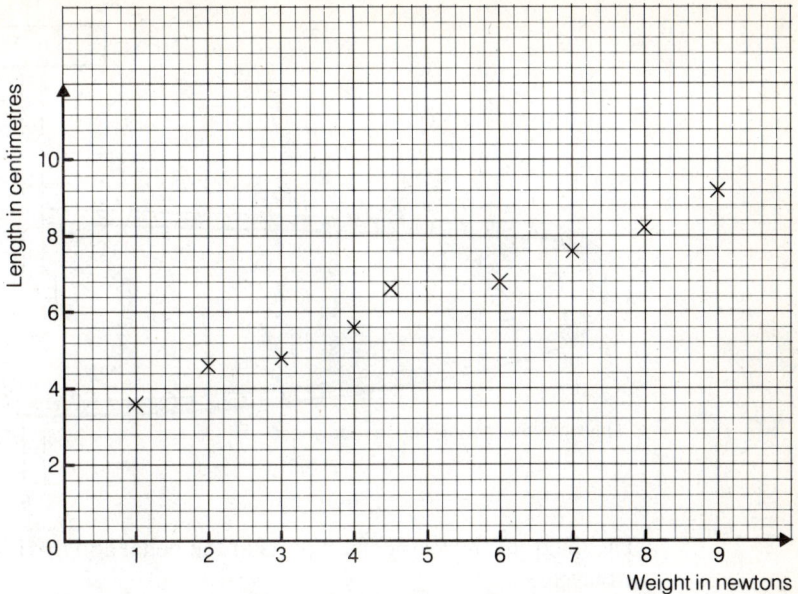

a) One of the points was plotted incorrectly. Which one?
b) What is the correct position for this point?
c) The points still do not lie on a perfectly straight line. Give one possible reason for this.
d) Plot the points on a piece of graph paper and draw the 'best' straight line for these results.
e) What was the 'unstretched' length of the spring?   [SWEB]

4. A load of 20 N is pulled 10 m up an inclined plane by a steady force of 5 N as shown in the diagram.

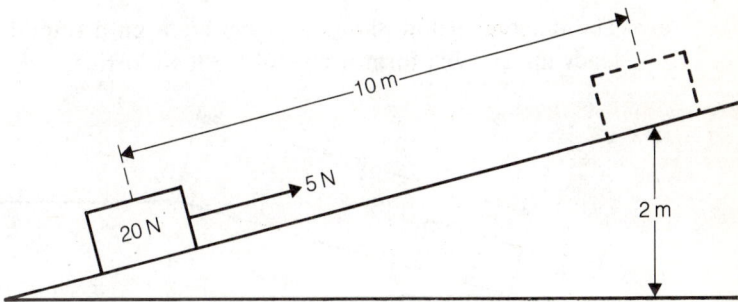

(i)   How much energy will the load have gained when it has been raised to a height of 2 m?
(ii) How much work is done in raising the load to this height?
(iii) What is the velocity ratio of the inclined plane?

[SWEB (part)]

5.

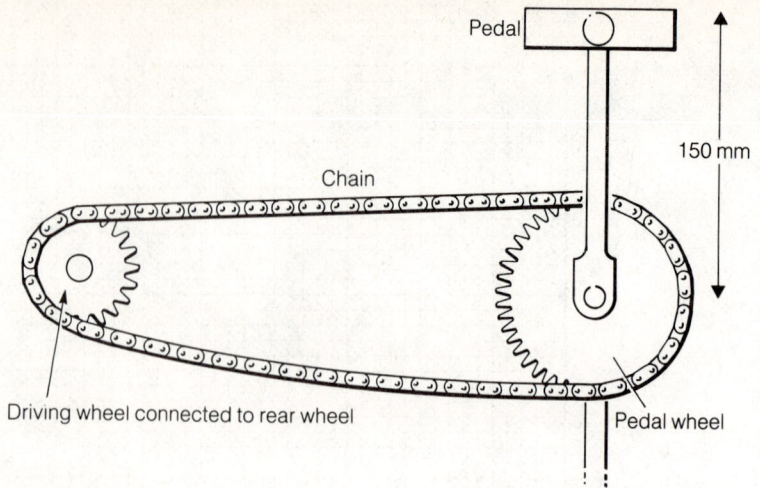

Chain

Pedal

150 mm

Driving wheel connected to rear wheel

Pedal wheel

The diagram shows the main parts of the pedal and driving wheels on a bicycle.

The pedal wheel has 50 teeth.

The driving wheel has 20 teeth.

(i) How many times does the rear wheel go round when the pedal goes round once?

(ii) The radius of the pedal crank is 150 mm (see diagram). The radius of the rear wheel (axle to tyre) is 250 mm. How many times is the rear wheel radius larger than the pedal crank radius?

(iii) Use your answers to parts (i) and (ii) to work out how far the bicycle moves forward when the pedal moves 1 metre.

[SWEB (part)]

6. The diagram below shows a heavy crate on a smooth slope which leads up to a platform used to help load lorries.

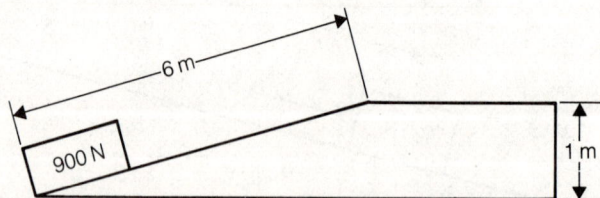

6 m

900 N

1 m

a) By using the ramp instead of lifting the box vertically on to the platform, what difference, if any, does this make to

(i) the force needed

(ii) the distance the box moves

(iii) the total work done on the box?

b) Which of the following is likely to be nearest in weight to 900 N?

   (i) A small child
   (ii) A large man
   (iii) A small car
   (iv) A heavy lorry.

c) By referring to your answer to b) suggest a suitable and appropriate motor driven machine which could be used to load the box directly on a lorry.

d) Calculate the minimum work needed to lift the crate vertically on to the loading platform. [LREB]

7. A 90 kg builder carries a 10 kg bucket of concrete up a ladder. He lifts himself and the bucket 5 m.
   a) Calculate the force (in newtons) the builder needs to exert to lift himself and the bucket.
   b) Calculate the work done by the builder.

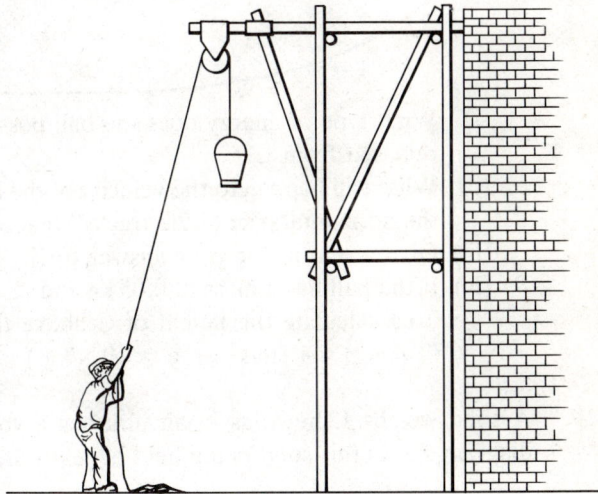

c) He could have lifted the bucket of concrete by using the pulley system shown. Explain why he would do less work in this way.
[SWEB]

8. a) The diagram below shows a see-saw of length 4 m which is pivoted at its mid-point. A small child of weight 200 N sits at one end of the see-saw at A.

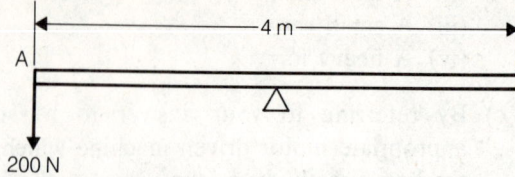

200 N

   (i)   Calculate how far from the centre of the see-saw the child's father must sit so that the see-saw balances horizontally if the father weighs 800 N.
   (ii) When the see-saw is fully tilted end A is 1.5 m above the ground. Calculate how much work is done in lifting the child from the ground through 1.5 m.

   b) Calculate the power developed in lifting a load of 200 N through a distance of 1.5 m in 4 seconds.

   c) Suppose that a ball bearing is released from point C down a frictionless track shaped as shown below.

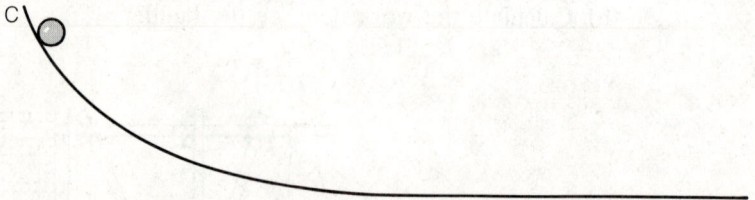

   (i)   What type of energy does the ball possess just before being released from C?
   (ii) What will happen to the velocity of the ball as it moves along the horizontal part of the track? (Ignore any air resistance.)
   (iii) Give a reason for your answer to (ii) above.
   (iv) If the ball has a mass of 0.05 kg and its stored energy at C is 0.1 J calculate the height of C above the ground.
         (Take $g = 10 \text{ m/s}^2$ or $g = 10 \text{ N/kg}$.)   [LREB (part)]

9. A solid weighs 12 newtons in air and has a volume 1000 cm³. The diagram shows this solid being held beneath the surface of a liquid.

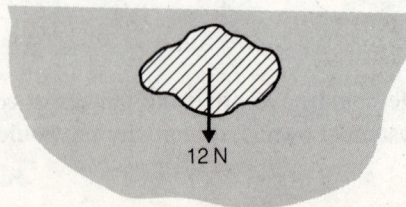

12 N

(i) What will happen to the solid, when released, if 1000 cm³ of the liquid weighs 8 N?

(ii) What will happen to the solid, when released, if 1000 cm³ of the liquid weighs 14 N?

(iii) Give a reason for your answer to part (ii) above.

[LREB (part)]

10. A steam engine which weighs 400 000 N climbs a slope which is 260 m long and rises a total vertical height of 10 m.

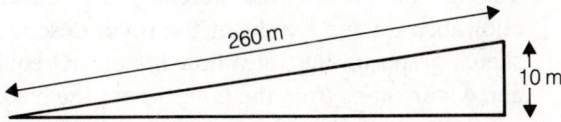

During the ascent the energy produced by the engine's furnace is 40 000 000 J.

(i) How much useful work is done on the engine during the ascent?

(ii) What is the percentage efficiency of the engine?

[LREB (part)]

11.

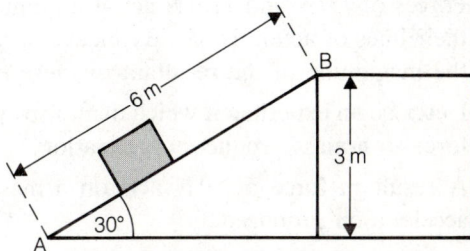

The diagram shows a packing case of weight 500 N on the inclined plane AB. Calculate how much work would be done in sliding the packing case up the inclined plane from A to B. The frictional force is 50 N.   [4]

State, giving your reason, whether the packing case would remain stationary if it were placed half-way up the inclined plane.   [2]

What effect would increasing the length of the inclined plane from B to the ground (keeping B at a height of 3 m above the ground) have on

(i) the velocity ratio, and

(ii) the efficiency of the inclined plane considered as a machine?

Give a reason for each of your answers. (You may assume that the frictional force does not change.)   [2, 2]

[London (part)]

12.   Draw a diagram of a wheel and axle arrangement which may be used for lifting heavy loads.   [3]

A wheel and axle arrangement is used to lift a bucket of water out of a well. Given that the wheel and axle have diameters of 1.40 m and 0.28 m respectively and that the greatest effort needed to lift 4 kg of water at a steady speed is 10 N, calculate

(i)   the velocity ratio,
(ii) the mechanical advantage,
(iii) the efficiency of the system.   [8]

Taking into account the weight of the bucket, and making some allowance for the weight of the rope, describe carefully (**or** draw a sketch graph to illustrate) how the effort required to lift the bucket and water varies from the point where the bucket is under the water, to where the full bucket is at the top of the well.   [5]
                                                                      [WJEC]

13.   Why is *force* referred to as a vector quantity?

Two forces acting at a point have magnitudes 5 N and 8 N. Explain why their resultant may have any magnitude between 3 N and 13 N.
                                                                        [4]

Forces of 7.0 N and 11.0 N act at a point so that the angle between their lines of action is 35°. By means of a scale diagram, determine the magnitude of the resultant of these two forces.   [4]

Describe an experiment which demonstrates that the application of a force to a mass produces acceleration.   [7]

A resultant force of 50 N acts on a mass of 4.0 kg. Calculate the acceleration produced.   [2]
                                                                  [Cambridge]

14.   a) A pupil performs an experiment to discover the effect of different forces on the length of a thin piece of elastic.
         Table 1 shows the results of his experiment.

                                TABLE 1

Length of elastic (cm)	15.3	20.0	24.7	29.4	34.1
Force pulling elastic (N)	0.00	0.10	0.20	0.30	0.40

         (i) Describe briefly how the pupil could have obtained the results in Table 1.

(ii) Draw a graph of 'length of elastic' against 'force pulling elastic' on graph paper. [4]

b) In a second experiment the pupil uses the same piece of elastic to measure the force which an air stream exerts on an aluminium sail.

An air track vehicle with an aluminium sail sits on a horizontal frictionless air track. The vehicle is attached to one end of the track by the piece of elastic and an air blower directs a steady stream of air onto the sail. The pupil measures the length of the stretched elastic.

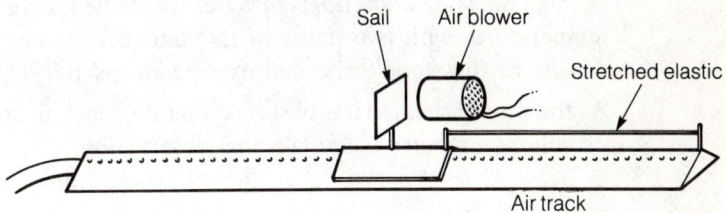

Table 2 shows the experimental results for sails of different area.

TABLE 2

Area of sail (cm^2)	20	50	80	100
Length of elastic (cm)	18.6	23.6	28.5	31.8
Force on sail (N)				

(i) Copy and complete Table 2 by writing down the force exerted by the air stream on each sail.
(ii) Use the results from Table 2 to show that the force on a sail varies directly as its area. [4]

c) In a final experiment the 100 cm^2 sail is bent backwards into a V-shape.

Is the length of the elastic again 31.8 cm? Explain your answer. [2]

[Scottish]

15. State Archimedes' Principle and describe an experiment you would perform to verify it. [3, 5]

A balloon with its contents has a mass of 1800 kg and occupies a volume of 2000 m³. It is held stationary, in still air, by a vertical rope fixed to the ground.
Determine
a) the upthrust on the balloon (take the density of the air surrounding the balloon to be 1.2 kg/m³), [2]
b) the tension in the rope, [2]
c) the initial acceleration of the balloon, if released. [3]

A small block of wood floats in water, contained in a beaker at room temperature, with two-thirds of its volume immersed. What is the density of the wood? The density of water is 1000 kg/m³.

As the water is heated it is observed that the block floats with more of its volume immersed. Explain this observation. [3]

[Oxford and Cambridge]

16. Draw a labelled diagram of a block and tackle pulley system which has two pulley wheels in each block. [4]

How would you measure the effort necessary to lift a load of 45 N using this system? Explain how far the effort would move if the load rises vertically by 20 cm. Calculate the efficiency of the system if an effort of 15 N is required. [7]

Why is the efficiency likely to be different for a much smaller load? State TWO methods by which the efficiency could be increased for a given load. [4]

[SWJB]

17. Define *moment of a force* and state a unit in which it may be measured. [3]

The diagram below shows a simple form of diving board.

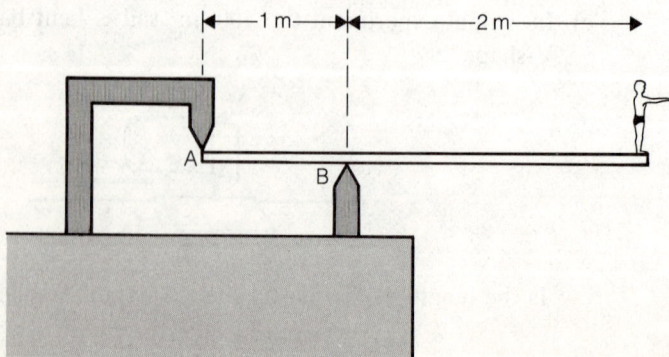

If the diver has a mass of 40 kg, calculate the magnitude and show the direction of the forces acting on the board at A and B if
(i) the mass of the board is negligible,
(ii) the board is uniform and has a mass of 20 kg. [9]

Describe, without calculation, what would happen to the forces at A and B if the diver were to walk towards B. [4]

[WJEC]

18. Describe how you would obtain, as accurately as possible, a series of readings for the load and corresponding extension of a spiral spring. [6]

A student obtained the following readings:

Load/N	0	1	2	3	4	5	6
Length of spring/cm	10.0	11.5	13.0	14.5	16.0	18.5	24.0

Using these results, plot a graph of load against extension and estimate the load beyond which Hooke's law is no longer obeyed. [7]

The spring is at rest with a mass of 0.2 kg on its lower end. It is then further extended by a finger exerting a vertical force of 0.5 N. Draw a diagram showing the forces acting on the mass in this position, giving the values of the forces. [3]

Describe the motion of the mass when the finger is removed. Make your description as precise as possible, by giving distances. State the position where the kinetic energy of the mass will be greatest. [4]

[London]

19. An inclined plane of length 4 m is used to raise a load of mass 20 kg through a vertical height of 1 m. It is found that an effort of 80 N is necessary to move the mass up the slope at a constant speed.
(i) Describe how you would apply the 80-N force. [2]
(ii) What is the velocity ratio of this inclined plane as a machine? [1]
(iii) Calculate the work done by the effort and the useful work done on the load. (Give your answers in joules.) [4]
Account for the difference between these two quantities and explain why they can never be equal in such a situation. [3]
(iv) Calculate the efficiency of this inclined plane as a system for raising loads. [2]

[London (part)]

20. a) Describe an experiment to show that for a body in equilibrium the sum of the clockwise moments about a point is equal to the sum of the anticlockwise moments about the same point. [6]

b)

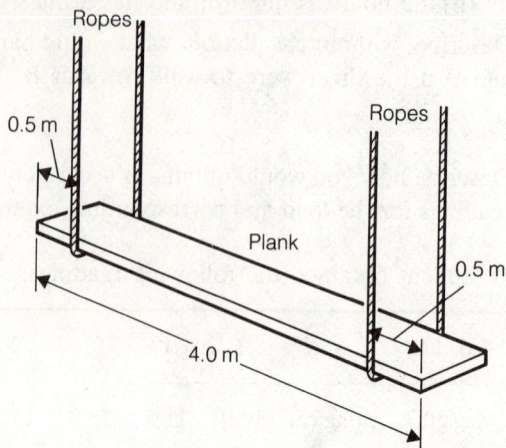

A painter stands on a uniform plank 4.0 m long and of mass 30 kg. The plank is suspended horizontally from vertical ropes attached 0.5 m from each end as shown in the diagram. The mass of the painter is 80 kg. Calculate the tensions in the ropes when the painter is 1.0 m from the centre of the platform. [8]

State briefly (no calculation required) how you would expect the tensions in the ropes to vary as the painter moves along the plank.

[2]

[London (part)]

21. State Archimedes' Principle. [3]

An irregularly shaped stone weighs 3.9 N in air, 2.4 N in water and 2.7 N in paraffin.

Find (i) the density of the stone, and (ii) the density of paraffin, assuming that the density of water is 1000 kg/m^3. [9]

A large polystyrene block is weighed using a spring balance. If the weighing could be repeated in a vacuum, would the weight be more, less or the same? Give **one** reason for your answer. [4]

[WJEC]

22. a) A uniform plank of length 4.4 m and weighing 200 N is placed horizontally and symmetrically on two supports which are 3.2 m apart. A man weighing 800 N stands on the plank over one of the supports.

Draw a diagram of the arrangement, showing clearly the forces acting on the plank. Calculate the force on each support. [7]

How far could the man move towards the nearer end of the plank before it starts to tip? [3]

b) An object moves in a circular path at uniform speed. Explain why its velocity is not uniform and a force is necessary to maintain it in this path. What is the direction of this force? [5]

[SWJB]

23.

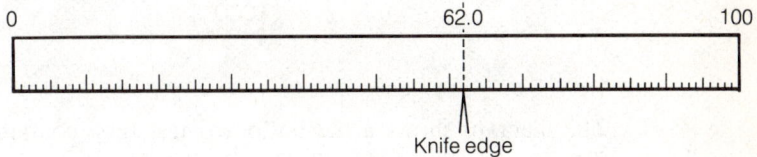

Knife edge

A knife edge is placed at the 62.0 cm mark of the *uniform* metre rule shown in the diagram. In order to balance the rule horizontally, a weight of 0.24 N is hung from one end. Show this weight on the diagram and also mark the weight W of the rule acting in the correct position.

Calculate the weight W of the rule. [Cambridge]

24. Explain what is meant by the term *centre of gravity*, and describe how it may be found for an irregularly shaped flat piece of cardboard. [6]

A uniform metre rule of mass 0.1 kg balances on a knife edge at its 40 cm mark when an unknown mass is placed over its 20 cm mark. Find the value of the unknown mass. [4]

After removing the unknown mass, the same metre rule is sawn through at its 20 cm mark and the short end is glued onto the rest of the rule as shown in the diagram (which is not drawn to scale).

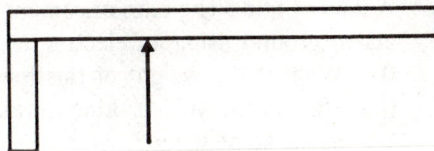

Find the point at which the rule will now balance. [6]

[WJEC]

25.

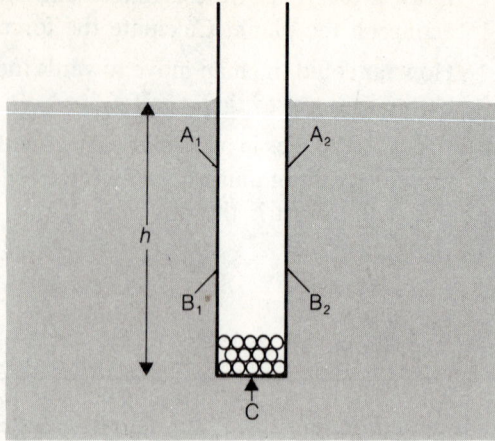

The diagram shows a flat-bottomed test tube containing lead shot floating upright in a liquid. Draw a diagram showing the forces per unit area acting on the test tube caused by the liquid at the points indicated by A_1, A_2, B_1, B_2 and C. (The relative sizes of the forces should be indicated.) [6]

The following readings were obtained for the total mass, M, of the test tube and lead shot, and the depth, h, of the test tube immersed as lead shot was added to the tube.

M(g)	48	55	60	65	73	77	84
h(cm)	8	9	10	11	12	13	14

Plot a graph of these readings. (You are advised to start your M axis at 40 g and your h axis at 8 cm.) [8]

From your graph find the depth immersed when M is 90 g. Use this result to find the area of the base of the test tube.
(Density of the liquid = 1.2 g/cm³, or 1200 kg m³.) [6]
[London]

26.   a) A load of five 50 kg bags of cement is raised to a scaffolding 20 m above ground using an electric motor and lifting tackle.
(i)   What is the weight of this load? [1]
(ii) How much work is done to raise the load to the scaffolding, at constant speed? [2]
(iii) If the load is raised in 25 seconds, what power is needed? [2]
(iv) If the efficiency of the electric motor and lifting tackle used is 40%, what must be the power of the motor? [3]

b) A boy raises one 50 kg bag of cement using a uniform plank 3 m long as a lever, as shown in the diagram. The bag of cement has its centre of mass 0.2 m from the end of the plank, and the pivot is 1 m from the same end of the plank. The boy applies a downward force at the other end to move the plank to a horizontal position.

(i) Neglecting the mass of the plank, calculate:
the distance of the centre of mass of the bag of cement from the pivot; [1]
the moment produced by the bag of cement about the pivot; [3]
the force applied by the boy. [2]

In practice, the mass of the plank is 10 kg.
(ii) Draw a diagram to show the positions and directions of all four forces acting on the plank to keep it horizontal. You need not show the values of the forces. [2]
(iii) Calculate the force applied by the boy, taking account of the mass of the plank. [4]

c) One 50 kg bag of cement falls 20 m from the scaffolding to the ground.
(i) Draw a graph to show how the potential energy of the bag of cement changes with height as it falls. Put accurate numerical scales on the axes. Label this graph P. [3]
(ii) Draw on the same figure a graph to show how the kinetic energy of the bag of cement changes with height as it falls. Label this graph K. [2]

[Oxford (part)]

27. A large tray containing water has a fine powder dusted onto its surface. A single drop of oil, of density 0.8 g/cm^3, is dropped onto the surface, where it spreads out into a circular film of radius 10 cm. The mass of 100 identical drops is found to be 0.04 g.
(i) What is the mass of one drop of oil? [1]
(ii) What is the volume of this drop? [2]
(iii) Calculate the area of the circular film of oil. [2]
(iv) Calculate the thickness of the oil film. [2]

[Oxford (part)]

28. A block of ice of mass 2 kg rests on top of a wet sheet of ice. Two strings attached to the block are pulled with horizontal forces at right angles of 3 N and 4 N respectively. The diagram shows a plan view. Frictional forces may be neglected.

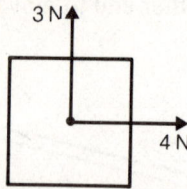

(i) What is the resultant force on the block? [2]
(ii) By scale drawing on the diagram (or by calculation) show the direction in which the block would move. [3]
(iii) Calculate the acceleration of the block. [2]

[Oxford (part)]

29. In a competition to take water from a well 7 m deep, Jack lifted 4 kg in 30 seconds and Jill lifted 5 kg in 40 seconds. The handle turned on a radius of 40 cm, whilst the radius of the axle was 5 cm, as illustrated in the diagram.

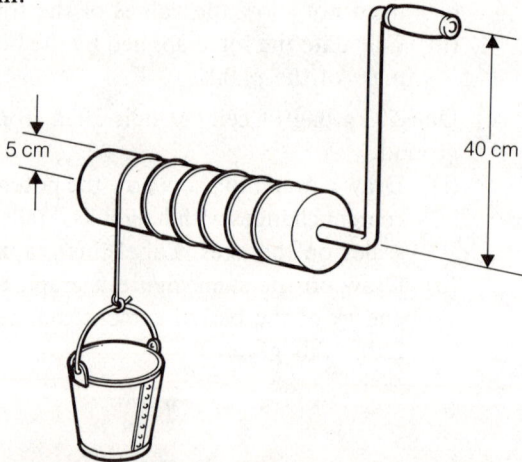

a) How much useful work was done by Jack, and how much useful power did he develop? [4, 2]
b) Who was the more powerful, Jack or Jill? Show your reasoning. [4]
c) Assuming 80% efficiency, calculate the size of the effort needed by Jack to turn the handle. [6]
d) Suggest two important reasons why both Jack and Jill had to expend more power than was actually used to lift the water. [4]

[Oxford]

30. Two similar springs obey Hooke's law. Each stretches by 40 mm (see diagram (i)) when hung from a rigid support and loaded with 300 g.

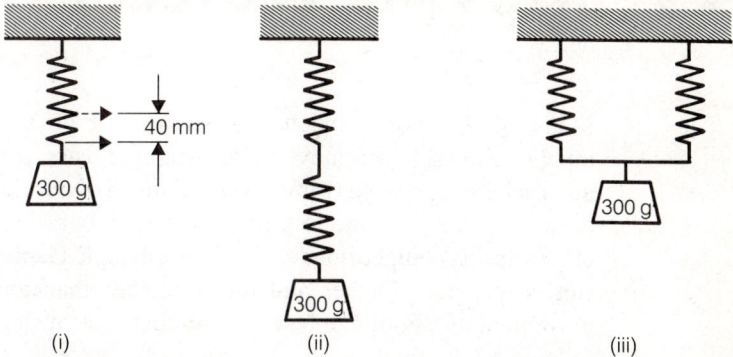

(i)   (ii)   (iii)

a) State Hooke's law.   [2]
b) What extension would be expected using a load of 360 g?   [2]
c) What load would give an extension of 16 mm?   [2]
d) What would be the total extension with one spring hung from the other and a load of 300 g on the bottom (see diagram (ii))? [2]
e) The springs are hung side by side and carry a load of 300 g between them as in diagram (iii). By how much does each spring extend?   [2]

[Oxford]

31. A uniform rule of length 1.0 m and mass 0.08 kg hangs freely from a pivot at one end and is pulled aside by a horizontal force F applied to the other end, so that the centre of mass C is at a horizontal distance of 0.4 m and a vertical distance of 0.3 m from the pivot, as shown in the diagram.

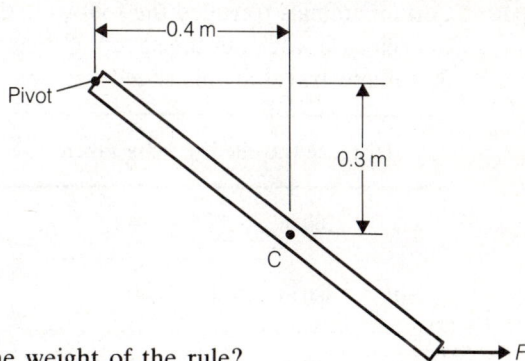

a) What is the weight of the rule?   [1]
b) What is the moment of this weight about the pivot?   [3]
c) What is the moment of the force F about the pivot?   [2]
d) Calculate the force F.   [2]
e) If the force F remained horizontal, but was increased until the rule was nearly horizontal, then F would have to be much larger than it is in the diagram. Explain this.   [2]

[Oxford]

4. Moving Objects

Many of the more obvious applications of physics in our world involve objects which move — for example, cars, trains, aeroplanes and rockets. In everyday life we spend much of our time moving from place to place — home to school, science laboratory to dining hall, etc. In sports competitions such as the Olympic Games athletes try to run faster, jump higher and throw further than anyone else. The movement of a body can be expressed in terms of some, or all, of the following quantities:

1. the distance it travels (or displacement)
2. its speed (or velocity)
3. its acceleration
4. the time during which the object is moving.

The problems which you will meet can be solved in two ways — either by drawing graphs or by using formulae. We shall look at both approaches so that, if you are given a choice, you can choose the method with which you feel happier. Before looking at either approach you need to know two definitions:

$$\text{Speed (or Velocity)} = \frac{\text{Distance travelled}}{\text{Time taken}}$$

Example Certain animals travelled the following distances in the times stated. In each case work out the speed of the animal and suggest an animal that might travel at this speed.

	Distance travelled	Time taken	Speed	Animal
a)	100 m	4 s		
b)	400 m	40 s		
c)	10 cm	2 min		

Method: The formula to use is:

$$\text{Speed} = \frac{\text{Distance travelled}}{\text{Time taken}}$$

The units of speed are given by the units of distance divided by the units of time.

Answers: a) 25 m/s (cheetah) **b)** 10 m/s (dog)
c) 5 cm/min (snail)

Note: You will often find the words speed and velocity written to mean the same thing. In most cases this will be true, but what you must remember is that velocity means 'speed in a particular direction'. Alternatively it may be written that speed is a scalar quantity and velocity is a vector quantity (see p.93).

The second definition you will need to know is:

$$\text{Acceleration} = \frac{\text{Change of velocity}}{\text{Time taken}}$$

Example A car is travelling at 10 miles per hour. The driver accelerates the car to 40 miles per hour. Work out the car's acceleration if this takes:

a) 5 s **b)** 6 s **c)** 20 s

Method: Using

$$\text{Acceleration} = \frac{\text{Change of velocity}}{\text{Time taken}}$$

First work out the change of velocity. The initial velocity is 10 miles/hour and the final velocity is 40 miles/h, so that the change of velocity is $(40 - 10)$ miles/h $= 30$ miles/h. The acceleration is then given by

$$\text{Acceleration} = \frac{30 \text{ miles/h}}{\text{Time taken}}$$

The units of acceleration are found by dividing the units of velocity by the units of time.

Answers: a) 6 miles/h/s **b)** 5 miles/h/s
c) 1.5 miles/h/s

Note: Like velocity, acceleration is a vector quantity. This means that it has a direction, but since the motion in the problems you will meet is nearly always in a straight line the direction is usually understood and so is not mentioned.

Having defined velocity and acceleration we are now in a position to look at graphical problems and then at calculations using formulae.

Graphical approach to problems

Distance–time graphs: (Distance is a scalar quantity — its vector equivalent is displacement.) The distances travelled by the object are plotted on the *y*-axis and the times taken to travel these distances are plotted on the *x*-axis. The gradient (or slope) of the graph is equal to the rate of change of distance with time, which is the same thing as the speed of the object. Because distances are usually in one direction the speed and velocity will be the same.

Example   The graph shows the distances travelled by an object in two-second intervals.

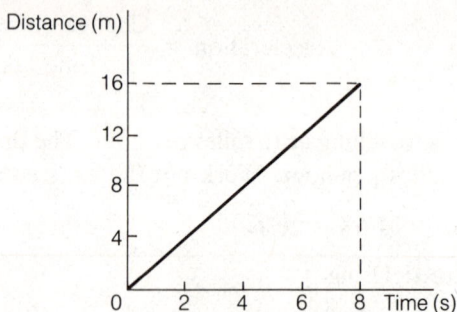

Calculate the speed of the object between:

a) 0 and 2 s   **b)** 0 and 4 s   **c)** 2 and 6 s   **d)** 2 and 8 s

Method: As already stated, the speed (or velocity) is given by

$$\text{Speed} = \frac{\text{Distance travelled}}{\text{Time taken}}$$

First look at the time interval being considered and read the corresponding distances travelled from the graph. Then work out the distance travelled in that time interval.

For example, if the time interval were 2–4 s, then the distance readings from the graph would be 4 m and 8 m, giving a distance travelled of $(8 - 4)\,\text{m} = 4\,\text{m}$. This would have taken $(4 - 2)\,\text{s} = 2\,\text{s}$, and so the speed of the object during this time period would have been

$$\text{Speed} = \frac{\text{Distance travelled}}{\text{Time taken}}$$

$$= \frac{4\,\text{m}}{2\,\text{s}}$$

$$= 2\,\text{m/s}$$

Answers: a) 2 m/s   **b)** 2 m/s   **c)** 2 m/s   **d)** 2 m/s

All of these answers are the same — this means that the object was travelling at a constant speed. Can you see a feature of the graph that might indicate that the speed is not changing?

The following example looks at distance–time graphs for objects whose speeds are not constant, i.e. they are either speeding up (*accelerating*) or slowing down (*decelerating*).

Example   Describe the motion of the body which produces each of the following distance–time graphs:

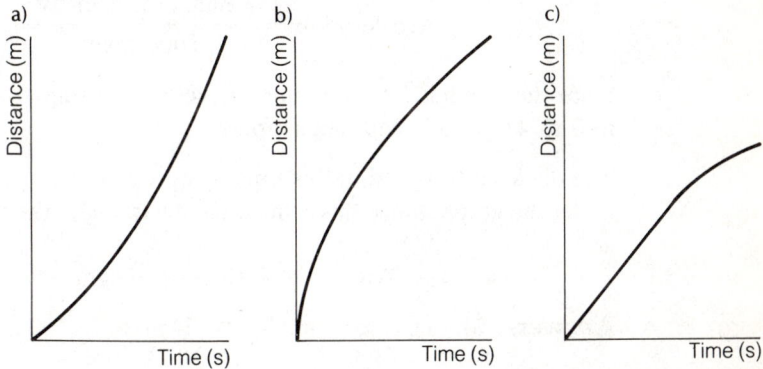

Method: Remember that the speed is the rate of change of distance with time and that this is given by the gradient of the graph. If the gradient is constant, then the body is travelling at constant speed. If the gradient is increasing, i.e. the graph is getting steeper, then the speed of the body is increasing (the body is accelerating). If the gradient is decreasing, i.e. the graph is getting less steep, then the body is slowing down (decelerating).

Answers: a) accelerating (speed increasing)   **b)** decelerating (speed decreasing)   **c)** constant speed, followed by deceleration.

Velocity–time graphs: This type of graph has the velocity of the object plotted on the y-axis and the corresponding time on the x-axis. The gradient of this graph is equal to the rate of change of velocity with time, which is the same as the acceleration of the object. The area under a velocity–time graph is equal to the distance travelled by the object.

Example Calculate the acceleration of the body whose motion is described by the graph shown. Also work out the distance it will have travelled after 4 s.

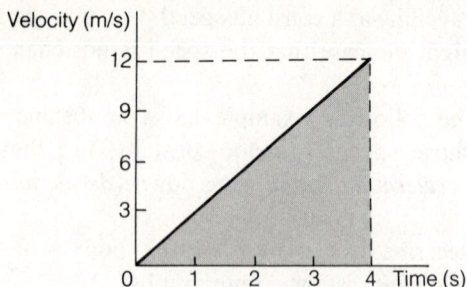

Method: The acceleration is given by the gradient of the graph, i.e.

$$\text{Acceleration} = \frac{\text{Change of velocity}}{\text{Time taken}}$$

Since the graph is a straight line the velocity change from 0 to 12 m/s in 0 to 4 s would seem appropriate.

The distance travelled in this time is represented by the shaded area under the graph. Since this is the area of a triangle, the formula to use is

$$\text{Area} = \tfrac{1}{2} \times \text{Base} \times \text{Height}$$

Answers: a) 3 m/s/s or 3 m/s^2 **b)** 24 m

Example One of the most common velocity–time graphs looks like this:

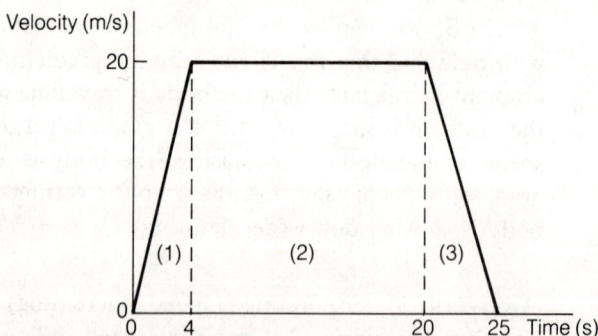

Can you see that this graph has three stages? First of all it shows an object whose velocity increases steadily (i.e. uniform acceleration) during the first 4 s. Then the object travels at constant velocity for the next 16 s (4–20 s). For the final 5 s it slows down steadily (i.e. uniform deceleration). We shall work out the acceleration during the three stages of the motion, the distance travelled during each stage, and also the average velocity during the whole 25 s for which the body is moving.

Stage 1 The acceleration is given by the gradient of the graph:

$$\text{Acceleration} = \frac{\text{Change of velocity}}{\text{Time taken}}$$

$$= \frac{20 - 0 \,\text{m/s}}{4 - 0 \,\text{s}}$$

$$= \frac{20}{4} = 5 \,\text{m/s/s or } 5 \,\text{m/s}^2$$

The distance travelled is the area under the graph:

$$\text{Distance} = \tfrac{1}{2} \times \text{Base} \times \text{Height}$$

$$= \tfrac{1}{2} \times (4 \,\text{s}) \times (20 \,\text{m/s})$$

$$= 40 \,\text{m}$$

Can you see how the units are obtained in both of these answers?

Stage 2 In this stage the velocity does not change and so the acceleration is zero. However, the object covers a distance travelled at this velocity and this distance is given by the area under the graph.

$$\text{Distance} = \text{Area of rectangle (between 4 s and 20 s)}$$

$$= 20 \times 16$$

$$= 320 \,\text{m}$$

Stage 3 The body is now slowing down (or decelerating) and its acceleration is given by the gradient:

$$\text{Acceleration} = \frac{\text{Change of velocity}}{\text{Time taken}}$$

$$= \frac{\text{Final velocity} - \text{Initial velocity}}{\text{Time taken}}$$

$$= \frac{0 - 20 \,\text{m/s}}{25 - 20 \,\text{s}}$$

$$= -\frac{20}{5} \,\text{m/s/s}$$

$$= -4 \,\text{m/s/s or } -4 \,\text{m/s}^2$$

(The negative sign indicates that the object is slowing down — the object has negative acceleration. However, its deceleration or retardation would be $+4$ m/s/s or $+4$ m/s^2.)

The distance travelled is the area under the graph:

$$\text{Distance} = \tfrac{1}{2} \times \text{Base} \times \text{Height}$$

$$= \tfrac{1}{2} \times (5 \,\text{s}) \times (20 \,\text{m/s})$$

$$= 50 \,\text{m}$$

The total distance travelled is found by adding together the distances travelled in each of the three stages, i.e.

Total distance = Stage (1) distance + Stage (2) distance + Stage (3) distance

$$= 40\,m + 320\,m + 50\,m$$

$$= 410\,m$$

The average velocity can then be calculated using the formula

$$\text{Average velocity} = \frac{\text{Total distance travelled}}{\text{Total time taken}}$$

$$= \frac{410\,m}{25\,s}$$

$$= 16.4\,m/s$$

Example A train leaves a station and accelerates from 0 m/s to 24 m/s in 3 minutes. It then travels at this steady speed for 10 minutes, before coming to rest at the next station in a further 4 minutes. Draw a velocity–time graph and work out the train's acceleration during each stage of the motion. Calculate the total distance travelled by the train and work out its average velocity during the motion.

Method: The question tells you that the maximum speed reached by the train is 24 m/s, and so this is the upper limit of the velocity axis. The total time between the two stations is (3 + 10 + 4) minutes = 17 minutes, and so this is the limit on the time axis. The graph can then be drawn:

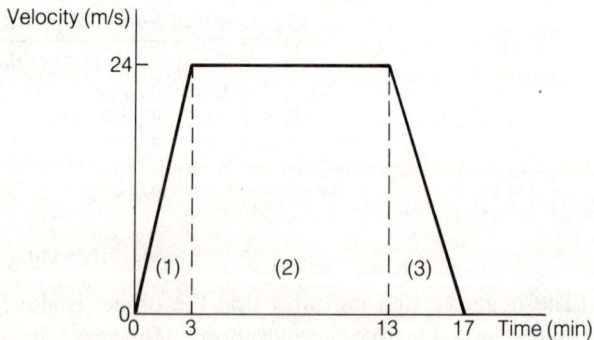

The acceleration at each stage can be calculated using the formula

$$\text{Acceleration} = \frac{\text{Change of velocity}}{\text{Time taken}}$$

and the distance travelled during each stage is given by

Distance = Area under the graph

Having done this for each of the three stages you can then work out the total distance travelled, and hence the average velocity using the formula:

$$\text{Average velocity} = \frac{\text{Total distance travelled}}{\text{Time taken}}$$

Note: Before calculating the distances you must convert the time to seconds.

Answers:

	Acceleration	Distance travelled
Stage (1)	8 m/s/min or 0.13 m/s^2	2 160 m
Stage (2)	0 m/s/min or 0 m/s^2	14 400 m
Stage (3)	−6 m/s/min or −0.10 m/s^2	2 880 m

Total distance travelled = 19 440 m
Average velocity = 1144 m/min = 19.1 m/s

Use of formulae to solve problems

If you have a more mathematical mind, you will probably find the use of formulae more straightforward than the graphical approach. You have already met the two main formulae in the previous section. However, some letters to represent the different terms are now introduced. These letters, with possible units in brackets, are:

u = initial velocity (m/s)
v = final velocity (m/s)
a = acceleration (m/s^2)
s = distance (m)
t = time (s)

The first equation is

$$\text{Acceleration} = \frac{\text{Change of velocity}}{\text{Time taken}}$$

$$= \frac{\text{Final velocity} - \text{Initial velocity}}{\text{Time taken}}$$

Introducing the appropriate letters gives

$$a = \frac{v - u}{t}$$

Rearranging gives

$$a \times t = v - u$$

or

$$v = u + a \times t \qquad [1]$$

The second equation is

Distance travelled = Average velocity × Time taken

$$= \frac{(\text{Initial velocity} + \text{Final velocity})}{2} \times \text{Time taken}$$

Introducing letters gives

$$s = \frac{(u + v)}{2} \times t \qquad [2]$$

You can use these two equations to solve any problem on motion in which the acceleration is uniform, but the solution may be made slightly easier by adding two more formulae.

$$s = (u \times t) + (\tfrac{1}{2} \times a \times t^2) \qquad [3]$$

$$v^2 - u^2 = 2 \times a \times s \qquad [4]$$

Before looking at some more complicated problems using these four formulae we shall try some direct substitutions into the equations. Remember at all times that if you are given three of the quantities you can always find the other two. Indeed, if you know three of the quantities there will always be an equation to find a fourth quantity.

Example A trolley starts from rest and accelerates at $2 \, m/s^2$. What will the velocity of the trolley be after:

a) 2 s   **b)** 6 s   **c)** 12 s?

Method: First write down those quantities which you are given, although one, the initial velocity, is not always obvious:

Initial velocity u = 0 m/s (the question states 'starts from rest')
Acceleration a = $2 \, m/s^2$
Time t = **a)** 2 s   **b)** 6 s   **c)** 12 s

The quantity you are asked to work out is the final velocity v. The formula to use is

$$v = u + a \times t$$

Substitute the values that you know:

$$v = 0 + 2 \times t$$
$$= 2 \times t$$

Answers: a) 4 m/s   **b)** 12 m/s   **c)** 24 m/s

Example   A sledge travelling at 3 m/s accelerates uniformly to 11 m/s. How far will the sledge have travelled if the acceleration lasts for:

a) 3 s   **b)** 5 s   **c)** 12 s?

Method: Write down the quantities given:

Initial velocity u = 3 m/s
Final velocity v = 11 m/s
Time t = **a)** 3 s   **b)** 5 s   **c)** 12 s

You are asked to work out the distance travelled, given by s, and so write down a formula which relates s, u, v and t. This is:

$$s = \frac{(u + v)}{2} \times t$$

Substituting the known quantities gives

$$s = \frac{(3 + 11)}{2} \times t$$
$$= \frac{(14)}{2} \times t$$
$$= 7 \times t$$

Answers: a) 21 m   **b)** 35 m   **c)** 84 m

Example   A car travelling at 13 m/s accelerates at 2 m/s². Calculate the distance travelled after:

a) 2 s   **b)** 3 s   **c)** 4 s

Method: Write down the quantities given:

Initial velocity u = 13 m/s
Acceleration a = 2 m/s²
Time t = **a)** 2 s   **b)** 3 s   **c)** 4 s

You want to work out the distance travelled, s, so write down the formula relating s, u, a and t. That equation is:

$$s = (u \times t) + (\tfrac{1}{2} \times a \times t^2)$$

Substituting the values given

$$s = 13 \times t + \tfrac{1}{2} \times 2 \times t^2$$
$$= 13 \times t + t^2$$

Note: It is a common mistake to square both t and a in the second term.

Answers: a) 30 m   **b)** 48 m   **c)** 68 m

Example   A motorcycle travels at 5 m/s and accelerates at 3 m/s². Calculate its velocity after it has travelled:

a) 4 m   **b)** 20 m   **c)** 100 m

Method: You are given the quantities:

Initial velocity u = 5 m/s
Acceleration a = 3 m/s²
Distance travelled s = **a)** 4 m   **b)** 20 m   **c)** 100 m

and you want to calculate the final velocity v. The equation relating v, u, a and s is

$$v^2 = u^2 + 2 \times a \times s$$

Substituting the values given

$$v^2 = 5^2 + 2 \times 3 \times s$$
$$= 25 + 6 \times s$$

When you have substituted the different values for s, remember that your equation will give you v^2. Calculate the square root to find the final velocity.

Answers: a) 7.0 m/s   **b)** 12.0 m/s   **c)** 25.0 m/s

Why is it unlikely that the motorcycle's acceleration would have been uniform over the longer distances in the example?

We are now in a position to attempt some more complicated examples.

Example   A train starts from rest and accelerates to 30 m/s in 6 s. It travels at this new velocity for 25 s, before decelerating to rest in 10 s.

Calculate:

a) the initial acceleration
b) the final acceleration (which is in fact a deceleration)
c) the total distance travelled by the train
d) the average velocity of the train.

Method: The problem could be approached graphically, and you may prefer to do this. Indeed, you could use it as a check for the calculations using the formulae. The problem must be divided into its three stages — the acceleration stage at the start, the constant velocity stage and the final deceleration stage.

Stage 1 You have to work out the acceleration in this stage and also the distance travelled. You are told:

Initial velocity u $= 0$ m/s   ('starts from rest')
Final velocity v $= 30$ m/s
Time t $= 6$ s

and you wish to calculate the acceleration a, and distance travelled s. The formula relating u, v, a and t is

$$v = u + a \times t$$

Substituting gives

$$30 = 0 + a \times 6$$
$$= 6 \times a$$

from which you can calculate a.

Any of three other equations can be used to calculate the distance travelled. The easiest equation is probably

$$s = \frac{(u + v)}{2} \times t$$

Substituting gives

$$s = \frac{(0 + 30)}{2} \times 6$$
$$= \frac{(30)}{2} \times 6$$
$$= 15 \times 6$$
$$= 90 \text{ m}$$

and so you have calculated the distance travelled in Stage 1.

Stage 2 In the second stage the train travels at constant velocity, but you can still work out the distance travelled using the formula

$$s = \frac{(u + v)}{2} \times t$$

because

Initial velocity u = Final velocity v = 30 m/s
Time t = 25 s

Substituting gives

$$s = \frac{(30 + 30)}{2} \times 25$$

$$= \frac{(60)}{2} \times 25$$

and so you have calculated the distance travelled in Stage 2.

In the third and final stage the train decelerates to rest. You know the following:

Initial velocity u = 30 m/s
Final velocity v = 0 m/s   ('decelerates to rest')
Time t = 10 s

The formula which involves these three quantities and the acceleration a is

$$v = u + a \times t$$

Substituting gives

$$0 = 30 + a \times 10$$
$$10 \times a = -30$$

and hence you can calculate a. Note that the acceleration is negative, indicating that the train is slowing down. Any of the other formulae can then be used to work out the distance travelled s during Stage 3. Again the easiest formula to use is probably:

$$s = \frac{(u + v)}{2} \times t$$

$$= \frac{(30 + 0)}{2} \times 10$$

$$= \frac{(30)}{2} \times 10$$

$$= 15 \times 10$$

and so you have calculated the distance travelled in Stage 3.

The total distance travelled during the motion of the train is found by adding together the distances travelled during each of the three stages of the motion.

The average velocity is calculated using the formula

$$\text{Average velocity} = \frac{\text{Total distance travelled}}{\text{Total time the train is in motion}}$$

Answers: a) 5 m/s²   **b)** −3 m/s²
c) 90 m + 750 m + 150 m = 990 m
d) 990 m/41 s = 24.1 m/s

In the second of these harder examples the acceleration due to gravity is introduced. This is the acceleration caused by the force of attraction between the Earth and any object relatively close to its surface. The accepted value of the acceleration due to gravity in this country is 9.81 m/s², but it is usually stated that you can use $g = 10$ m/s².

Example A circus clown juggles with three balls, each of which rises 2 m into the air on each throw. If the acceleration due to gravity is 10 m/s², calculate **a)** the velocity with which the ball leaves the clown's hand, and **b)** the total time each ball spends in flight.

Method: This type of problem should be divided into two stages — the ball rising to its maximum height, and the ball returning to the clown's other hand.

In the first stage, the following quantities are known:

Distance travelled s = 2 m
Acceleration a = $-g$ = -10 m/s² (the ball decelerates as it rises)
Final velocity v = 0 m/s   (the ball stops momentarily at the top of the flight)

You are asked to calculate the initial velocity u and so the equation to use is

$$v^2 = u^2 + 2 \times a \times s$$

Substituting gives

$$0 = u^2 - 2 \times 10 \times 2$$

from which you can work out u^2 and so u.

Having calculated u, you can then use any of the other equations to calculate the time t taken to rise to the 2 m height, but possibly the easiest equation to use is

$$s = \frac{(u + v)}{2} \times t$$

Rearranging gives

$$t = \frac{2 \times s}{(u + v)}$$

The motion is in fact symmetrical, so that it will take the same length of time for the ball to return to the clown's other hand. However, you may like to check this by repeating the calculation, and remembering that in the second stage:

Initial velocity u = 0 m/s (at the top of the flight)

Acceleration a = g = +10 m/s² (because the ball gets faster as it comes down)

Distance travelled s = 2 m

You can also work out that the ball returns to the clown's hand with the same speed that it left the other hand. Although the speeds are the same, the velocities are different — can you see why this might be?

Answers: a) 6.3 m/s **b)** 2 × 0.63 = 1.26 s

Newton's laws of motion

Sir Isaac Newton (1642–1727) proposed three laws of motion. The first can be written:

1. Any body will remain at rest or, if already moving, will continue to move at a constant speed in a straight line, unless an external force acts on the body.

In his second law, Newton looked at the part played by the external force:

2. The external force is proportional to the rate of change of momentum of the body.

Momentum: Momentum is defined by the equation

Momentum = Mass × Velocity

In the third law, Newton moved his attention from the body which experienced the force to whatever was producing the force.

3. For any action, there will be an equal and opposite reaction.

Example Work out the momentum of a 5 kg mass travelling at a constant velocity of:

a) 2 m/s   **b)** 3 m/s   **c)** 10 m/s

Method: Use the formula for momentum and substitute the values given.

Answers: a) 10 kg m/s   **b)** 15 kg m/s   **c)** 50 kg m/s

Newton's second law can then be written mathematically:

$$\text{External force} \propto \frac{\text{Change of momentum}}{\text{Time taken}}$$

$$\propto \frac{\text{Final momentum} - \text{Initial momentum}}{\text{Time taken}}$$

$$\propto \frac{\text{Mass} \times \text{Final velocity} - \text{Mass} \times \text{Initial velocity}}{\text{Time taken}}$$

$$\propto \frac{m \times v - m \times u}{t}$$

$$\propto m \times \left(\frac{v - u}{t} \right)$$

where m = mass, v = final velocity, u = initial velocity, t = time.

You will remember the equation of motion

$$v = u + a \times t$$

(see p.130)

which can be rearranged to give

$$a = \frac{v - u}{t}$$

Newton's second law can then be written:

External force $\propto$ Mass × Acceleration

If the force is measured in newtons, the mass in kilograms and acceleration in metres/second/second, then this becomes an equation which is used extensively at all levels of physics:

External, or applied, force = Mass × Acceleration

or

$$F = m \times a$$

You would *not* be required to prove this formula.

Example Complete the following table:

	Force (N)	Mass (kg)	Acceleration (m/s²)
a)	—	2	7
b)	80	20	—
c)	100	—	12

Method: Using the formula

$$F = m \times a$$

substitute the two quantities you are given, and then, if necessary, rearrange the equation before working out your answer.

Answers: a) 14 N   **b)** 4 m/s²   **c)** 8.3 kg

Conservation of momentum

Momentum is a vector quantity and so has both a magnitude and a direction. In any collision momentum is conserved. This means that the total momentum before a collision is equal to the total momentum after the collision. You will discover at a more advanced level that this can be explained by Newton's third law.

Example A trolley of mass 1 kg travels at 6 m/s. It collides with a stationary trolley and the two trolleys join and move off together. Calculate the combined velocity of the trolleys if the second trolley has a mass of:

a) 1 kg   **b)** 2 kg   **c)** 5 kg

Method: To solve this sort of problem it may be helpful to draw diagrams of the situations 'before' and 'after' the collision. Mark the known information on them, e.g.

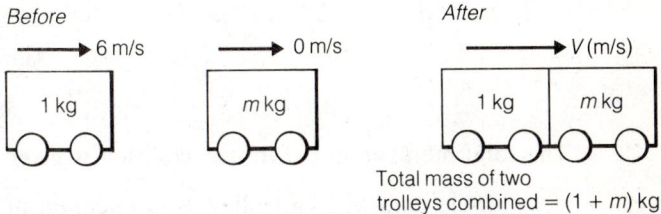

Before

→ 6 m/s   → 0 m/s

1 kg m kg

After

→ V (m/s)

1 kg m kg

Total mass of two
trolleys combined = $(1 + m)$ kg

Write down the momentum before and after the collision:

$$\text{Momentum before} = \text{Momentum after}$$

or

(Momentum of 1 kg trolley + Momentum of m kg trolley) before
$$= \text{(Momentum of combined trolleys) after}$$

$$1 \text{ kg} \times 6 \text{ m/s} + m \text{ kg} \times 0 \text{ m/s} = (1 + m) \text{ kg} \times v \text{ m/s}$$

or

$$6 \text{ kg m/s} = (1 + m) \times v \text{ kg m/s}$$

$$\therefore v = \frac{6}{(1 + m)} \text{ m/s}$$

Substitute the different mass values for the trolley which was stationary before the collision.

Answers: a) 3 m/s   **b)** 2 m/s   **c)** 1 m/s

Momentum problems are made rather more difficult when the trolleys are travelling in opposite directions. This is because momentum is a vector, and you must then consider the direction of the momentum as well as its magnitude.

Example   A trolley of mass 2 kg is travelling at 10 m/s when it collides with a trolley of mass 3 kg travelling at 2 m/s in the opposite direction. If the two trolleys stick together in collision, what will be their joint velocity after the collision?

Method: As before it is easier to draw 'before' and 'after' diagrams, marking on the known quantities. Because we do not know the direction of the trolleys after the collision, let us suppose they travel in the same direction as the 2 kg trolley was travelling before the collision. If this is an incorrect assumption it will appear during the calculation.

Before

→ 10 m/s   2 m/s ←

2 kg   3 kg

After

→ V (m/s)

2 kg | 3 kg

Total mass = 5 kg

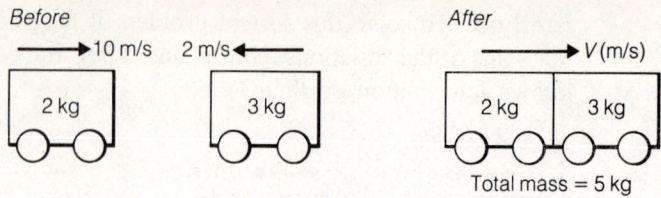

The total momentum before the collision is given by

Momentum of 2 kg trolley + Momentum of 3 kg trolley
$$= 2 \text{ kg} \times 10 \text{ m/s} + 3 \text{ kg} \times (-2 \text{ m/s})$$

The negative sign is introduced to the velocity because the trolley is moving in the opposite direction, i.e. movement to the right is positive and movement to the left is negative.

The total momentum after the collision is given by

Momentum of combined trolleys $= (2 \text{ kg} + 3 \text{ kg}) \times v \text{ m/s}$

Because momentum is conserved

Total momentum before collision = Total momentum after collision
$$20 - 6 = 5 \times v$$
$$14 = 5 \times v$$

Answer: $v = 2.8$ m/s.

If the total momentum before the collision had been a negative quantity, then v would have worked out as a negative number, i.e. a velocity to the left.

Kinetic energy

We have already seen that moving bodies possess momentum. They also have energy because work must be done to stop them. This energy of motion is called kinetic energy and is calculated using the formula

Kinetic energy $= \frac{1}{2} \times$ Mass $\times$ (Velocity)^2

Being a form of energy, kinetic energy is measured in joules and is a scalar quantity, i.e. it has size only and does not depend on the direction in which the body is moving.

Example Calculate the kinetic energy of a 3 kg mass if it is travelling at:

a) 2 m/s   **b)** 7 m/s   **c)** 20 m/s

Method: The formula to use is

$$KE = \tfrac{1}{2} \times m \times v^2$$

Substitute the values given, remembering to square the speed.

Answers: a) 6 J   **b)** 73.5 J   **c)** 600 J

Note: Unlike momentum, which is always conserved during collisions, kinetic energy is only conserved in molecular collisions.

In the world as we know it the *total* energy before and after a collision will be the same, but some of the kinetic energy before the collision will be converted into heat (due to friction) and sound during the collision. As a result the total kinetic energy of the bodies in the collision will be less after the collision.

Example   The following results were obtained during an experiment with two trolleys:

Mass of trolley A = 0.8 kg
Mass of trolley B = 2.4 kg
Velocity of trolley A before collision = 40 cm/s
Velocity of trolley B before collision = 0 cm/s
Velocity of trolleys A and B after collision = 10 cm/s

Work out **a)** the total momentum, and **b)** kinetic energy before and after the collision and comment on your results.

Method: It is helpful to draw 'before' and 'after' diagrams, marking the relevant quantities on each:

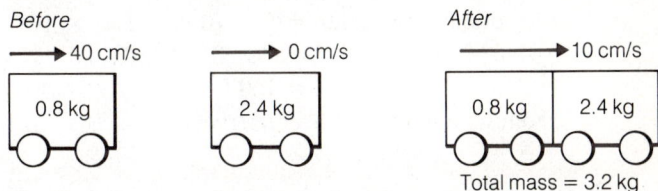

Before   → 40 cm/s   → 0 cm/s   *After*   → 10 cm/s
0.8 kg   2.4 kg   0.8 kg 2.4 kg
Total mass = 3.2 kg

The total momentum before the collision is given by

$$
\begin{pmatrix}\text{Momentum} \\ \text{of} \\ \text{trolley A}\end{pmatrix} + \begin{pmatrix}\text{Momentum} \\ \text{of} \\ \text{trolley B}\end{pmatrix} = \begin{pmatrix}\text{Mass} & \text{Velocity} \\ \text{of} \times \text{of} \\ \text{trolley A} & \text{trolley A}\end{pmatrix} + \begin{pmatrix}\text{Mass} & \text{Velocity} \\ \text{of} \times \text{of} \\ \text{trolley B} & \text{trolley B}\end{pmatrix}
$$

The total momentum after the collision is given by

$$
\begin{pmatrix}\text{Momentum of trolleys} \\ \text{A and B combined}\end{pmatrix} = \begin{pmatrix}\text{Combined masses of} \\ \text{trolleys A and B}\end{pmatrix} \times \begin{pmatrix}\text{Velocity of} \\ \text{trolleys A and B}\end{pmatrix}
$$

According to the law of conservation of momentum, the total momentum before the collision should be equal to the total momentum after the collision.

The total kinetic energy before the collision is given by

$$
\begin{Bmatrix} \text{Kinetic} \\ \text{energy of} \\ \text{trolley A} \end{Bmatrix} + \begin{Bmatrix} \text{Kinetic} \\ \text{energy of} \\ \text{trolley B} \end{Bmatrix} = \left\{ \frac{1}{2} \times \begin{array}{c} \text{Mass} \\ \text{of} \\ \text{trolley A} \end{array} \times \left(\begin{array}{c} \text{Velocity} \\ \text{of} \\ \text{trolley A} \end{array} \right)^2 \right\}
$$

$$
+ \left\{ \frac{1}{2} \times \begin{array}{c} \text{Mass} \\ \text{of} \\ \text{trolley B} \end{array} \times \left(\begin{array}{c} \text{Velocity} \\ \text{of} \\ \text{trolley B} \end{array} \right)^2 \right\}
$$

The total kinetic energy after the collision is given by

$$
\begin{array}{c} \text{Kinetic energy of} \\ \text{trolleys A and B} \\ \text{combined} \end{array} = \frac{1}{2} \times \begin{array}{c} \text{Combined masses of} \\ \text{trolleys A and B} \end{array} \times \left(\begin{array}{c} \text{Velocity of} \\ \text{trolleys A and B} \end{array} \right)^2
$$

Because some of the kinetic energy is converted into heat and sound, the second value should be less than the first.

Answers: a) Momentum before $= 0.8 \times 40 + 2.4 \times 0$

$$= 32 + 0$$
$$= 32 \text{ kg m/s}$$

Momentum after $= (0.8 + 2.4) \times 10$

$$= 3.2 \times 10$$
$$= 32 \text{ kg m/s}$$

$\therefore$ Momentum is conserved.

b) Kinetic energy before $= \frac{1}{2} \times 0.8 \times (40)^2 + \frac{1}{2} \times 2.4 \times (0)^2$

$$= 640 + 0$$
$$= 640 \text{ J}$$

Kinetic energy after $= \frac{1}{2} \times (0.8 + 2.4) \times 10^2$

$$= \frac{1}{2} \times 3.2 \times 10^2$$
$$= 160 \text{ J}$$

$\therefore$ Kinetic energy is not conserved.

Motion in a circle

Motion in a circle is important because it helps us to understand more about our solar system (planets moving around the Sun) and our galaxy (stars moving around a common centre).

At the other end of our thinking it helps to explain the motion of electrons around the nucleus of the atom. (You should remember that these are somewhat simple views because the motion is not necessarily circular but can be *elliptical*, but at the level of accuracy required for most school physics the approximation to circular paths is perfectly adequate.)

Dealing more in the world with which we are familiar, circular motion is used in our understanding of cars cornering and when objects on strings are swung around one's head, for example the bolas used by South American cowboys to catch cattle.

We usually consider the object to be moving at constant speed. However, its velocity (which is a vector quantity) is continually changing, because the *direction* is always changing. You will remember that if a body's velocity is changing, then it must be accelerating. It can be shown that the acceleration is directed *towards the centre* of the circle. For this reason it is called a *centripetal* ('centre-seeking') *acceleration*.

For there to be an acceleration, there must be a force and this, too, is directed towards the centre of the circle. The force is called the *centripetal force*.

The centripetal acceleration is given by the formula

$$\text{Centripetal acceleration} = \frac{v^2}{r}$$

where v is the speed or velocity magnitude and r is the distance of the object from the centre of the circle, i.e. the radius of the path.

Example What is the centripetal acceleration of an object, travelling in a circle of radius 3 m, if it has a speed of:

a) 2 m/s   **b)** 4 m/s   **c)** 7 m/s?

Method: Use

$$\text{Centripetal acceleration} = \frac{v^2}{r}$$

and substitute the given values. Remember to square only the speed.

Answers: a) 1.33 m/s²   **b)** 5.33 m/s²   **c)** 16.33 m/s²

The centripetal force is given by the equation

$$\text{Force} = \text{Mass} \times \text{Acceleration}$$

or $\text{Centripetal force} = \text{Mass} \times \text{Centripetal acceleration}$

$$F = m \times \frac{v^2}{r}$$

Example Calculate the centripetal force needed to keep a body of mass 3 kg travelling at 4 m/s in a circular path of radius:

a) 0.5 m   **b)** 2 m   **c)** 3 m

Method: Use

$$F = m \times \frac{v^2}{r}$$

Substituting the values given leads to

$$F = 3 \times \frac{4^2}{r}$$

$$= 3 \times \frac{16}{r}$$

$$= \frac{48}{r}$$

Then substitute the values for r.

Answers: a) 96 N   **b)** 24 N   **c)** 16 N

Questions

Information for these questions: acceleration due to gravity = 1000 cm/s² = 10 m/s².

1. A car starts from rest (0 m/s) and reaches a speed of 12 m/s in 20 s.
    a) What is its acceleration?
    b) What might its speed be after 60 s?
    c) What might the speed be after 600 s?
    Why is c) unlikely to be correct? Suggest a reason for this.

2. A spaceship is launched with an acceleration of 20 m/s/s. What speed does it reach after 1 minute (= 60 s)?

3. A car travelling at 42 m/s brakes with a deceleration of 6 m/s/s (i.e. slows down at 6 m/s/s).
    a) How long will it take to come to rest?
    b) If the car hits a lorry after braking for 5 s, how fast will it be going just before the crash?

4. Convert:
    a) 45 km/h into km/min
    b) 45 km/h into km/s
    c) 45 km/h into m/s (1 km = 1000 m)

5. Convert:
    a) 30 m/s into m/h
    b) 30 m/s into km/h

6. An athlete covers 100 m in 10 s.
   a) What is his average speed?
   b) Why is your answer only an average?
   c) Why could the athlete not keep up this speed for a 1500 m race?

7. In a 4×100 m relay, the first runner runs at 9 m/s, the second at 10 m/s, the third at 7.5 m/s and the fourth at 8 m/s. How long does the team take to complete the race?

8. An aircraft travelling at 600 km/h accelerates steadily at 10 km/h/s. If the speed of sound is 1100 km/hour at the aircraft's altitude, how long will it take to reach the sound barrier?

9. Water, which flows over a weir at a rate of 900 kg/s, takes 1.5 s to fall vertically into the stream below.
   a) (i) What is the speed with which the falling water hits the stream?
      (ii) What is the height through which the water falls?
   b) Calculate
      (i) the weight of water falling over the weir in 5.0 s,
      (ii) the work which has been done on this weight of water when it hits the stream below the weir.
   c) Calculate the power of the falling water at the instant it hits the stream.
   d) State the energy transformations which occur as the water falls from the weir into the stream below.

   Take acceleration of free fall to be 10 m/s^2 (10 N/kg).

   [Cambridge]

10. Draw sketch graphs of y = velocity against x = time for each of the following situations. Make sure that you label the axes and mark on any relevant values.
    a) A car travelling at a constant velocity of 20 m/s for 10 s.
    b) A train accelerating from rest (0 m/s) up to 12 m/s in 6 s.
    c) A ball being thrown upwards from the ground at an initial velocity of 30 m/s. (Remember that the acceleration due to gravity is 10 m/s^2 *downwards* and that the ball will be momentarily at rest at its highest point.)
    d) An object starting from rest and accelerating at 4 m/s^2 for 5 s; travelling at the velocity reached for 20 s; and decelerating to rest in a further 10 s.

11. A student carried out two experiments using a ticker timer, ticker tape, a set of weights and a trolley.

a) In the first experiment he kept the mass of the trolley constant and applied different forces to it. He used ticker tape to measure the acceleration on each occasion. The following table of results was obtained:

Force (N)	Acceleration (cm/s²)
2	17
4	33
6	52
8	68
10	85
12	100

Start your graph at $y = 0$, $x = 0$ and plot a graph of y = force against x = acceleration.

What is your conclusion from the graph?

b) In the second experiment he kept a constant force and varied the mass of the trolley by placing extra masses on top of the trolley.

Mass (kg)	Acceleration (cm/s²)
1	35
2	17
3	12
4	8.5
5	7

He then worked out $1/m$ and plotted a graph of y = acceleration against x = 1/mass. Draw this graph starting at $x = 0$, $y = 0$. What are your conclusions?

12.   Cars on a motorway evenly spaced 30 m apart (centre to centre) pass a fixed point at the rate of 50 per minute. Calculate the speed of the cars.   [WJEC]

13.   a) Calculate the work done in lifting a box of mass 2 kg through a vertical height of 3 m.
      b) The box is then released. Calculate the kinetic energy, speed and momentum of the box just before it hits the ground.

14.   Draw sketch graphs of y = distance against x = time for each of the following situations. Make sure that you label the axes and mark on any relevant values.
      a) A motorcycle travelling at a constant velocity of 10 m/s.
      b) A car accelerating from rest at 3 m/s² for 5 s.
      c) A train decelerating from 20 m/s to rest in 10 s.

15.   Calculate the acceleration (or deceleration) and the distance travelled by objects which have the following velocity–time graphs.

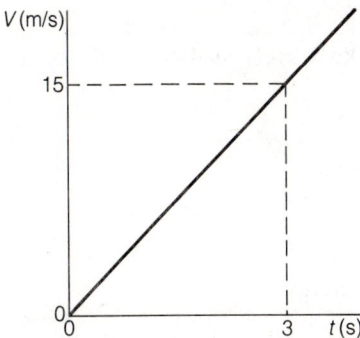

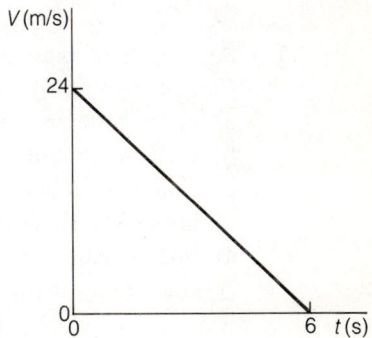

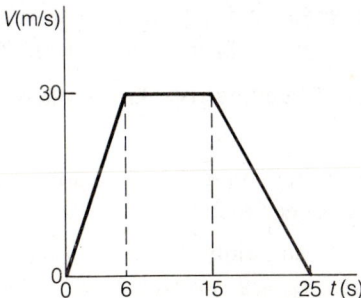

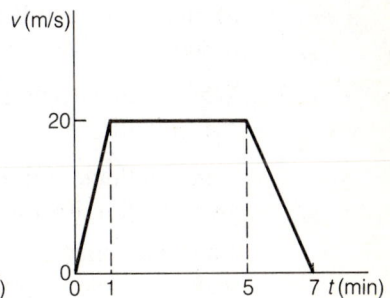

16. Complete the following table which involves the kinetic energy and momentum of different objects.

	Mass (kg)	Velocity (m/s)	Momentum (kg m/s)	Kinetic energy (J)
a)	5	4	—	—
b)	3	20	—	—
c)	2	—	20	—
d)	6	—	—	90
e)	—	6	24	—
f)	—	3	—	180
g)	—	—	100	200

17. An object of mass 3 kg travels at 4 m/s and accelerates to 10 m/s. Calculate the object's
a) initial momentum
b) final momentum
c) change in momentum
d) initial kinetic energy
e) final kinetic energy
f) change in kinetic energy.

18. A girl of weight 500 N jumps off a wall. Her velocity is 20 m/s just before she hits the ground. Calculate the force exerted on her if she:
a) does not bend her knees and is brought to rest in 0.1 s
b) does bend her knees and is brought to rest in 1 s.

What is the advantage of bending your knees when you jump on to the ground?

Can you think of three other situations when a force can be reduced by spreading it over a longer time?

Can you think of three situations where a force is increased by making it last as short a time as possible?

19. Complete the following table, which gives details of an object changing its velocity when a force is applied. You can assume uniform acceleration.

	Mass (kg)	Initial velocity (m/s)	Final velocity (m/s)	Time (s)	Acceleration (m/s^2)	Force (N)
a)	3	0	12	2	—	—
b)	2	0	—	4	—	8
c)	—	2	22	—	5	20
d)	10	—	24	6	3	—
e)	6	2	17	3	—	—
f)	—	3	—	7	3	60
g)	—	—	60	5	10	80

20. Complete the following table of values, which involves the distance travelled s; the initial velocity u; the final velocity v; the time t; and the acceleration a.

	s (cm)	u (cm/s)	v (cm/s)	t (s)	a (cm/s^2)
a)	—	2	12	3	—
b)	—	8	20	—	2
c)	100	2	8	—	—
d)	200	0	—	10	—
e)	20	—	13	—	3
f)	—	—	35	8	4

21.   A ball is dropped from a cliff. What is the total distance fallen after
      a) 1 s   b) 2 s   c) 6 s   d) 10 s,
      if the acceleration due to gravity is 10 m/s²?

22.   a) Calculate the work done in lifting a sphere of weight 100 N
         through a vertical height of 2.0 m from the floor.

      b) The sphere is then released. What is its velocity immediately
         before it hits the ground?

      c) The sphere rebounds to a height of 1.5 m. Calculate the 'loss' of
         energy of the sphere.
         Where do you think the 'lost' energy might have gone?

23.   A snooker ball of mass 0.1 kg makes an impact with an identical
      stationary ball. Before the impact the moving ball has a velocity of
      1.5 m/s and it follows along the same path with a velocity of 0.5 m/s
      after the impact. Calculate:

      a) the velocity of the second ball after the impact

      b) the change in kinetic energy of the first ball as a result of the
         impact.

24.   A bullet of mass 20 g (0.02 kg) travelling at 300 m/s, hits and imbeds
      itself in a 1.98 kg block of wood, which is hanging on a length of
      string. Calculate:

      a) the combined velocity of the block and bullet after the collision

      b) the kinetic energy of the block and bullet after the collision

      c) the vertical height to which the block and bullet will rise after the
         collision. ($g = 10$ m/s².)

25.   A gun of mass 10 kg fires a bullet of mass 30 g. Calculate the recoil
      velocity of the gun if the bullet has a velocity of:

      a) 200 m/s   b) 300 m/s   c) 400 m/s

      What effect might this have on the person firing the gun?

26.   A package is dropped from an aeroplane which is travelling at
      250 m/s parallel to the ground and 1000 m above it. If the acceleration
      due to gravity is 10 m/s² and air resistance can be ignored, calculate:

      a) the time the package takes to hit the ground

      b) the horizontal distance the package has travelled when it hits the
         ground.

27. Complete the following table, which deals with objects travelling in circular paths.

	Centripetal force (N)	Mass (kg)	Speed (m/s)	Radius of paths (m)	Centripetal acceleration (m/s^2)
a)	20	2	—	5	—
b)	8	—	2	—	4
c)	—	3	6	2	—
d)	12	0.4	2.5	—	—

Past examination questions

1. A ticker-timer produces 50 dots per second on a tape which is pulled through it. The tape shown below is drawn to actual size.

   a) How can you tell that the tape was pulled through the ticker-timer at a constant speed?

   b) Take measurements from the tape shown so that you can calculate the average size of the gaps between the dots. Show your working.

   c) Calculate the speed at which the tape was pulled. Show your working.   [SWEB]

2. A space rocket is launched from Earth and reaches its maximum speed of 15000 m/s after 500 s.

   a) Calculate the average acceleration of the rocket.

   b) At the speed of 15000 m/s, how long does it take the rocket to travel 6000 km?

   c) The rocket motor exerts a constant force from launching but the acceleration of the rocket increases. State three reasons accounting for this.   [SREB]

3. A girl wearing a parachute jumps from a helicopter. She does not open the parachute straight away. The table shows her speed during the 9 seconds after she jumps.

Time in seconds	0	1	2	3	4	5	6	7	8	9
Speed in m/s	0	10		30	40	25	17	12	10	10

a) Complete the table by writing down the speed at 2 seconds.
b) Plot a graph of speed in m/s on the vertical axis against time in seconds on the horizontal axis.
c) How many seconds after she jumped did the girl open her parachute?
How do the results show this?
d) (i) What force pulls the girl down?
(ii) What force acts upwards?
(iii) Which of these two forces is larger:
at 3 seconds?
at 6 seconds?
at 9 seconds?
e) How will the graph continue after 9 seconds if she is still falling?
f) The girl makes a second jump with a *larger area* parachute. She falls through the air for the same time before opening her new parachute.
How will this affect the graph:
(i) during the first 4 seconds?
(ii) after this? [SWEB]

4. A car of mass 1000 kg accelerates from rest at 2 m/s^2.
a) How much force is accelerating the car? Show your working.
b) What will the speed of the car be after 4 seconds? Show your working.
c) How long will it take the car to reach a speed of 12 m/s?
[SWEB]

5. a) Diagram 1

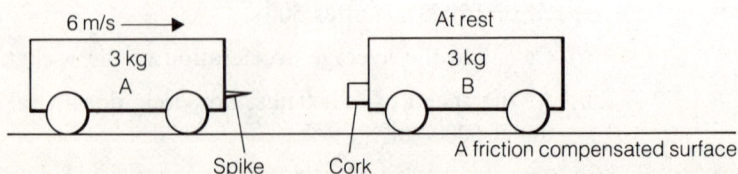

Trolley 'A', mass 3 kg, was travelling at 6 m/s when it collided with the stationary trolley 'B' — as shown in diagram 1.

(i)   What was the momentum of trolley 'A' before the collision?

(ii) The trolleys collide and move on together. What is their combined velocity?

(iii) What would the combined velocity of the two trolleys be if the mass of trolley 'B' were 6 kg instead of 3 kg?

b) Diagram 2

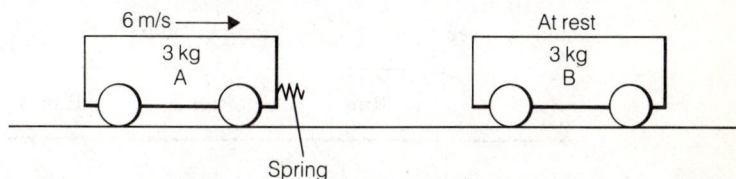

The first experiment is repeated with a spring instead of a spike. In this experiment trolley 'A' came to a stop. Again there is no loss of momentum.

(i) What would be the velocity of trolley 'B' after the collision shown in diagram 2?

(ii) The collision in diagram 2 creates forces on both trolleys. Compare these forces for size and direction. Give a reason for your answers.

   1. Size of force on 'A' compared to 'B'.

   2. Direction of force on 'A' compared to 'B'   [SREB]

6.

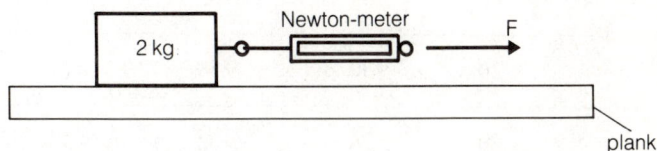

The diagram shows a 2 kg block on a plank pulled by a force F measured on a newton-meter (spring balance). The block accelerates at 3 m/s^2.

a) What force F would be shown on the newton-meter if there were *no friction* between the block and the plank? Show your working.

It is found that the newton-meter reading is 10 newtons at first, falling to 8 newtons when the block is moving.

b) Why does the newton-meter reading fall?

c) Calculate the *force of friction* acting on the *moving* block. Show your working.

d) What will be the *velocity* of the block, in metres/sec, if it continues to accelerate at 3 m/s^2 for 3 seconds, starting from rest?

e) What will be the momentum of the block after 3 seconds?

[SREB (part)]

7. This was an experiment to investigate the air and frictional resistance due to the movement of a car. The car was accelerated to 112 km/h (70 mph) and then allowed to freewheel along a reasonably straight and level line. The data in the table were obtained in these runs, runs 1 and 3 in the same direction, run 2 in the opposite direction.

Time min – sec	Speed (km per hour)			Mean speed (km/h)
	Run 1	Run 2	Run 3	
0	112	112	112	112
10	96	90	93	93
20	79	78	79	79
30	65	67	62	65
40	57	57	55	56
50	48	50	48	49
1 – 00	39	43	40	41
10	30	38	30	33
20	26	32	25	28
30	22	30	20	24
40	20	25	16	20
50	10	8	12	10
2 – 00	5	3	5	4

(i) Is it good experimental practice to repeat the runs in this experiment? Write two reasons for your answer.
(ii) Plot a graph of mean speed (km/h) on the vertical axis against time on the horizontal axis.
Draw a smooth curve, to all the points **except** the last two.

(iii) What evidence is there for thinking that the car's speedometer is inaccurate at speeds below 20 km/h?

(iv) Assume that the readings below 20 km/h are inaccurate and draw a dotted line on the graph where you think the correct readings would take it.

(v) What is there about the graph that suggests that resistance to movement increases with speed?   [SREB]

8. a) Write down the equations which define velocity and acceleration.

A firework rocket starts from rest and accelerates uniformly upwards to a velocity of 20 m/s in 0.5 s. It maintains this velocity for a further 0.5 s and finally decelerates uniformly to rest after a further 2.0 s.

b) (i) Name the *two* main forces which act on the rocket in the first 0.5 s and state the direction of each.

(ii) Which is the larger force? Give a reason for this answer.

c) Plot a graph of velocity in m/s on the vertical axis against time in s on the horizontal axis for the rocket's motion.

d) (i) In which direction is the rocket travelling during the time shown on the graph?

(ii) What energy changes occur during the flight?
The .... energy of the fuel has changed into .... energy and .... energy at the top of the flight.

e) During the first 0.5 s:
(i) calculate the acceleration (in m/s^2).
(ii) calculate the average velocity (in m/s).

f) How far does the rocket travel while its velocity is constant?

g) At what time does the rocket reach its maximum height?

h) Calculate the maximum height.   [SWEB]

9. State Newton's second law of motion.

For a body of fixed mass, show how its acceleration may be related to the applied force. Define the newton.   [6]

A car of mass 1000 kg accelerates uniformly from rest to 15 m/sec in 2 minutes. Calculate

(i) its acceleration,

(ii) its final kinetic energy,

(iii) its final momentum.   [10]
            [WJEC]

10. Give the meaning of the term *momentum*.

A model railway truck of mass 0.25 kg is pushed along a straight track so that it collides with and rebounds from buffers at the end of the track. Its speed just before hitting the buffers is 1.2 m/s and it leaves the buffers travelling with a speed of 1.1 m/s in the opposite direction. The time for which truck and buffers are in contact is 0.50 s.

Find:
(i)   the initial momentum of the truck,   [2]
(ii) the momentum of the truck as it leaves the buffers,   [2]
(iii) the change in momentum of the truck,   [2]
(iv) the force exerted on the truck by the buffers,   [3]
(v)   the force exerted on the buffers by the truck.   [2]

How does the principle of conservation of momentum apply to this collision?   [3]

In terms of momentum changes explain how, according to the kinetic model, a gas molecule exerts a force on the walls of its container.
                                                                            [4]
[Oxford and Cambridge]

11.

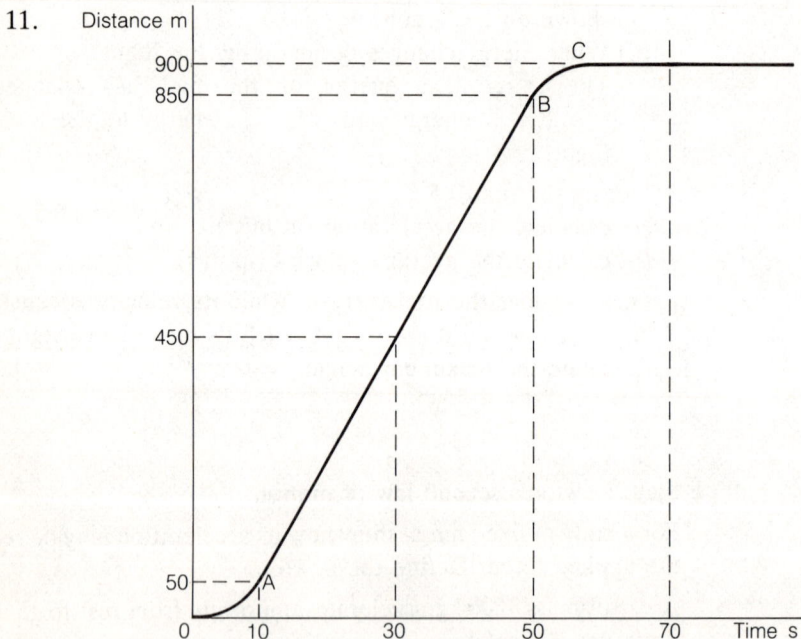

The graph represents a car journey.
a) Briefly describe the motion represented by OA, AB, BC on the graph.

b) What is the car's average speed during the first 10 seconds?
c) What is the speed of the car after 30 seconds?
d) What is the speed of the car after 70 seconds?
e) What is the total distance travelled? [10]

[JMB]

12.

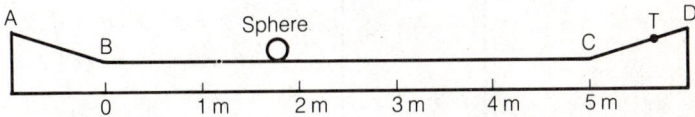

The horizontal section BC (of length 5.0 m) of the smooth track ABCD shown in the diagram was calibrated in metres. A steel sphere of mass 0.3 kg was released from a point on the slope AB and it rolled towards the end D of the track. A short time after the sphere had passed B a stopwatch was started and the times at which the sphere passed various calibration marks were noted and recorded in the following table.

Distance from B/m	2.0	3.0	4.0	5.0
Time/s	3.5	6.0	8.5	11.0

a) Using graph paper, draw a distance–time graph for the sphere. [4]
b) Calculate the average speed of the sphere as it rolled between the 3.0 m and 4.0 m marks. [2]
c) Assuming that the sphere rolled freely after it left the slope AB, calculate the distance of the sphere from B when the stopwatch was started. [2]
d) What is the acceleration of the sphere as it rolled along BC? Explain your reasoning. [2]
e) When the sphere met the sloping part CD of the track it slowed down until it stopped at the point T. The sphere reached T 13.0 s after the stopwatch was started. Calculate the deceleration of the sphere as it rolled up the slope CD. [3]
f) State any energy changes that occur as the sphere rolls along the track from C to T. [2]
g) Using the principle of conservation of energy, calculate the vertical height of T above the point C. [5]

[London]

13.

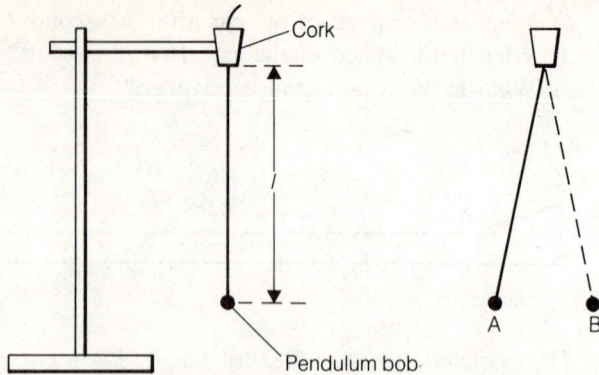

Cork

Pendulum bob

Using a stopwatch and the apparatus shown above, a student found the time taken for one complete oscillation of the pendulum bob (i.e. from A to B and back to A) for differing lengths, l, of the pendulum and produced the set of results shown in the table.

Time for one oscillation in s	2.82	2.38	2.01	1.62	1.20
l in m	1.96	1.44	1.00	0.64	0.36
$\sqrt{l}$ in $\sqrt{m}$	1.40	1.20	1.00	0.80	0.60

a) Plot a graph having *time for one oscillation* as the vertical axis and $\sqrt{l}$ as the horizontal axis. Draw the best straight line through your points.
b) Calculate the gradient (slope) of the line, showing clearly how you have obtained your answer.
c) Given that the acceleration due to gravity, g, can be obtained using the formula

$$g = \frac{40}{(\text{gradient})^2}$$

calculate g.

[15]
[AEB 1982]

14. a) A ball of mass 0.2 kg is fired vertically from the Earth's surface with a velocity of $40\,\text{ms}^{-1}$. Calculate:
(i)   the initial kinetic energy of the ball;
(ii) the greatest height reached;
(iii) the time to reach the ground again.   [6]

Would the results of the above calculations be different if the same procedure was repeated from the surface of the Moon? Explain any differences as fully as you can.   [4]

b) An object is projected parallel to the Earth's surface from a point well above it. Indicate on a diagram the possible paths of the object for various speeds of projection.

If the object remains in an orbital path, indicate the direction of its acceleration at some point in the path and name the force causing this acceleration. [5]

[SUJB]

15. The speed of a train which is hauled by a locomotive varies as shown below as it travels between two stations along a straight horizontal track.

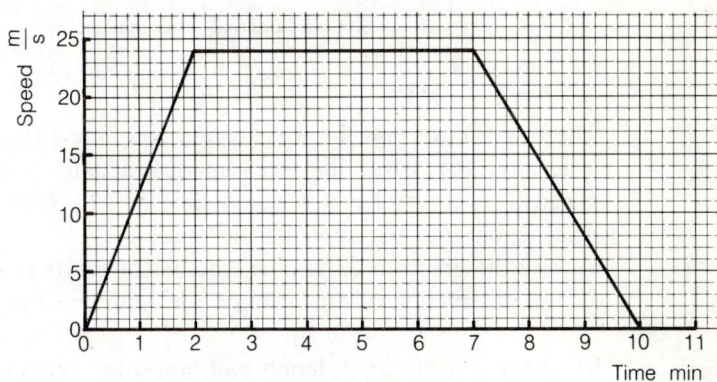

Use the graph to determine
a) the maximum speed of the train,
b) the acceleration, in m/s^2, of the train during the first 2 minutes of the journey,
c) the time during which the train is slowing down,
d) the total distance, in metres, between the two stations along the line,
e) the average speed, in m/s, of the train. [14]

Explain why the pull of the locomotive on the train during the first 2 minutes of the journey must be greater than the pull during the next 5 minutes of the journey. [3]

Is there any part of the journey when the pull of the locomotive is equal to the resistive forces acting on the train? Explain your answer.

[3]

[London]

16.

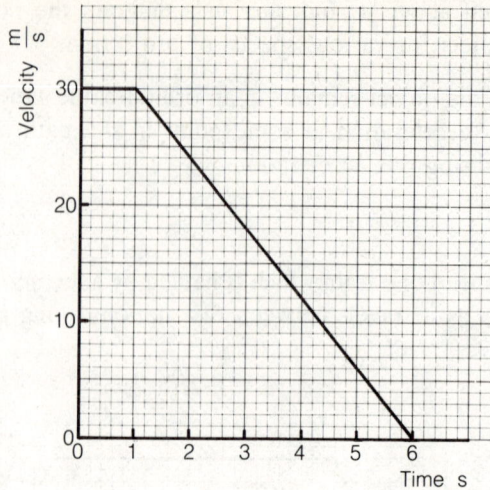

The graph shows how the velocity of a car of mass 1500 kg varies with time after the driver first sees an obstruction on the road 106 m ahead. The driver has a reaction time of 1.0 s between seeing the obstruction and first applying the brakes.

a) Use the graph to determine whether or not the car collides with the obstruction. (Show clearly how you arrive at your answer.) [4]

b) Determine the retardation and hence the braking force experienced by the car while it is slowing down. [4]

c) Explain why the driver tends to be thrown forward in the car as it slows down. [4]

d) Calculate the kinetic energy of the car when travelling at a velocity of 30 m/s. [3]

e) Explain why, if the car had been travelling at 15 m/s, the braking distance would have been greater than $\frac{1}{4}$ of the braking distance when the velocity was 30 m/s.

(You may assume that the same braking force was applied.) [5]

[London]

17. a) A car moves along a straight level road with a uniform acceleration of 2 m s^{-2}. What does this tell you about the speed of the car? [2]

b) The driver in a car travelling at 18 m s^{-1} sees a child run out into the road ahead. He brakes as hard as possible. The speed–time graph for the car, starting from the instant the driver sees the child, is shown.

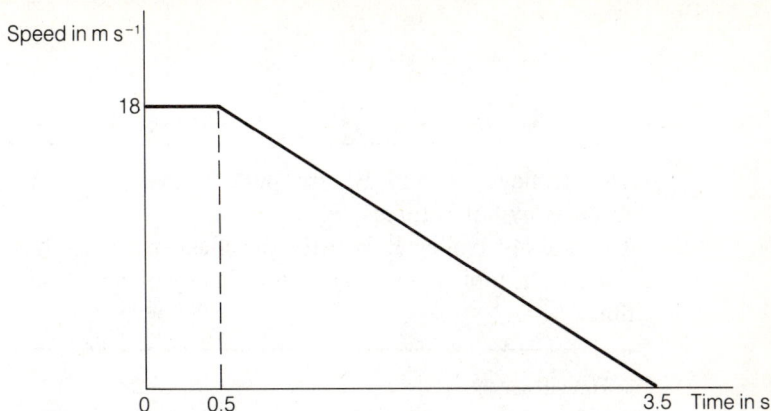

(i) Explain why the graph is in two distinct parts.

(ii) Calculate the total distance travelled by the car before it stops.

(iii) Safety tests require the foot brakes of a car to be able to decelerate it at a rate equal to, or better than, $5\,\text{ms}^{-2}$. Show, by calculation, whether or not this car would pass such a brake test.

(iv) Give **one** factor, apart from the braking system of the car, which affects the braking distance and explain its effect on this distance.   [8]

[Scottish]

18. A small steel ball of mass 60 g is released from rest from a height of 0.80 m above a rigid horizontal metal plate. After hitting the plate the ball rises vertically to a height of 0.55 m above it. Calculate:

a) the velocity of the ball just before impact;

b) the kinetic energy of the ball just after impact;

c) the loss of kinetic energy on impact. Give reasons for the energy loss.   [9]

Suggest some practical arrangements in such an experiment

(i) to release the ball carefully at the desired height,

(ii) to estimate the height of rise accurately.   [6]

[SUJB]

19.

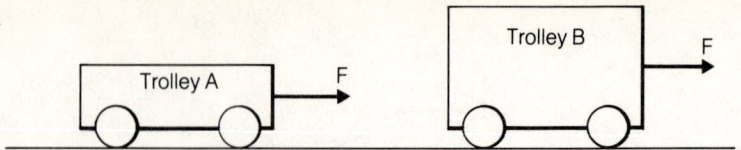

Two trolleys, A and B, are pulled across friction compensated surfaces by equal forces, F.

The mass of trolley B = twice the mass of trolley A.

The results table below shows the velocity of each trolley at different times.

Time in seconds	0	1	2	3	4	5
Velocity of trolley A in m/s	0	1.2	2.3	3.7	4.8	6.0
Velocity of trolley B in m/s	0	0.6	1.3	1.7	2.4	3.0

a) Plot on the same piece of graph paper a graph for each trolley of the above results. Plot velocity on the y-axis against time on the x-axis. Draw a best straight line through each set of points.

b) (i)   Which trolley has the greater acceleration?

   (ii) From your graphs find the acceleration of each trolley showing clearly how you obtained your answers and giving correct units.

   (iii) On your graph in part a), draw the graph you might expect to obtain for a third trolley, C, which has a mass three times that of trolley A, and is also pulled by an equal force, F.

   [LREB]

20.   Defining the symbols used, write down formulae for *potential energy*, *kinetic energy* and *momentum*.   [4]

In a fairground ride a train of mass 2000 kg does a 'loop-the-loop' on its track.

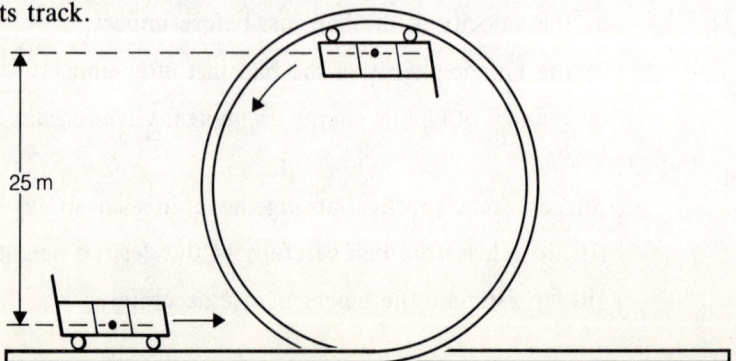

25 m

If the train enters the loop at 30 m/s, calculate

(i) its initial kinetic energy,

(ii) its initial momentum. [4]

Assuming no energy losses, calculate

(iii) the kinetic energy of the train when it is at its highest point,

(iv) the momentum of the train when it is at its highest point. [4]

Calculate the change in momentum of the train between entering the loop at the bottom, and being at the top of the loop. On a sketch diagram show the direction of the single force which could produce this change in momentum. [4]

[WJEC]

21. A ball is allowed to roll from rest down an inclined grooved runway. The ball is released from the 0 cm mark and its positions at various times are recorded. The inclination of the runway is θ to the horizontal.

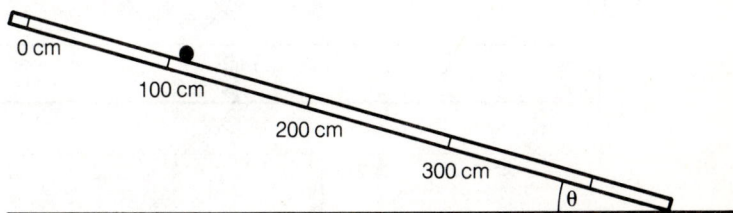

For one value of θ, the following readings were obtained.

Position s/cm	0	25	100	225	400
Time t/s	0	1.0	2.0	3.0	4.0

a) Plot a graph of the position, s, (y-axis) against time squared, t^2, (x-axis). [8]
   What deduction can be made from the graph about the relationship between s and t^2? Give your reasons.

b) Using the information that the acceleration of the ball down the runway is twice the slope of the graph, find a value for the acceleration. [5]

c) (i) Explain why the ball moves down the runway when released.
   (ii) If the angle θ is increased does the acceleration of the ball increase or decrease? Give a reason for your answer. [4]

[London]

22.

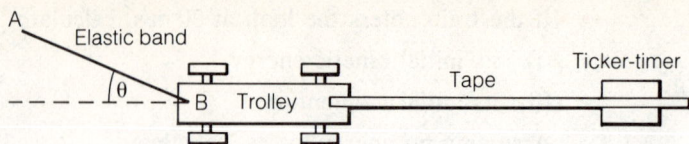

A

Elastic band

θ

B   Trolley

Tape

Ticker-timer

The diagram above shows the view from above of a trolley being pulled using an elastic band AB and moving over a friction-compensated slope. A tape attached to the trolley passes through a ticker-timer.

A student carried out a series of experiments in which the elastic band AB was stretched to the same length each time but the angle θ was varied. On each occasion a tape was produced from which the results shown in c) were obtained.

a) (i)   Describe a test which can be carried out to show that the slope is friction-compensated.

(ii)   Why did the student stretch the elastic band to the same length each time?   [4]

b)

Tape

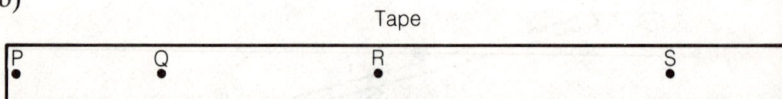

P   Q   R   S

Scale with 2-mm divisions

The diagram shows one of the tapes obtained. The time interval between each dot shown is 0.2 s. By taking measurements from the tape using the scale provided, determine

(i)   the average speed in cm/s over the distance PQ,

(ii)   the acceleration in cm/s^2 over the distance PS if the average speed over RS is 26 cm/s.

Which end of the tape was fastened to the trolley? Give a reason.   [6]

c)

Angle θ/°	20	40	50	60	70	80
cos θ		0.94	0.77	0.64	0.50	0.34	0.17
Acceleration $\left| \dfrac{cm}{s^2} \right.$		61	50	42	24	22	11

The table shows the results as recorded by the student. However, on one occasion the student made an error in calculating the acceleration.

(i) Plot a graph of $\cos\theta$ (*y*-axis) against acceleration (*x*-axis)

(ii) Use the graph to determine
    (1) which acceleration was calculated incorrectly,
    (2) the correct value of this acceleration,
    (3) the acceleration of the trolley when the elastic band is parallel to the longer side of the trolley. [7]

[London]

23. a) What is meant by saying that momentum is a *vector* quantity? [2]

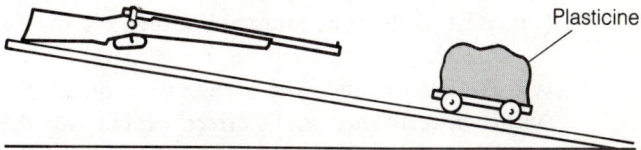
Plasticine

b) In an experiment to determine the speed of the shot from an air-rifle, a shot is fired from the rifle into a piece of plasticine mounted securely on a small truck. The truck runs on rails which are inclined to the horizontal in order to compensate for the effect of friction. How would you determine experimentally the correct inclination of the rails and the speed of the trolley? [7]

In such an experiment in which the shot remained embedded in the plasticine after impact, the following results were obtained:

    Mass of shot = 0.005 kg
    Mass of truck, plasticine and shot = 0.50 kg.
    Speed of truck down the incline after impact = 2.0 m/s.

Using these values, calculate:
    (i) the momentum of the loaded truck after impact, [3]
    (ii) the velocity of the shot at impact, [2]
    (iii) the kinetic energy of the loaded truck after impact, [3]
    (iv) the kinetic energy of the shot before impact. [1]

Explain why the answers you have calculated in (iii) and (iv) differ. [2]

[Oxford and Cambridge]

24. A small ball-bearing is dropped beside a vertical metre rule. It is photographed in light flashing at a frequency of 20 flashes per second.

An accurate diagram of the photograph is shown.

The rule is marked in mm (100, 200, 300, etc.).

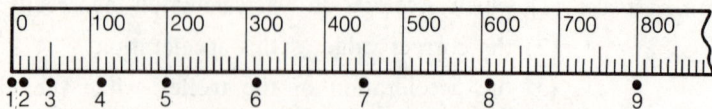

(i)   What is the time-interval between each flash? [1]
(ii) How far did the ball-bearing fall between the third flash and the fourth flash? [1]
(iii) How far did the ball-bearing fall between the eighth flash and the ninth flash? [1]
(iv) Calculate the average velocity between:
      the third and fourth flashes; [2]
      the eighth and ninth flashes. [1]
(v)   What is the time interval between the third flash and the eighth flash? [1]
(vi) Hence, calculate the acceleration of the ball-bearing. [3]
(vii) If air resistance has no effect, explain why the distances fallen by the ball-bearing would be the same whatever its mass. [3]

[Oxford (part)]

25. a) A thin strip of paper tape pulled by a trolley has a dot made on it every $\frac{1}{50}$ second by a stationary vibrator (ticker-tape timer). The diagram shows at full size a length of this tape with dots made as the trolley rolls down a gentle slope.

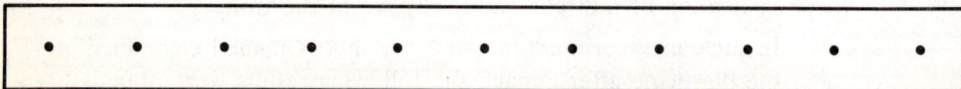

(i)   What sort of motion does the tape represent? [1]
(ii) How far has the trolley moved between the first and the eleventh dots? [2]
(iii) What is the time interval between the first and the eleventh dots? [1]
(iv) What value does this give for the trolley's speed? [2]

b) The trolley is replaced at the top of the track and pulled down it by a constant force. The tape is then cut up into 5-dot lengths. These lengths are glued to paper, as shown, to produce a block graph.

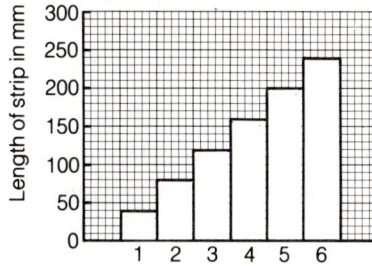

(i)   How long does it take for each strip to receive 5 dots? [1]
(ii) How far did the trolley travel for:
      strip 1;   [1]
      strip 6?   [1]
(iii) What was the average velocity of the trolley during the time
      taken for:
      strip 1;   [2]
      strip 6?   [1]
(iv) What was the increase in velocity between the times for strip
      1 and strip 6?   [2]
(v)   What was the acceleration of the trolley?   [2]

[Oxford (part)]

26. A car, initially at rest, is uniformly accelerated at 0.5 m/s^2 for 20 s,
     and is then kept at constant velocity for a further 10 s.
     (i)   Draw a velocity–time graph for this motion of the car. Label the
           axes and show the scales clearly.   [4]
     (ii) From the graph, calculate the total distance travelled in the 30 s.
           Explain how you have done this.   [3]
     (iii) Explain how a passenger could tell from the car's speedometer
           that the acceleration is uniform during the first 20 s. [2]
     (iv) Describe how he could determine this acceleration by watching
           the speedometer.   [3]

[Oxford (part)]

27. A coin rests on a record-player turntable at a distance of 90 mm from
     the centre. The turntable is rotating at $33\frac{1}{3}$ revolutions per minute.
     a) Calculate the speed of the coin.   [6]
     b) Apart from friction and air resistance, what forces act on the
        coin? In which directions do they act?   [4]
     c) In which direction must friction act on the coin? Explain. [4]
     d) Explain why the coin might slide off:
        (i)   if the turntable went faster;   [3]
        (ii) if the turntable was stopped suddenly.   [3]

[Oxford]

28. a) A sloping ramp of length 10 m is used to slide a block of ice of mass 50 kg up to a shelf 2 m above the ground. A force of 120 N parallel to the ramp is used to pull it slowly up to the shelf.

   (i)   What is the weight of the ice?   [1]

   (ii) How much work would be required to lift the block vertically up to the shelf without using the ramp?   [2]

   (iii) How much work is done by the applied force in pulling the block up the ramp?   [2]

   (iv) Why is less force needed to raise the block of ice by the ramp than to lift it vertically?   [2]

   (v)   What force parallel to the ramp would be needed if there were no frictional force to overcome?   [2]

   (vi) What is therefore the frictional force on the block in this case?   [1]

   b) The block of ice of mass 50 kg slips down the ramp onto the floor where it collides at a velocity of 5 m/s with a stationary block of ice of mass 40 kg. After the collision the 50 kg block continues in the same direction at 2 m/s.

   Calculate the following:

   (i)   the momentum of the 50 kg block just before the collision;   [2]

   (ii)   the momentum of this block just after the collision;   [2]

   (iii) the loss in momentum of the 50 kg block due to the collision;   [1]

   (iv)   the gain in momentum of the 40 kg block due to the collision;   [2]

   (v)   the velocity of the 40 kg block just after the collision; [2]

   (vi)   the kinetic energy lost by the 50 kg block due to the collision;   [2]

   (vii) the kinetic energy gained by the 40 kg block.   [2]

   (viii) Explain why the answers to (vi) and (vii) are not the same.   [2]

   [Oxford (part)]

29. A small lead sphere is suspended on a thin string from a stand so that the length of its suspension can be varied. The arrangement is indicated in the diagram opposite.

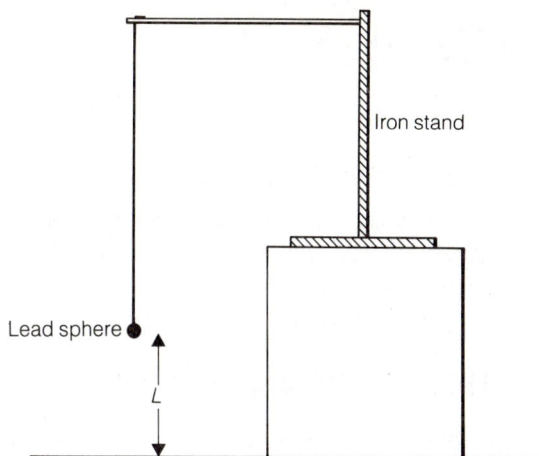

The distance L from the bottom of the sphere to the ground is measured and the sphere is pulled to one side through an angle of approximately 5° and released. It then swings from side to side carrying out oscillations.

The period T of such an oscillation is the time between the instants at which the bob passes a particular point in its swing *travelling in the same direction*. Describe in detail how you would measure L and obtain as accurately as possible a value for the period of these oscillations.   [6]

The timing is repeated for a number of different lengths of the string. *The support is kept fixed throughout.* The following values for T^2 and L are obtained.

T^2/s^2	5.95	5.67	5.02	4.10	3.47	2.95
L/m	0.124	0.200	0.353	0.575	0.740	0.875

Plot a graph of T^2 against L. L is to be plotted along the x-axis with scale beginning at zero and extending to 1.0 m. The scale for T^2 along the y-axis should be chosen to cover the range from 2.0 s^2 to 7.0 s^2.   [5]

Determine the gradient of your graph making clear the particular values of T^2 and L you have used. Also use your graph to deduce the height of the bottom of the bob above the ground to give a period of 2.5 s.   [4]

[Cambridge]

5. Electricity

This chapter is divided into two main sections: static electricity (electrostatics) and current electricity. We shall consider electrostatics first, but nearly all the mathematical problems arise in the area of current electricity.

Electrostatics (static electricity)

The quantity of charge Q which can be stored by an object is related to the capacitance C of the object and the difference in potential V between it and its surrounds. The three quantities are related by the equation

$$\text{Charge} = \text{Capacitance} \times \text{Potential difference}$$

or

$$Q = C \times V$$

Q is measured in coulombs, C in farads, and V in volts. A body which has the ability to store charge is called a capacitor.

Example A capacitor has a capacitance of 20 µF. How much charge will be stored on each plate when the following potential difference is applied across it:

a) 2 V   **b)** 10 V   **c)** 15 V

Method: Use

$$Q = C \times V$$

Remember when substituting that $1\ \mu F = 1 \times 10^{-6}\ F$ or $0.000001\ F$

Answers: a) $4 \times 10^{-5}\ C$ **b)** $2 \times 10^{-4}\ C$ **c)** $3 \times 10^{-4}\ C$

You are unlikely to meet any other formulae to do with capacitors although you should remember that, for a parallel plate capacitor, the capacitance depends on the overlapping plate area A, the plate separation d and the substance between the plates, represented by the dielectric constant for the substance ϵ. The formula relating these is

$$C = \epsilon \frac{A}{d}$$

Current electricity

A flow of electric charge between two points is called an electric current. The size of the current depends on the amount of charge and also how fast the charge flows. The formula relating charge Q, current I, and time t, in seconds, is

$$Q = I \times t$$

Example 6000 coulombs of electric charge flow between two points. Calculate the electric current if this charge flows in:

a) 1000 s   **b)** 3000 s   **c)** 12 000 s

Method: You must make the current I the subject of the equation. Rearranging give

$$I = \frac{Q}{t}$$

Answers: a) 6 A   **b)** 2 A   **c)** 0.5 A

For electric charge to flow there must be a complete circuit and the charge must be given energy to make it move around the circuit. The energy may be provided by a chemical source such as a cell or battery of cells. The 'push' behind the current is called the *electromotive force* (e.m.f.) which is measured in volts. Within the circuit there will be some opposition to the flow and this is called *resistance*. For any component in an electric circuit its resistance is given by the formula

$$\text{Resistance} = \frac{\text{Potential difference across it}}{\text{Current flowing through it}}$$

or

$$R = \frac{V}{I}$$

Example

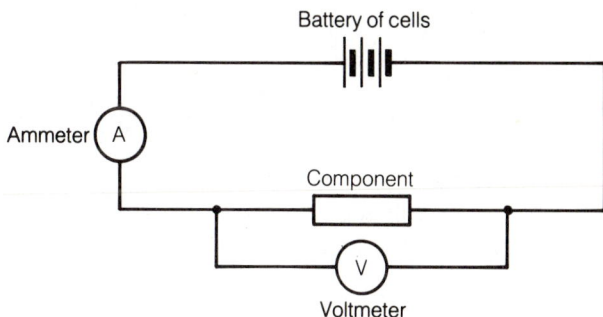

Calculate the resistance of the component if the current reading on the ammeter A and the potential difference reading on the voltmeter V are:

	Ammeter reading (A)	Voltmeter reading (V)
a)	2.0	12.0
b)	3.0	6.0
c)	4.5	18.0

Method: The ammeter reads the current flowing through the circuit *and* through the component. The voltmeter measures the potential difference across the component.
Using

$$R = \frac{V}{I}$$

work out the resistance. Resistance is measured in ohms (Ω).

Answers: a) $6\,\Omega$ **b)** $2\,\Omega$ **c)** $4\,\Omega$

If there is more than one resistor in a circuit, then the resistors may be arranged in more than one way. We shall look at resistors in series and resistors in parallel.

Resistors in series

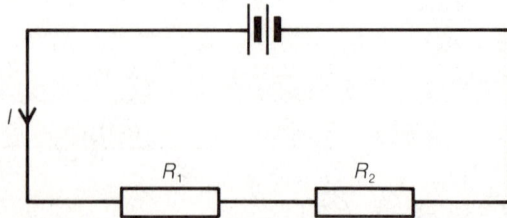

In the circuit shown the current I will flow through both the resistors before it returns to the battery of cells. The total resistance met by the current is found by adding the resistances of the resistors together, i.e.

$$\text{Total resistance} = \text{Resistance}_1 + \text{Resistance}_2$$

or
$$R_{\text{total}} = R_1 + R_2$$

Example Calculate the total resistance in the circuit shown if the values of the two resistors are:

	R_1 (Ω)	R_2 (Ω)
a)	3	6
b)	6	6
c)	12	24

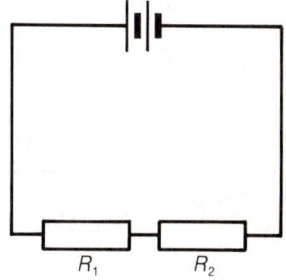

Method: Use

$$R_{\text{total}} = R_1 + R_2$$

Answers: a) $9\,\Omega$ **b)** $12\,\Omega$ **c)** $36\,\Omega$

Resistors in parallel

The resistors could also have been arranged in parallel (see diagram). This means that the current I can flow through either of the resistors, e.g. I_1 flowing through R_1 and I_2 through R_2. Remember that $I = I_1 + I_2$. In this case the total resistance of the pair of resistors is given by

$$\frac{1}{R_{\text{total}}} = \frac{1}{R_1} + \frac{1}{R_2}$$

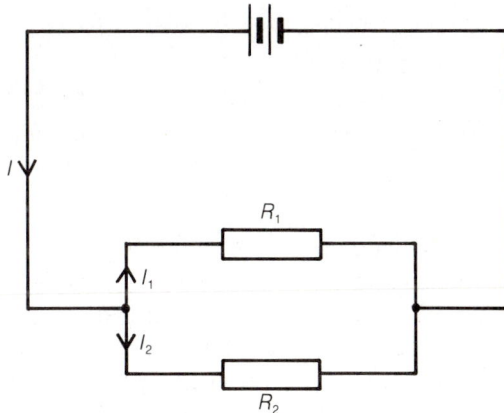

Example   Calculate the total resistance in the circuit shown if the values of the two resistors are

	R_1 (Ω)	R_2 (Ω)
a)	3	6
b)	6	6
c)	12	24

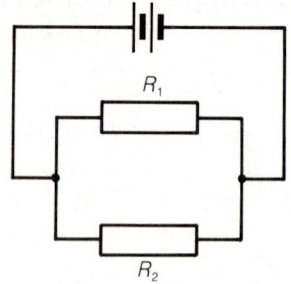

Method: Using

$$\frac{1}{R_{\text{total}}} = \frac{1}{R_1} + \frac{1}{R_2}$$

let us look at part **a)** in its entirety:

$$\frac{1}{R_{\text{total}}} = \frac{1}{3} + \frac{1}{6}$$

$$= \frac{2 + 1}{6} \quad \left(\text{because } \frac{1}{3} = \frac{2}{6}\right)$$

$$= \frac{3}{6}$$

$$= \frac{1}{2}$$

$$\therefore R_{\text{total}} = \frac{2}{1} = 2\,\Omega$$

Answers: b) $3\,\Omega$ **c)** $8\,\Omega$

Note: For two (or more) resistors in parallel the total, or effective, resistance is always *less* than the values of the individual resistors.

The situation becomes more complicated when there are series and parallel arrangements within the same circuit. In these cases calculate the effective resistance of each part of the circuit before adding the effective resistances as if they were all in series. In any electric circuit always try to replace networks of resistors by their equivalent resistance until you have achieved as simple a circuit as possible.

Example What is the effective resistance in the following circuit?

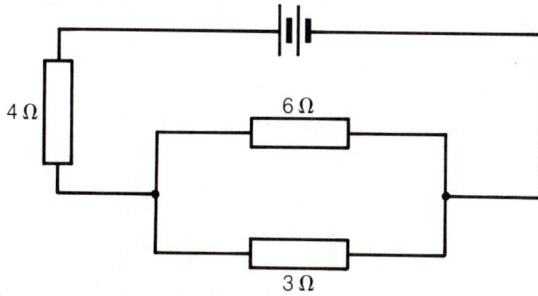

Method: First replace the parallel network by a single resistor to give

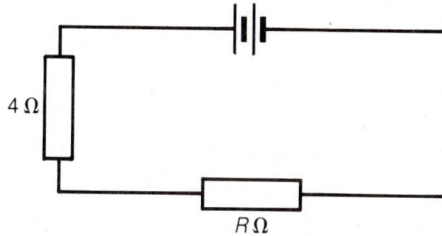

To find R use

$$\frac{1}{R_{\text{total}}} = \frac{1}{R_1} + \frac{1}{R_2}$$

$$= \frac{1}{6} + \frac{1}{3}$$

$$= \frac{1 + 2}{6}$$

$$= \frac{3}{6} = \frac{1}{2}$$

$$\therefore R = 2\,\Omega$$

You now have a series circuit:

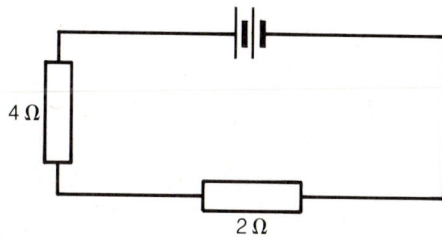

These two resistors can be replaced by a single resistor, using

$$R_{total} = R_1 + R_2$$
$$= 4 + 2$$
$$= 6\,\Omega$$

giving a final equivalent circuit:

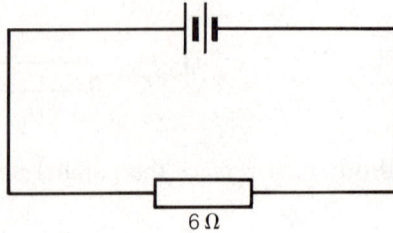

$6\,\Omega$

Example   Calculate the effective resistance of the following networks:

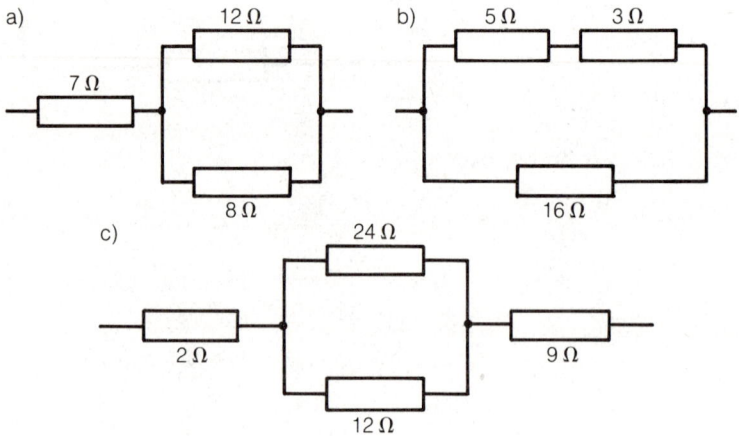

a)

$12\,\Omega$

$7\,\Omega$

$8\,\Omega$

b)

$5\,\Omega$ $3\,\Omega$

$16\,\Omega$

c)

$24\,\Omega$

$2\,\Omega$ $9\,\Omega$

$12\,\Omega$

Method: Simplify the circuit a stage at a time, working out equivalent resistances at each stage. The two formulae to use are

$$R_{total} = R_1 + R_2 \text{ for a series network}$$

and

$$\frac{1}{R_{total}} = \frac{1}{R_1} + \frac{1}{R_2} \text{ for a parallel network}$$

In **a)** work out the parallel network, and then treat the problem as two resistors in series.

In **b)** first solve the upper part of the network by taking the two resistors in series and then calculate the equivalent of the parallel network.

In **c)** first work out the equivalent resistance of the parallel network and then treat the problem as three resistors in series.

Answers: a) 11.8 Ω   **b)** 5.3 Ω   **c)** 19.0 Ω

In the following problem the situation is made more complicated because you have not only to consider a parallel network but you are also asked to work out the current flowing through each resistor.

Example Calculate the currents I_1 and I_2 when R_1 and R_2 have the following values:

$R_1(\Omega)$	12	30	4
$R_2(\Omega)$	6	10	6

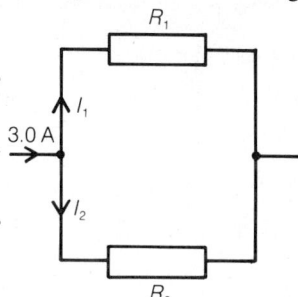

Method: Several approaches are possible. The method adopted here is to calculate the effective resistance using

$$\frac{1}{R_{total}} = \frac{1}{R_1} + \frac{1}{R_2}$$

Having obtained a value for R_{total} work out the potential difference V across the network using

$$V = I \times R_{total}$$

where R_{total} is the effective resistance.

This is the potential difference across both R_1 and R_2 and so you can write

$$V = I_1 \times R_1 \text{ and } V = I_2 \times R_2$$

Rearranging gives

$$I_1 = \frac{V}{R_1} \text{ and } I_2 = \frac{V}{R_2}$$

As a check you should find that the current flowing into the parallel network is equal to $I_1 + I_2$. You will also see that the larger current flows through the smaller resistor. You would expect this because there is less resistance to oppose the flow of current.

Answers:

	a	b	c
$I_1(A)$	1.0	0.75	1.8
$I_2(A)$	2.0	2.25	1.2

Example   In the circuit shown, calculate the current readings on the ammeters A_1, A_2 and A_3 and the potential difference readings on the voltmeters V_1 and V_2.

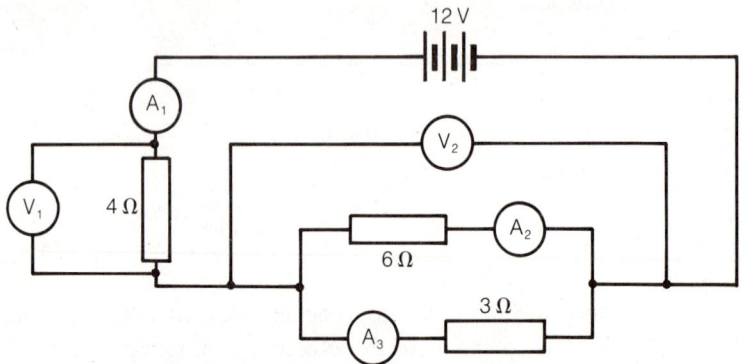

Method: You may feel happy to solve the problem with the meters included in the circuit, but it is easier to redraw the circuit with the meters removed:

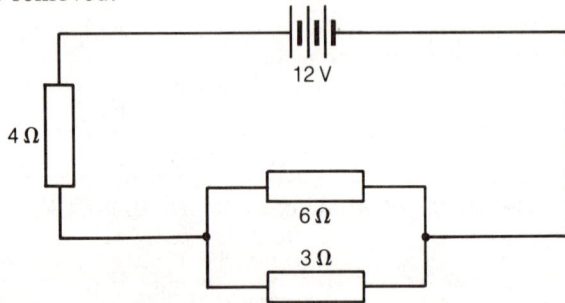

First find the equivalent resistance R of the parallel network and then the total resistance in the circuit by considering $R\,\Omega$ and $4\,\Omega$ in series.

Having found the total resistance, work out the current leaving the battery of cells. This will flow through A_1 and the $4\,\Omega$ resistor. The reading on V_1 can be found using

$$V = I \times R$$

where $R = 4\,\Omega$

When the current reaches the junction of the parallel network some of it will flow through the 3 Ω resistor and the remainder through the 6 Ω resistor. The potential difference, read on V_2, across both the resistors is the same, and is the same as the potential difference across the equivalent resistor R. You can calculate this using the same formula $V = I \times R$. (Check that $V_1 + V_2 = 12$ V.)

Having calculated the potential difference reading V_2, work out the readings on A_2 and A_3 using

$$V = I \times R$$

and substituting the appropriate meter readings.

$V_2 = A_2 \times R$ with $R = 6\,\Omega$

and

$V_2 = A_3 \times R$ with $R = 3\,\Omega$

Having worked out the readings on A_2 and A_3 check that $A_1 = A_2 + A_3$

Answers: $V_1 = 8$ V $V_2 = 4$ V
$A_1 = 2$ A $A_2 = \frac{2}{3}$ A $A_3 = \frac{4}{3}$ A

Conversion of galvanometer to ammeter and voltmeter

A galvanometer measures very small currents. Electric current is measured using an ammeter and electrical potential difference is measured using a voltmeter. Both of these meters are galvanometers which have been converted for particular purposes.

Conversion of galvanometer to ammeter

Example A galvanometer has a resistance of 5 Ω and experiences a full-scale deflection when a current of 15 mA flows through it. How might it be converted to an ammeter to read a current of:

a) 1.5 A   **b)** 3.0 A   **c)** 5.0 A?

Method: Remember that an ammeter must be placed in series with the component or branch in a circuit. We can then measure the current flowing *through* that part of the circuit. If we look at part **a)** of the question, a current of 1.5 A will flow towards the galvanometer.

The galvanometer however can take a maximum current of only 15 mA (= 0.015 A). In the same way that a bypass takes much of the flow of traffic *around* a town, a low resistance shunt resistor is connected in parallel with the galvanometer:

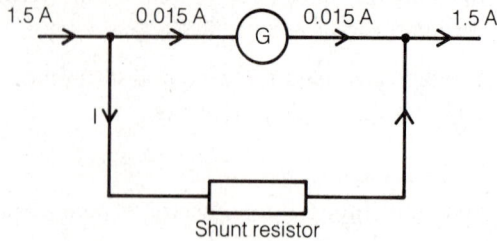

The shunted current I is $(1.5 \, \text{A} - 0.015 \, \text{A}) = 1.485 \, \text{A}$. To calculate the resistance of the shunt resistor redraw the previous diagram and add some extra information:

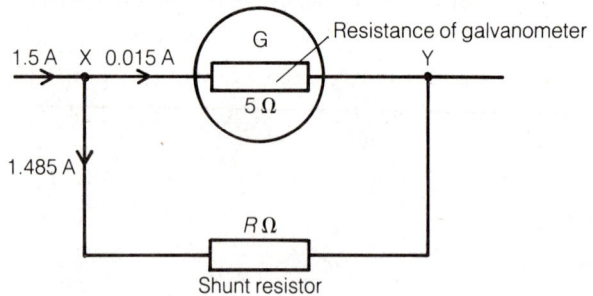

The potential difference between X and Y must be the same whether you consider the 0.015 A flowing through the 5 Ω resistor, or whether you consider the 1.485 A flowing through the $R \, \Omega$ shunt.

Using $V = I \times R$, for the upper path

$$V_{XY} = 0.015 \times 5$$
$$= 0.075 \, \text{V} \qquad [1]$$

and for the lower path

$$V_{XY} = 1.485 \times R \qquad [2]$$

Equations [1] and [2] must be equivalent because V_{XY} is the same, and so

$$0.075 = 1.485 \times R$$

or
$$R = \frac{0.075}{1.485}$$

$$= 0.051 \, \Omega$$

To convert the galvanometer into an ammeter to read up to 1.5 A (or 1.5 A full-scale deflection) you would put a 0.051 Ω resistor in parallel with the galvanometer.

Now attempt parts **b)** and **c)**.

Answers: b) 0.025 Ω   **c)** 0.015 Ω, both in parallel.

Note that the effective resistance of the ammeter is now small (see the work on resistors in parallel), so that the ammeter is now more like a perfect ammeter which should have no resistance so that it does not disturb the circuit in which it is placed.

Conversion of galvanometer to voltmeter

Example A galvanometer has a resistance of 10 Ω and experiences a full-scale deflection when a current of 5 mA flows through it. How might it be converted to a voltmeter to read potential differences of

a) 5 V   **b)** 10 V   **c)** 15 V?

Method: Remember that a voltmeter must be placed in parallel with the component or part of a circuit, the potential difference *across* which we wish to measure. If we look at part **a)** of the question, we see that the potential difference across the galvanometer is given by

$$V = I \times R$$
$$= 0.005 \times 10$$
$$= 0.05 \text{ V}$$

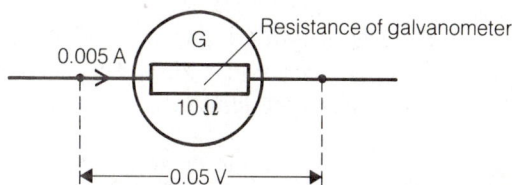

In order that a potential difference of 5 V is measured then an 'extra' (5 V − 0.05 V) = 4.95 V must be dropped across the galvanometer. To do this a resistor (sometimes called a bobbin or multiplier) is placed in series with the galvanometer. To calculate the resistance of the added resistor redraw the previous diagram and add some extra information:

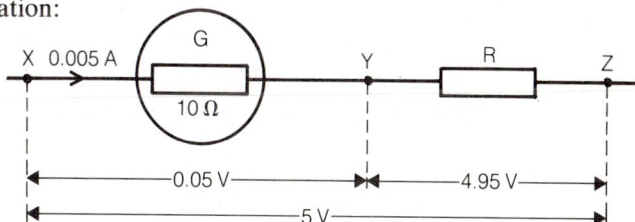

The current flowing through the resistor R is 0.005 A and so

$$R = \frac{V}{I}$$

$$= \frac{4.95}{0.005}$$

$$= 990\,\Omega$$

To convert the galvanometer into a voltmeter to read up to 5 V (or 5 V full-scale deflection) a 990 Ω resistor is connected in series with the galvanometer.

Now attempt parts **b)** and **c)**.

Answers: b) 1990 Ω **c)** 2990 Ω, both in series.

Note: The effective resistance of the voltmeter is now large (see the work on resistors in series) so that the voltmeter is more like a perfect voltmeter, which should have infinite resistance so that it draws no current from the component across which it is connected.

Factors affecting resistance

Nearly everything will oppose the flow of electric current and therefore has some resistance. The problems that you meet may be to do with pieces of wire. There are three factors that affect the resistance of a piece of wire:

1. The length of the wire. This may be considered as several resistors placed in series. This means that the resistance is proportional to the length:

$$R \propto L$$

2. The cross-sectional area of the wire. This can be considered as several resistors in parallel. This means that the resistance is inversely proportional to the cross-sectional area:

$$R \propto \frac{1}{A}$$

3. The material from which the wire is made. The quantity which represents this is called the *resistivity* and is usually given the symbol ρ.

Combining all three factors gives

$$\text{Resistance} = \text{Resistivity} \times \frac{\text{Length}}{\text{Cross-sectional area}}$$

or

$$R = \rho \times \frac{L}{A}$$

$$\Omega \quad \Omega\,\text{m} \quad \frac{\text{m}}{\text{m}^2} = \frac{1}{\text{m}}$$

Remember in calculations using this formula that the length and cross-sectional area must both be in the same basic unit, e.g. m and m^2 or mm and mm^2, and this must tie in with the unit of length included in the resistivity units.

Example   The resistivity of manganin is $5.0 \times 10^{-7}\,\Omega$ m. Calculate the resistance of resistors made from manganin which have the following lengths and cross-sectional areas:

	a	b	c
L	2 m	1000 cm	150 mm
A	$2.0 \times 10^{-5}\,\text{m}^2$	$0.007\,\text{cm}^2$	$0.3\,\text{mm}^2$

Method: The formula to use is

$$R = \rho \times \frac{L}{A}$$

The units must be consistent. In part **a)** the length is in m, the cross-sectional area in m^2 and the resistivity in Ω m. Then substitute the numbers as they are. However, in **b)** and **c)** the units are 'mixed' since the lengths and cross-sectional areas are in cm or mm and cm^2 or mm^2 respectively. You can convert these into m and m^2, but you may find the mathematics easier if you convert the resistivity into Ω cm and Ω mm. This is done by multiplying the resistivity value by 10^2 and 10^3 respectively.

Answers: a) $0.05\,\Omega$ **b)** $7.14\,\Omega$ **c)** $0.25\,\Omega$

These problems are sometimes made harder by giving the radius or diameter of the wire, so that you have to calculate the cross-sectional area first. To do this remember that $A = \pi \times r^2$.

Potentiometer

You have already seen that for a wire of given cross-sectional area, the resistance of the wire is proportional to the length. This fact is used in a device called a *potentiometer*. It usually consists of a cell, or battery of cells, and a length of uniform wire AB (usually 1 m long) as shown.

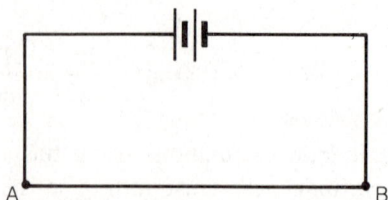

Example If the potential difference across AB is 2.0 V and AB is 1 m long, what would be the potential difference across the following lengths of wire?

a) 25 cm   **b)** 50 cm   **c)** 60 cm

Method: 1 m or 100 cm is equivalent to a potential difference of 2 V. Therefore 1 cm is equivalent to $\frac{1}{100} \times 2\,V = 0.02\,V$. 25 cm is then equivalent to $0.02 \times 25 = 0.5\,V$.

Answers: a) 0.5 V   **b)** 1.0 V   **c)** 1.2 V

If a cell E_1 is then connected as shown, a movable contact can be made on the potentiometer wire AB using a sharp-edged contact called a *jockey* or *rider*.

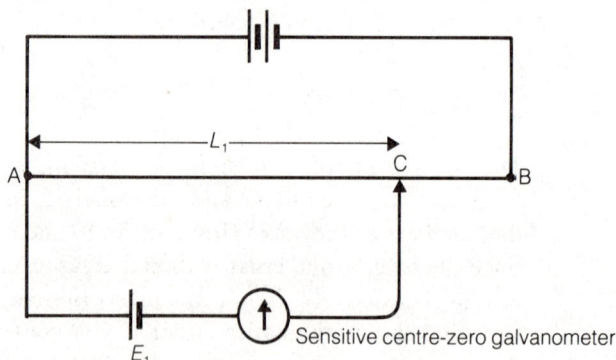

Sensitive centre-zero galvanometer

When the jockey is at the point C the centre-zero galvanometer shows no deflection. If the jockey is moved towards A, the galvanometer pointer will move in one direction. If it is moved towards B, the pointer will move in the opposite direction. The balance position C is where the e.m.f. of the cell E_1 is equal to the potential difference between A and C. This is because the potential of the negative terminal of E is the same as the potential at C. If the two are at the same potential then there is no potential difference between them and so no current flows through the galvanometer. The potential of the positive terminal of E_1 is the same as the potential of A because the two are connected.

Therefore E_1 is proportional to the length AC or

$$E_1 \propto L_1 \qquad\qquad [1]$$

A second cell E_2 can then be used to replace E_1 and its balance length L_2 found, i.e.

$$E_2 \propto L_2 \qquad\qquad [2]$$

Equations [1] and [2] can be combined to give

$$\frac{E_1}{E_2} = \frac{L_1}{L_2}$$

Knowing L_1 and L_2 you can calculate the ratio of the e.m.f.s of E_1 and E_2, and if you know either E_1 or E_2 you can calculate the other.

Example If E_2 is 1.5 V and gives a balance length of 75 cm, calculate the e.m.f. of a cell E_1 which gives a balance length of:

a) 30 cm   **b)** 50 cm   **c)** 90 cm

Method: Rearrange

$$\frac{E_1}{E_2} = \frac{L_1}{L_2}$$

to make E_1 the subject. This gives

$$E_1 = E_2 \times \frac{L_1}{L_2}$$

Substitute the values given:

$$E_1 = 1.5 \times \frac{L_1}{75}$$

Answers: a) 0.6 V   **b)** 1.0 V   **c)** 1.8 V

The potentiometer is an ideal voltmeter.

Wheatstone bridge

This is similar to the potentiometer in that, at balance, no current flows through a galvanometer. There are two possible arrangements:

a)   **b)**

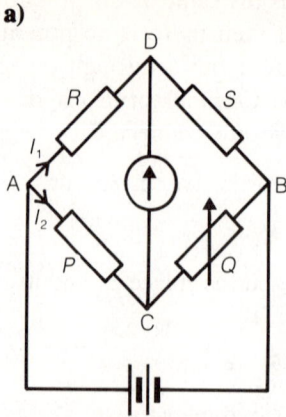

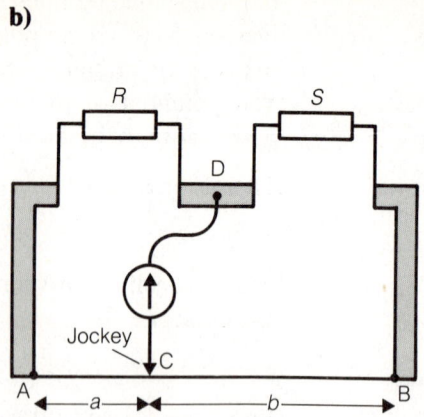

The labels correspond in both diagrams so that you can see that the two circuits are the same. The bridge is balanced by varying Q or by moving the jockey along the wire. The galvanometer shows no deflection when the bridge is balanced. At balance the potentials at D and C must be the same, otherwise a current would flow through the galvanometer. If this is the case, then in the first arrangement a):

$$\text{p.d. across } R = \text{p.d. across } P$$

$$I_1 \times R = I_2 \times P$$

$$\therefore \quad \frac{R}{P} = \frac{I_2}{I_1} \qquad\qquad [1]$$

also

$$\text{p.d. across } S = \text{p.d. across } Q$$

$$I_1 \times S = I_2 \times Q$$

$$\therefore \quad \frac{S}{Q} = \frac{I_2}{I_1} \qquad\qquad [2]$$

Equating [1] and [2] gives

$$\frac{R}{P} = \frac{S}{Q}$$

Example If $S = 4\,\Omega$ and $Q = 8\,\Omega$, calculate the value of R which gives a balance when P is:

a) $2\,\Omega$ **b)** $5\,\Omega$ **c)** $7\,\Omega$

Method: Substitute the given values in

$$\frac{R}{P} = \frac{S}{Q}$$

to give
$$\frac{R}{P} = \frac{4}{8} = \frac{1}{2}$$

or
$$R = \frac{P}{2}$$

Answers: a) $1\,\Omega$ **b)** $2.5\,\Omega$ **c)** $3.5\,\Omega$

In the second arrangement b) with the meter bridge:

$$\text{p.d. across } R = \text{p.d. across AC}$$

or
$$R \propto a \qquad\qquad [1]$$

also
$$\text{p.d. across } S = \text{p.d. across CB}$$

or
$$S \propto b \qquad\qquad [2]$$

Dividing [1] by [2] gives

$$\frac{R}{S} = \frac{a}{b}$$

Example   Calculate the value of R which would give a balance on the meter bridge for an S value of $10\,\Omega$ when a is:

a) 20 cm   **b)** 45 cm   **c)** 75 cm.

Method: If a is known, then the value for b can be found from $100 - a$. Therefore

$$\frac{R}{S} = \frac{a}{(100 - a)}$$

or
$$R = S \times \frac{a}{(100 - a)}$$

$$= 10 \times \frac{a}{(100 - a)}$$

Answers: a) $2.5\,\Omega$ **b)** $8.2\,\Omega$ **c)** $30\,\Omega$

Internal resistance of cells and batteries

Earlier we met the idea of the electromotive force of a cell or battery of cells. If a very high resistance voltmeter, i.e. one which draws minimal current, is connected across the cell, then the reading on it gives the e.m.f. of the cell. However, as soon as an external circuit is connected to the cell, the voltmeter reading drops. The new reading is called the terminal potential difference or t.p.d. This drop can be explained if the internal resistance of the cell is considered. Some potential difference within the cell is necessary if the current flowing in the circuit is also to flow through the cell — which it must to complete the circuit. These so-called 'lost volts' are the difference between the e.m.f. and the t.p.d.

Example   **a)**   **b)**

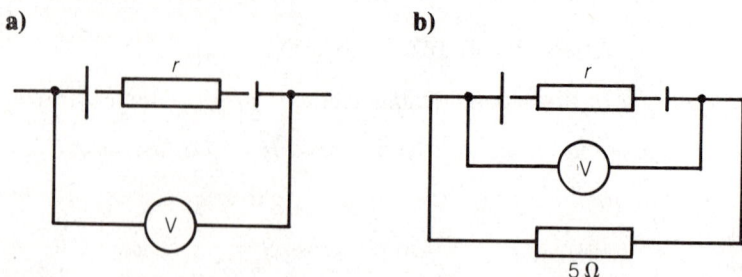

5 Ω

When a voltmeter is connected across a dry cell on open circuit, as shown in circuit a) above, it reads 1.5 V. Calculate the internal resistance of the cell if, when a 5 Ω resistor is connected across the cell as shown in circuit b), the voltmeter reading drops to:

a) 1.2 V   **b)** 1.0 V   **c)** 0.5 V

Method: In fig. a) the cell is on open circuit, i.e. no current leaves or enters the cell, and so the internal resistance has no effect on the circuit. In fig. b) the external resistor causes a current to flow and the circuit equation becomes

$$E = I \times (r + R) \tag{1}$$

where E is the e.m.f. of the cell and R is the external resistance.

By looking at the circuit in fig. b) again you will see that the voltmeter is reading the potential difference across the external resistor R. This is also the potential difference across the terminals of the cell. This fact will enable you to calculate I because $I = \dfrac{V}{R}$.

You can then work out the total resistance in the circuit, because

$$I = \frac{E}{(r + R)} \text{ (Equation [1] rearranged)}$$

Further rearrangement gives

$$r + R = \frac{E}{I}$$

or $$r = \frac{E}{I} - R$$

Answers: a) 1.25 Ω   **b)** 2.5 Ω   **c)** 10 Ω

Electrical power and electrical heating

One of the most common uses of electricity is to provide some sort of heating, e.g. in an electric cooker, toaster or kettle. When an electric current passes through *any* object, e.g. a resistor, then that may well heat up also. The formulae to use are:

$$\begin{aligned}
\text{Electrical power} &= \text{Current} \times \text{Potential difference} = (I \times V)\\
\text{in watts} &= (\text{Current})^2 \times (\text{Resistance}) = (I^2R)\\
&= \frac{(\text{Potential difference})^2}{\text{Resistance}} = \left(\frac{V^2}{R}\right)
\end{aligned}$$

and

$$\begin{aligned}
\text{Heat energy} &= \text{Power} \times \text{Time in seconds}\\
\text{in joules} &= I \times V \times t\\
&= I^2 \times R \times t\\
&= \frac{V^2}{R} \times t
\end{aligned}$$

Example   Given the power ratings shown, calculate the current flowing through the following domestic appliances when connected to the 240 V mains:

Appliance	Power (W)
a) Kettle	2500
b) Light bulb	60
c) Freezer	1000
d) Power drill	500
e) Cooker	6500

Method: The formula to use is

$$P = I \times V$$

Rearranging gives

$$I = \frac{P}{V} = \frac{P}{240}$$

Answers: a) 10.4 A   **b)** 0.25 A   **c)** 4.17 A   **d)** 2.08 A
e) 27.1 A

Example The previous example can be further developed by working out the resistance of the heating coils within the appliances.

Method: In this case the formula to use is

$$P = \frac{V^2}{R}$$

or
$$R = \frac{V^2}{P} = \frac{240^2}{P}$$

Answers: a) 23.0 Ω   **b)** 960 Ω   **c)** 57.6 Ω   **d)** 115 Ω
e) 8.86 Ω

Alternatively, in this question you could have used the equation

$$P = I^2 \times R$$

rearranging it to give

$$R = \frac{P}{I^2}$$

In all of these problems, to find the energy converted from electricity to heat use the formula:

Energy = Power × Time in seconds

and you should refer to the chapter on heat for examples of the use of this formula.

Fuses: Another useful application of the formula $P = I \times V$ is to work out the size of fuse which should be included in the circuit operating a device — either in the plug or in the equipment itself.

Example You are given the following fuses: 3 A, 5 A, 10 A, 13 A. Which fuse would you use for the following pieces of electrical equipment when they are connected to the 240 V mains?

a) an electric heater rated at 2500 W
b) a black and white television rated at 120 W
c) an electric kettle rated at 1300 W
d) an electric iron, rated at 800 W.

Method: A fuse will 'blow' and break the circuit if too large a current passes through it. Knowing the power and the voltage (or potential difference) you can work out the operating current of the equipment using

$$P = I \times V$$

Rearranging gives

$$I = \frac{P}{V}$$

$$= \frac{P}{240}$$

The fuse must have a fusing value which is bigger than the operating current. Choose the fuse with the nearest, but larger, fuse current value.

Answers: a) 13 A fuse   **b)** 3 A fuse   **c)** 10 A fuse
d) 5 A fuse

The kilowatt-hour: When electricity boards are working out electricity bills they need to know how much electrical energy has been used by the consumer. This could be calculated in joules, but the 'unit' used by the boards is the kilowatt-hour. This is the amount of energy used by an electrical device rated at 1 kilowatt if it is operating for 1 hour. The number of joules used is vast and could present the electricity boards with administrative problems.

Example How many kilowatt-hours of electrical energy are used by the following devices operating for 3 hours?

a) a light bulb rated at 60 W
b) an electric fire rated at 3 kW
c) a television rated at 300 W.

Method: The formula to use is

Energy in kilowatt-hours = Power in kilowatts × Time in hours

Remember to convert the power to kilowatts,
e.g. 60 watts = 0.06 kilowatts.

In this example the time is given in hours, but if it were not you should always remember to convert it to hours.

Answers: a) 0.18 kW h   **b)** 9.0 kW h   **c)** 0.9 kW h

The electricity boards charge a certain price for every kilowatt-hour used and from this they calculate how much money the consumer must pay.

Example Calculate the cost of running the following devices for the times indicated, if the cost of each unit is 5p.

Device	Power	Time
a) Light bulb	100 W	6 h
b) Immersion heater	3000 W	2 h
c) Kettle	1500 W	3 min
d) Refrigerator	120 W	1 week

Method: The formula to use to work out the cost is:

$$\text{Cost} = \text{Number of units} \times \text{Cost of one unit}$$
$$= \text{Power} \times \text{Time} \times \text{Cost of one unit}$$

Remember that the power must be converted to kilowatts and the time to hours.

Answers: a) 3p   **b)** 30p   **c)** 0.38p   **d)** 100.8p

The answer to **d)** is much higher than the actual cost of running the refrigerator. Can you think why the refrigerator is much cheaper to run?

Electrolysis

So far, this chapter has concentrated on electric currents flowing in solids. However electricity can also flow in liquids and gases.

Liquids which conduct electric currents under normal conditions are called electrolytes. They include salt solutions, dilute acids and alkalis, liquid metals and molten salts. During the flow of current through an electrolyte chemical changes may take place within the electrolyte. For example, a metal salt may liberate the metal, or an acid may liberate hydrogen. When such substances are liberated, the mass which is released depends both on the amount of electrical charge passed through the electrolyte and on the particular substance which is being liberated.

Experiments have shown that the following formula is valid:

$$\text{Mass liberated} = \text{Constant} \times \text{Electrical charge passed}$$

or $$m = Z \times Q$$

where the constant Z is called the electrochemical equivalent of the substance.

You will remember that

Electrical charge = Current × Time in seconds

or $$Q = I \times t$$

so that the mass liberated is given by

$$m = Z \times I \times t$$

Example The electrochemical equivalent of copper is 3.3×10^{-7} kg/C. Calculate the mass of copper deposited during electrolysis if the following currents are passed for the length of time shown:

	Current	Time
a)	0.5 A	10 min
b)	1.2 A	50 min
c)	0.8 A	5 min

Method: The mass is calculated using

$$m = Z \times I \times t$$

but remember that t is in seconds.

Answers: a) 9.9×10^{-5} kg   **b)** 1.19×10^{-3} kg
c) 7.92×10^{-5} kg

Example A current of 2 A is passed for 30 minutes through solutions of different metal salts. Given the following electrochemical equivalents (Z), work out the mass of metal liberated from each solution:

a) silver, $Z = 1.12 \times 10^{-6}$ kg/C
b) copper, $Z = 3.3 \times 10^{-7}$ kg/C
c) nickel, $Z = 3.0 \times 10^{-7}$ kg/C

Method: Again use

$$m = Z \times I \times t$$

which becomes

$$m = Z \times 2 \times 30 \times 60$$
$$= Z \times 3600$$

By substituting the different values of Z given, you will be able to find the mass liberated.

Answers: a) 4.032×10^{-3} kg   **b)** 1.188×10^{-3} kg
c) 1.08×10^{-3} kg

Transformers

These are used to increase or decrease alternating voltages and currents from one value to another. For example, the mains voltage at the socket in your home is 240 V AC (alternating current) and yet your cassette tape recorder is likely to work on voltages between 6 V and 12 V. The mains voltage has to be *stepped down* to these lower voltages. Transformers at power stations *step up* the voltage which is generated by the dynamo or generator to a much higher voltage (perhaps 375 000 V for transmission on the National Grid). A transformer consists of three main parts — an input, or primary, coil, a soft iron core, and an output, or secondary, coil.

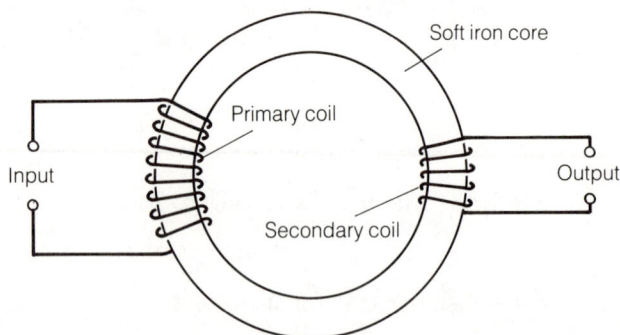

Assuming that the transformer is 100% efficient, then the following formulae can be used:

$$\frac{\text{Voltage across primary coil}}{\text{Voltage across secondary coil}} = \frac{\text{Number of turns on the primary coil}}{\text{Number of turns on the secondary coil}}$$

or

$$\frac{V_\text{p}}{V_\text{s}} = \frac{n_\text{p}}{n_\text{s}}$$

Example Calculate the secondary voltage produced for a 240 V primary input, for the following transformer turns ratios:

a) 100:1   **b)** 1:10   **c)** 24:1

Method: The 'turns ratio' is another way of writing

$$\frac{\text{Number of turns on the primary coil}}{\text{Number of turns on the secondary coil}}$$

Using

$$\frac{V_p}{V_s} = \frac{n_p}{n_s}$$

Substitute the value for V_p. Rearrangement gives

$$V_s = \frac{V_p}{n_p/n_s} = \frac{240}{n_p/n_s}$$

Answers: a) 2.4 V   **b)** 2400 V   **c)** 10 V

If the voltage across the secondary coil is less than the voltage across the primary coil, then the transformer is a step-down device. The reverse makes it a step-up transformer.

If the voltage is stepped up, then the current is stepped down. This can be seen by looking at the input and output powers. If the transformer is 100% efficient (which it usually is in exam calculations), then

$$\text{Input power} = \text{Output power}$$

or $$I_p \times V_p = I_s \times V_s$$

This can be rearranged to give

$$\frac{V_p}{V_s} = \frac{I_s}{I_p}$$

But

$$\frac{V_p}{V_s} = \frac{n_p}{n_s}$$

so that

$$\frac{I_s}{I_p} = \frac{n_p}{n_s}$$

Example If there are 100 turns on the primary coil and the primary current is 2 A, calculate the number of turns on the secondary coil to produce a secondary current of:

a) 2 mA   **b)** 50 A   **c)** 0.4 A

Method: Use

$$\frac{I_s}{I_p} = \frac{n_p}{n_s}$$

Substitute the values given:

$$\frac{I_s}{2} = \frac{100}{n_s}$$

and rearrange to give

$$n_s = \frac{100 \times 2}{I_s} = \frac{200}{I_s}$$

Remember that $1\,\text{mA} = 0.001\,\text{A}$.

Answers: a) 100 000   **b)** 4   **c)** 500

Note: If the voltage is stepped up, then the current is stepped down and vice versa.

Stepping up the voltage is important at power stations because this means that low currents are used to transmit the electrical energy along the transmission cables. The power loss on the cable is given by I^2R where R is the resistance of the cable, and so a low current value reduces the power losses.

Example

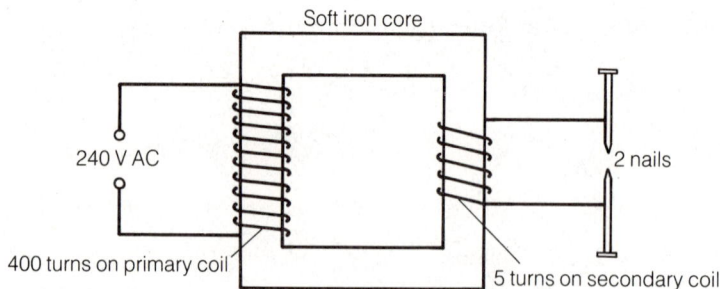

Soft iron core

240 V AC

2 nails

400 turns on primary coil

5 turns on secondary coil

a) Calculate the secondary voltage across the two nails in the transformer shown.

b) If the primary current is 0.5 A, what will the current be in the secondary circuit when the two nails are pressed together?

c) What effect will this current have on the nails?

Method: The secondary voltage can be worked out using

$$\frac{V_p}{V_s} = \frac{n_p}{n_s}$$

Substitute the values given:

$$\frac{240}{V_s} = \frac{400}{5} = \frac{80}{1}$$

Rearranging to make V_s the subject gives

$$V_s = \frac{240}{80}$$

The voltage is stepped down, and so you should expect to find that the current is stepped up. Using

$$\frac{I_s}{I_p} = \frac{n_p}{n_s}$$

and substituting gives

$$\frac{I_s}{0.5} = \frac{240}{5} = \frac{80}{1}$$

or
$$I_s = 0.5 \times 80$$

Answers: a) 3 V   **b)** 40 A   **c)** A current of this size is likely to melt the ends of the nails and weld them together (the process of spot welding).

Questions

1.

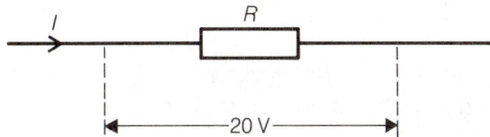

Calculate the current I flowing through the resistor R when R is:

a) 4 Ω   b) 10 Ω   c) 40 Ω

2. Calculate the effective resistance of the following resistors when they are placed a) in series, and b) in parallel:

(i)   3 Ω and 6 Ω

(ii) 3 Ω and 12 Ω

(iii) 5 Ω and 20 Ω

3. Calculate the current which flows when 2000 C of charge pass a point in a circuit in:

a) 20 s   b) 400 s   c) 15 min

4.   Complete the following table of values:

	Power (W)	Current (A)	Potential difference (V)	Resistance (Ω)
a)	1000	5	—	—
b)	40	—	240	—
c)	3000	—	—	15
d)	—	12	240	—
e)	—	—	12	2
f)	—	10	—	16

5.   Calculate the heat energy generated when a 1500 W heater is switched on for:

   a) 20 s   b) 1 min   c) 30 min

6.   If one unit of electrical energy (1 kW h) costs 5p, calculate the cost of running the following appliances for the stated time:

Appliance	Power	Time
Light bulb	60 W	3 h
Power drill	330 W	1 min
Kettle	2 kW	3 min
Immersion heater	3 kW	2 h

7.   The following results were obtained in an experiment to find how the current passing through a resistor varied with the potential difference across the resistor.

Potential difference (V)	Current (A)
0	0
2.0	0.15
4.0	0.32
6.0	0.47
8.0	0.62
10.0	0.78
12.0	0.94
14.0	1.10
16.0	1.26

a) Draw a diagram of a circuit which could have been set up to obtain these results.
b) Plot a graph of potential difference on the y-axis against current on the x-axis.
c) What conclusions can you reach from the graph?
d) What is the current value when the potential difference is 7 V?
e) What is the potential difference value which gives a current of 1.0 A?

8. Calculate the effective resistance of the following arrangements:

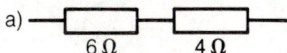

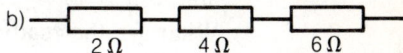

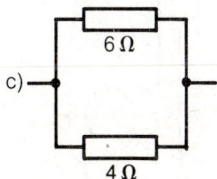

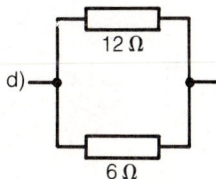

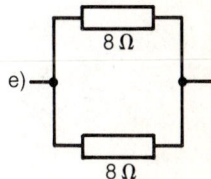

a) 6 Ω, 4 Ω

b) 2 Ω, 4 Ω, 6 Ω

c) 6 Ω, 4 Ω

d) 12 Ω, 6 Ω

e) 8 Ω, 8 Ω

9. a) Calculate the total resistance in the circuit.
    b) Calculate the reading on A.
    c) Calculate the readings on V_1 and V_2.
    d) Can you see any relationship between V_1, V_2 and the driving voltage of the battery?

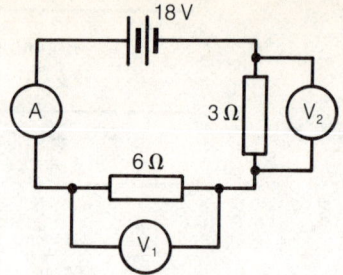

10. a) Calculate the readings on A.
    b) What is the reading on V?

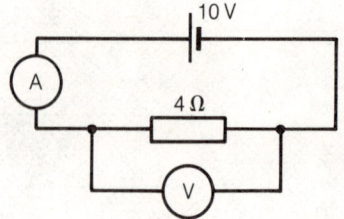

11. a) What is the effective resistance in the circuit?
    b) Calculate the reading on A_1.
    c) What is the reading on V?
    d) Calculate the readings on A_2 and A_3.
    e) Can you see any relationship between the three ammeter readings?

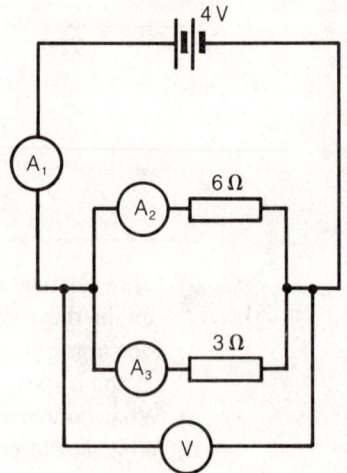

12. a) What is the effective resistance of the circuit?
    b) Calculate the reading on A_1.
    c) Calculate the readings on V_1 and V_2.
    d) What are the readings on A_2 and A_3?

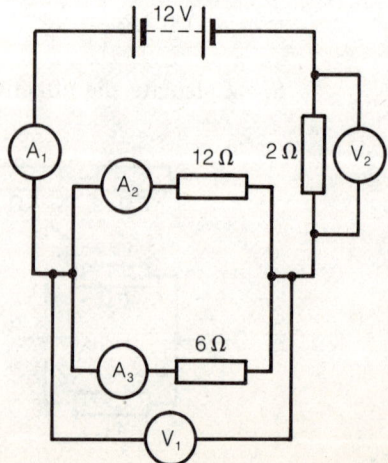

13. Calculate the resistance of 15 m of copper (resistivity of copper $= 1.72 \times 10^{-8}\,\Omega$ m) if the cross-sectional area is $3.14 \times 10^{-6}\,m^2$.

14. What length of resistance wire of cross-sectional area $0.6 \times 10^{-7}\,m^2$ and resistivity $1.1 \times 10^{-6}\,\Omega$ m, would you cut from a reel to make a $44\,\Omega$ resistor?

15. A student obtained the following results during an electrolysis experiment when different currents were passed through a solution of a metal salt:

Charge passed (C)	Mass deposited (g)
0	0
200	0.41
400	0.85
600	1.25
800	1.70
1000	2.05
1200	2.50
1400	2.95
1600	3.30
1800	3.75
2000	4.20

a) Draw a graph of y = mass deposited against x = charge. From the graph, or otherwise, determine the electrochemical equivalent of the element deposited.

b) On the *same* graph, draw with a dotted line, the expected graph if an element of electrochemical equivalent = 0.000 125 g/C had been used.

16. A power cable is made of steel (resistivity $2.32 \times 10^{-3}\,\Omega.\text{m}$) of radius 3 cm ($= 3 \times 10^{-2}\,\text{m}$). Calculate the resistance of 50 m of the cable. If the current flowing through it is $10^{-2}\,\text{A}$, calculate the power loss from the cable.

17. Compare the resistance of 1 m of aluminium and copper wires of the same mass per unit length.

Resistivity of copper	$= 1.7 \times 10^{-8}\,\Omega\,\text{m}$
Density of copper	$= 8.9 \times 10^{3}\,\text{kg/m}^3$
Resistivity of aluminium	$= 2.8 \times 10^{-8}\,\Omega\,\text{m}$
Density of aluminium	$= 2.7 \times 10^{3}\,\text{kg/m}^3$

18. A wire 1 m long and radius $0.5 \times 10^{-3}\,\text{m}$ has a resistance of $0.6\,\Omega$. What is the resistance of a wire of the same material 1.5 m long and $0.25 \times 10^{-3}\,\text{m}$ radius?

19. A current of 2.0 A is passed through a solution of copper sulphate for 4 hours 27 minutes. What thickness of copper will be deposited on the side of a copper cathode measuring 5 cm $\times$ 12 cm? (Electrochemical equivalent of copper $= 0.00033\,\text{g/C}$, Density $=$ Mass/Volume $= 8.9\,\text{g/cm}^3$.)

20.

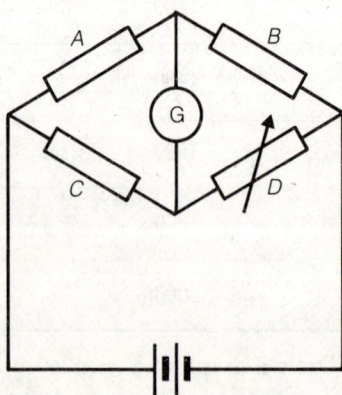

The resistor D is varied until the Wheatstone bridge network is balanced, i.e. no current is registered on the galvanometer G. Complete the following table of results for this balance arrangement:

	A (Ω)	B (Ω)	C (Ω)	D (Ω)
a)	6	3	—	2
b)	10	—	7	4
c)	2	5	4	—
d)	—	6	10	5

21. The metre bridge shown was used to compare the two resistors X and Y. The rider is tapped along the wire until the bridge is balanced, i.e. no current flows through the galvanometer G.

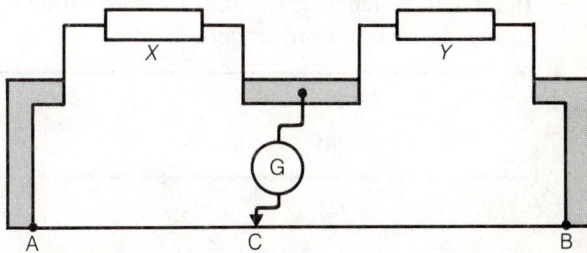

Calculate the length AC for the following values of X and Y:

	X (Ω)	Y (Ω)
a)	2	2
b)	2	3
c)	2	4
d)	3	5
e)	6	4
f)	1	2

22.

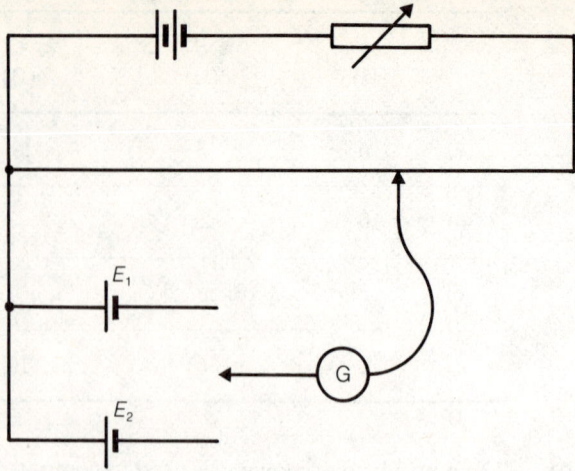

The variable resistor was set to its highest value and balance lengths L_1 and L_2 were found for the cells E_1 and E_2 respectively. The variable resistor was then adjusted and for each set of adjustments the balance lengths L_1 and L_2 were found for both cells. The following results were obtained:

L_1 cm	L_2 cm
90	66
80	59
70	51
60	44
50	37
40	29

a) For each set of values work out the value of L_1/L_2 and hence find an average value for E_1/E_2.
b) If $E_2 = 1.5\,\text{V}$, what is the value for E_1?
c) If $E_1 = 0.8\,\text{V}$, what is the value for E_2?
d) Plot a graph of $y = L_1$ against $x = L_2$, and find the gradient of the graph.
e) How does this gradient compare with the values obtained in part a)?

Past examination questions

1. a) (i) What do you understand by the term *electrical resistance*?
   (ii) Knowing the voltage applied across the ends of a conductor and the current flowing through it, state in words how the resistance is calculated.
   (iii) State *Ohm's Law* fully for an ordinary electrical conductor.
   (iv) A conductor obeys Ohm's Law.
   The current is 1 amp when the voltage is 2 volts.
   Find: the current when the voltage doubles to 4 volts.
   Find out what happens to the value of the resistance of the conductor.

   b) (i) What is the purpose of the fuse in a 13 A plug?
   (ii) A fuse can just withstand a current of 3 amps passing through it.
   Its resistance to this current is 10 milliohms (= 0.01 ohms).
   Find the voltage across the fuse, in millivolts.
   (iii) A voltage of 8 millivolts across the same fuse gives a current of 1 amp.
   Find the resistance of the fuse to this current.
   (iv) Give a physical reason why the value in (iii) is different from the 10 milliohms of (ii).   [SREB (part)]

2.

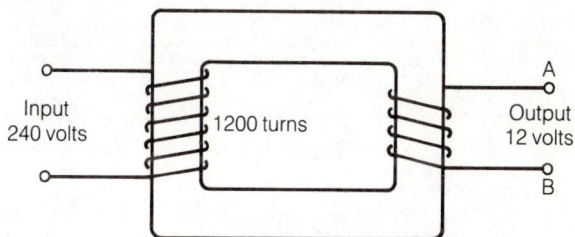

The diagram shows the main features of a transformer.
a) How many turns between A and B will be needed to give an output of 12 volts between A and B? Show your working.
b) If the transformer is 100% efficient, what current in amps will be taken from the input when a 12 volt, 24 watt lamp is connected between A and B? Show your working.   [SREB (part)]

3. If the cost of electricity is 5p per kilowatt-hour, how much will it cost:
   a) to use a 3 kW electric fire for 1 hour?
   b) to use a 100 W lamp for 25 hours?   [SWEB]

4. An 800 W immersion heater is put in a saucepan containing 2 kg of water.

    a) How much energy does the heater give the water in
       (i)   1 second?
       (ii) 50 seconds?

    b) Calculate the temperature rise of the water in 50 seconds. (It takes 4000 J of heat to raise the temperature of 1 kg of water by 1°C.)   [SWEB]

5. a) This is the circuit symbol for a resistor:

    Draw the symbol for:
    (i)   a variable resistor;
    (ii) a battery.

    Claire wants to find the resistance of the wire in an immersion heater. She gets the following results:

Potential difference across heater in volts	Current through heater in amps
0	0
1.0	0.5
2.0	1.0
3.0	1.4
4.0	1.8
5.0	2.2
6.0	2.5
7.0	2.7
8.0	2.9
9.0	3.0

b) Draw a circuit diagram of the circuit she used to obtain these results. Her supply was a 12 V battery.

c) Assuming that the results in the above table are accurate: calculate the resistance of the immersion heater:
   (i)   when the p.d. is 1 V;
   (ii) when the p.d. is 9 V.

d) Andrew looks at her table of results and says that as the p.d. gets larger so does the current. So a graph of the results would look like this:

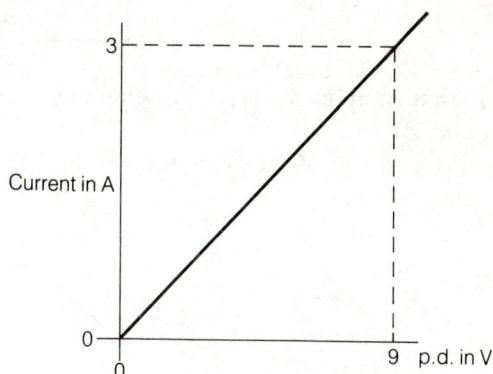

Draw this graph on graph paper and on the axes show roughly the shape of the graph from Claire's results.

e) Use the table of results to calculate the power of the immersion heater:
   (i)   when the p.d. is 1 V;
   (ii) when the p.d. is 9 V.

f) Explain why Claire's results do not give the straight line which Andrew suggested.   [SWEB]

6. a) Describe fully how you would check the 0.5-A graduation of an ammeter using a copper voltameter, if you were told that 1 coulomb of charge deposits 0.00033 g of copper,

                                                                    [10]

   Would it be advisable to try to check a 10-A graduation by the same means?   [2]

   b) Two heating coils dissipate heat at the rate of 40 W and 60 W respectively when connected in parallel to a 12-V DC supply of negligible internal resistance. Calculate the resistances of the coils.   [4]

   Assuming that these resistances remain constant, what would be their rates of dissipation of heat when connected together in series with the same supply as before?   [4]

                                                                 [London]

7. The circuit below is used to measure the electrical resistance of the component labelled 'C'.

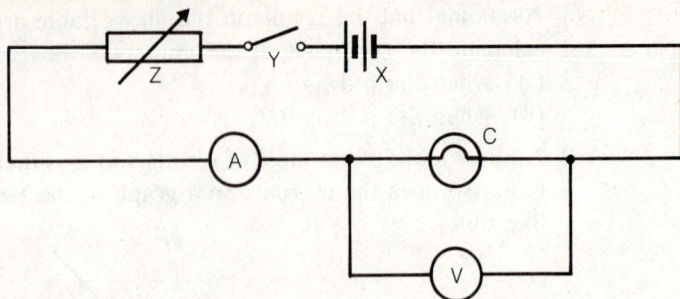

a) What components are represented by the symbols lettered X, Y and Z?
b) The readings of the ammeter and the voltmeter in the circuit are shown below:

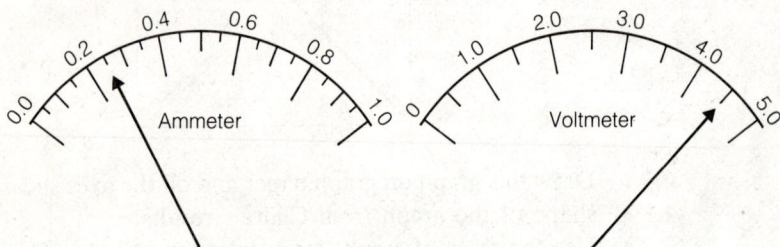

(i) What is the reading shown on the ammeter?
(ii) What is the reading shown on the voltmeter?

c) Calculate the resistance of the component C.
d) Calculate the power developed in component C.
e) If the current through C is doubled by about how many times will the power increase?
f) Name a suitable material to use for each of the following:
(i) a fuse wire;
(ii) a lamp filament.   [LREB]

8. a)

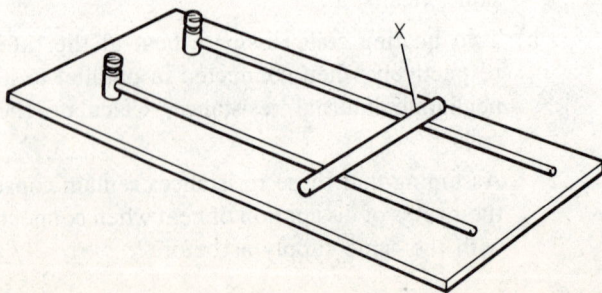

The diagram shows two pieces of bare wire connected to terminals on a piece of insulating material. A third piece of bare wire X rests on the wires and is free to move. You are given a number of dry cells each of e.m.f. 1.5 V and two bar magnets and are asked to use these to make the wire X move.

(i) How would you use the dry cells to produce a battery of 6 V?

(ii) Show, by diagram, how you would use this battery and the magnets to make X move away from the terminals. [5]

b)

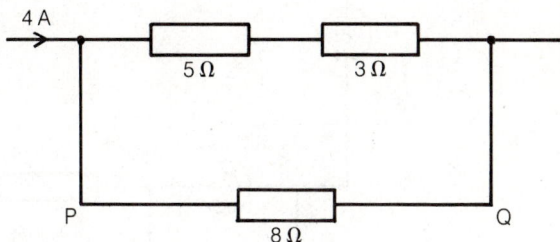

The diagram shows a network of resistors.

(i) If a current of 4 A enters the network as shown, what is the current in the branch PQ?

(ii) Calculate the voltage across the 5 Ω resistor. [3]

c) Draw a labelled diagram of a moving-coil loudspeaker and explain in detail how it works. [7]

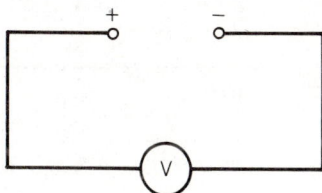

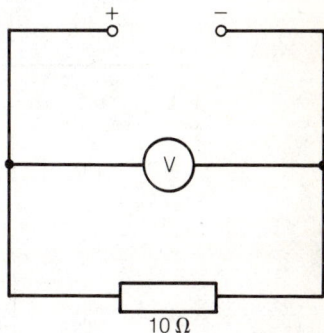

d)

The diagram shows two identical high resistance voltmeters connected across two identical DC power sources. The left-hand voltmeter reads 6.0 V but the right-hand voltmeter reads 4.0 V.

(i) Suggest why there is a difference between the readings of the two voltmeters.

(ii) What would be the reading on the voltmeter if the 10 Ω resistor were replaced by a 15 Ω resistor? [6]

[AEB]

9.   A pupil connects a 3 volt battery in series with an ammeter, a small 2.5 volt bulb and a rheostat (variable resistor), with a voltmeter in parallel with the bulb as in the diagram. The rheostat is adjusted to produce different voltages across the bulb.

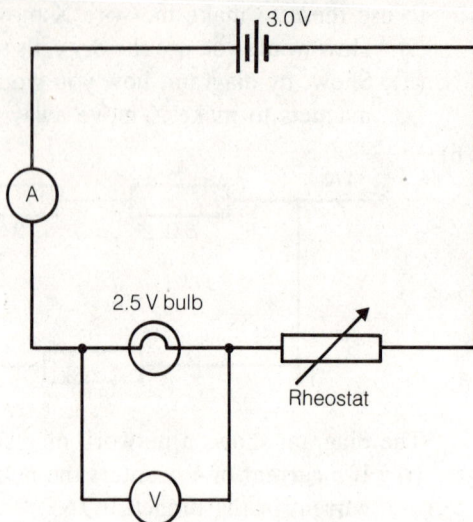

The currents and voltages were measured and recorded as follows:

	Voltage, V volts	Current, I amps	$\dfrac{\text{Voltage}}{\text{Current}}, \dfrac{V}{I}$	Voltage × Current V × I	Expected brightness of bulb
1	0.5	0.15	3.3	0.075	
2	1.0	0.3			
3	1.5	0.42	3.55	0.63	
4	2.0	0.5			
5	2.5	0.55	4.55	1.4	
6	3.0	0.6			

(i)   Copy out and complete the table by calculating the missing values of 'volts × amps' (V × I) and $\dfrac{\text{volts}}{\text{amps}}\left(\dfrac{V}{I}\right)$.

Fill in the final column headed 'expected brightness of bulb' using words from this list:

dim, normal, less bright than normal, very bright.

(ii) Plot a graph of 'volts/amps' (V/I) on the vertical axis, against volts × amps (V × I) on the horizontal axis.

(iii) The value of $\dfrac{\text{volts}}{\text{amps}}$ $\dfrac{V}{I}$ gives the *resistance* of the bulb.

Use your graph to find how the *resistance* changes as the value of volts × amps changes.

(iv) The value of volts × amps measures the *power* given to the bulb. An increase in *power* raises the temperature of the bulb's filament.

Use your graph to find how the resistance of the bulb varies with its temperature. [SREB]

10.

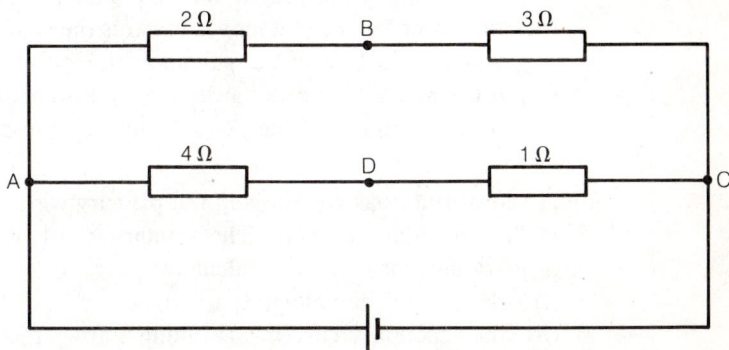

The diagram shows four resistors connected to an accumulator of e.m.f. 2.0 V and negligible internal resistance. The resistances of the individual resistors are shown on the diagram.

Calculate the total current flowing from the accumulator.

The points B and D are now joined by a wire. Indicate, with a reason, the direction in which you would expect current to flow in the wire BD. [Cambridge]

11. a) An electric fire is rated at 1000 watt. Calculate the current it uses when connected to a 250-volt supply. Show your working.

b) Using your answer to a), write down the fuse rating you would use to put in the plug connected to the fire. Choose from these values: 1 A, 3 A, 5 A, 7 A, 10 A, 13 A. Give a reason for your choice. [SREB (part)]

12.   a)

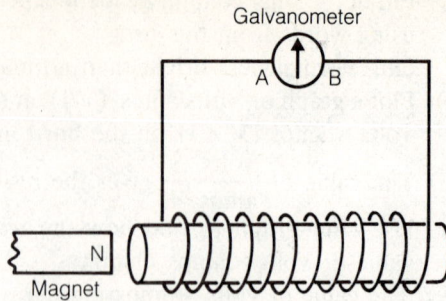

Galvanometer

A B

N

Magnet

The diagram shows a solenoid connected to a galvanometer. Explain why

(i)   if the magnet is held stationary at the end of the coil, there is no deflection of the galvanometer pointer,

(ii) if the magnet is moved towards the solenoid there is a deflection of the galvanometer pointer,

(iii) the faster the magnet moves towards the solenoid the greater is the deflection of the galvanometer pointer,

(iv) if the magnet is moved away from the solenoid the direction of the current is from A to B through the galvanometer.
[10]

b) A transformer has 400 turns in the primary winding and 10 turns in the secondary winding. The primary e.m.f. is 250 V and the primary current is 2.0 A. Calculate

(i)   the secondary voltage, and

(ii) the secondary current, assuming 100% efficiency.   [6]

Transformers are usually designed so that their efficiency is as close to 100% as possible. Why is this?

Describe *two* features in transformer design which help to achieve high efficiency.   [4]
[London]

13.   Draw a diagram of a sensitive moving coil instrument which may be used to measure small electric currents. List, or indicate on the diagram, those features which are incorporated to produce a linear scale.   [8]

Such a meter has a resistance of 30 ohms, and its needle is at the maximum reading when 0.2 A passes through it. A 6 ohm resistor is now connected in parallel with the meter. Calculate

(i)   the combined resistance of the meter and 6 ohm resistor in parallel,

(ii) the total current taken by the combination from a 6 V source,

(iii) the ratio of the currents in the meter and 6 ohm resistor.   [8]
[WJEC]

14. A manufacturer's catalogue gives information on a semiconductor diode, in the form of the graph shown below.

a) (i) Sketch a circuit you could use to check the information on the graph.

(ii) State how the resistance of the diode changes as the potential difference across it is increased. [3]

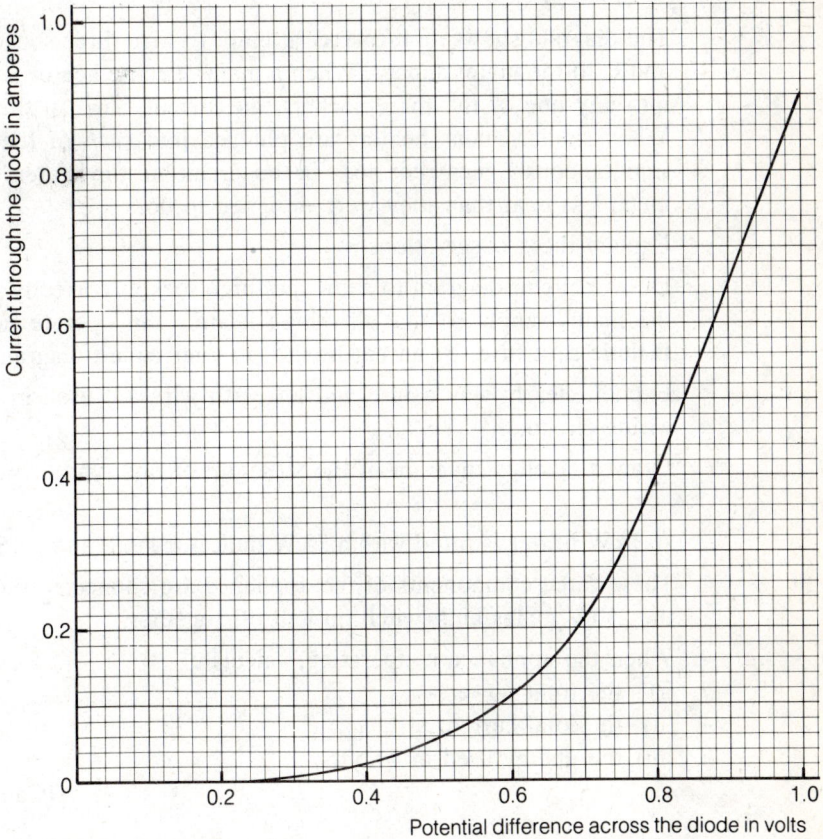

Potential difference across the diode in volts

b) The diode is connected into the circuit shown below.

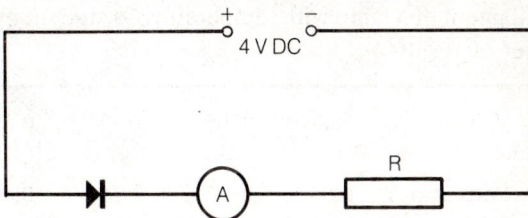

(i) If the ammeter reads 0.40 amps, what is the resistance of resistor R?

(ii) What would be the reading on the ammeter if the diode was reversed? [4]

[Scottish]

15.

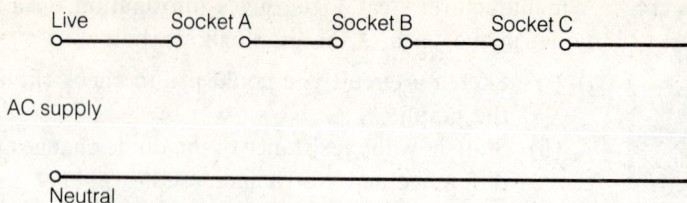

The diagram shows an **incorrect** attempt to wire three sockets A, B and C to the mains supply. When a mains electric heater is plugged into any one of the three sockets, no current flows in the circuit. When similar mains heaters are plugged into *each* of the sockets simultaneously, a current flows in the circuit but the heaters give out much less heat than they were designed to do.

Explain these observations.

Draw a circuit diagram to show the three sockets correctly wired to the mains supply so that the three heaters can operate normally. Include a) a fuse, b) an earth wire, in your circuit diagram.   [7]

Explain clearly why a fuse and an earth wire are used in a mains wiring circuit.

Draw a labelled diagram of the structure of one type of fuse.

[4]

A 3 kW heater is fitted with a 35 W indicator lamp and a 15 W fan.

These three components of the appliance are connected directly to the 250 V mains and switch on and off together.

When the appliance is operating, calculate
(i)   the total power,
(ii) the total current,
(iii) the energy used in 4 hours.   [6]

[Cambridge]

16.   In an experiment to investigate the variation of the resistance of the filament of a lamp with temperature, a student obtained the following set of results.

Voltage in V	0.01	0.05	0.13	0.38	1.08	2.10
Current in A	0.05	0.15	0.25	0.40	0.60	0.75

a) Calculate the resistance, R, of the filament for each value of the current.
b) Plot a graph having resistance as the vertical axis and current as the horizontal axis. Draw a smooth curve through your points.

c) Use your graph to estimate the value of *R* when the current is zero.

d) What information concerning the variation of resistance with current can you deduce from the graph? [13]

[AEB]

17. Draw a diagram of a simple DC motor and explain how it works. [9]

A 12 V DC motor takes 2 A when lifting a 1 kg mass vertically at a steady speed of 1.8 m/s. Calculate

(i) the electrical power used by the motor,

(ii) the power used in raising the load,

(iii) the efficiency of the motor. [7]

[WJEC]

18. State Ohm's Law.

Sketch graphs showing how the current varies with voltage for

(i) a resistor at constant temperature,

(ii) a thermionic diode.

Explain the shapes of the graphs obtained. [10]

In the circuit diagram below, the battery has an e.m.f. of 12 V and negligible internal resistance. Calculate the current flowing from the battery when

(i) switches S_1 and S_2 are open,

(ii) switch S_1 is closed but S_2 is open,

(iii) switch S_1 is open but S_2 is closed,

(iv) both switches are closed. [6]

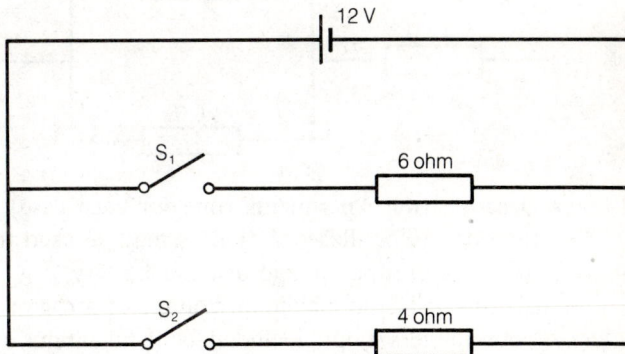

[WJEC]

19. a) Write down the formula for
        (i) the equivalent resistance of two different resistors in series, and
        (ii) the equivalent resistance of two different resistors in parallel.
                                                                          [2]

        Suppose you were given three resistors of 3 Ω, 6 Ω and 6 Ω, an accumulator, voltmeter, ammeter, rheostat, switch, and connecting wire. Describe in detail, giving sketches of the circuits you would employ, how you would test the formula you have written down in (ii) above. (More than one test is required.)   [10]

     b) A cell of e.m.f. 1.5 V and internal resistance 3 Ω is connected in series with a cell of e.m.f. 2.0 V and internal resistance r so that the cells assist each other. When this arrangement is joined across the ends of a resistor of constant resistance 10 Ω, a current of 0.25 A is produced. Determine
        (i) the value of r, and   [4]
        (ii) the heat which would be produced in the 10 Ω resistor if the current were maintained for a continuous period of 4 min.
                                                                          [4]
                                                                    [London]

20. State **two** fundamentally different effects which can be produced by the passage of an electric current.   [2]

     Describe an experiment which may be performed to demonstrate **one** of these effects.   [5]

     The resistance combination shown below is connected across a steady 12 V supply. Calculate the current through each component and the power supplied by the source.

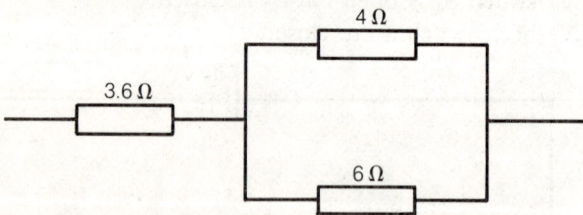

                                                                          [9]
                                                                      [WJEC]

21. a) Describe **two** experiments (one for each case), to show how a cathode ray oscilloscope (CRO) may be used to
        (i) measure the voltage of a car battery,
        (ii) measure the maximum voltage of a car or cycle dynamo.
        Your answers should include labelled diagrams of the circuits you would use and an indication of the values you might obtain. You should **not** draw or attempt to explain how the CRO works.
                                                                         [14]

b) A moving-coil galvanometer (milliammeter) has a resistance of 5 ohms and will give a full-scale deflection when a current of 0.015 A flows through it.
Calculate

   (i)   the potential difference across the meter when a current of 0.015 A flows through it,

   (ii) the value of the resistance which would convert the meter into an ammeter reading up to 3 A, showing how the resistance would be connected to the galvanometer,

   (iii) the value of the resistance which would convert the meter into a voltmeter reading up to 15 V, showing how the resistance would be connected to the galvanometer. [11]

[JMB]

22. An electric cooker has the following specification:

Item	No. of items	Power of item (W)
Ceramic hob, *small* heating area	2	1250
Ceramic hob, *large* heating area	2	1500
Grill	1	2000
Oven	1	2500

Calculate how much energy (in kW h) the cooker will use in 30 minutes when all the items are used simultaneously.

How much will it cost to run the cooker during this time if electrical energy costs 6p for 1 kW h?

Calculate the maximum current that will be carried by the cable connecting this cooker to a 250 V mains supply. [8]

[London (part)]

23. Describe the construction of a **diode** and briefly explain its action. [5]

Explain the difference between **alternating** and **direct** current and draw a circuit diagram or describe how a diode may be used to convert AC to DC. [4]

Draw a diagram of a simple transformer. Such a transformer working at 90% efficiency takes 0.1 A from the 240 V mains. Calculate the current supplied at the 12 V tappings. [7]

[WJEC]

24. a) When a 12 V car battery is connected to an electric motor, it is found that the initial current which flows is very large. As the motor speeds up the current decreases to a lower steady value. If the car battery is replaced by eight dry cells each of e.m.f. 1.5 V connected in series the motor does not work at all.

   (i) Draw a diagram showing the essential features of a DC motor. [6]

   (ii) Explain why the initial current through the motor is large when it is first connected to the battery, and suggest a reason for its decrease as the motor speeds up. [6]

   (iii) Draw a circuit diagram representing the eight dry cells in series and calculate their combined e.m.f. [2]

   (iv) Suggest a reason for the motor not working when connected to the dry cells. [2]

   b) When a voltmeter is connected across a dry cell it reads 1.5 V. If a 5 Ω resistor is now connected across the cell the voltmeter reading decreases to 0.5 V. Calculate the internal resistance of the cell. [4]

   [London]

25. a)

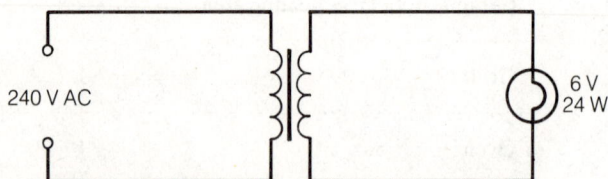

   It is required to run a 6 V, 24 W lamp from a 240 V AC mains using a transformer as shown above.

   (i) Calculate the current that would be taken by the lamp when operating normally. [2]

   (ii) Calculate the turns ratio of the transformer you would use. [2]

   (iii) Calculate the current taken by the primary coil of the transformer, assuming it to be 100% efficient. [2]

   (iv) Why, in practice, is the efficiency of the transformer less than 100%? [3]

   b) Alternatively the 6 V, 24 W lamp can be operated normally from a 240 V DC supply using a suitable fixed resistor, R, as below.

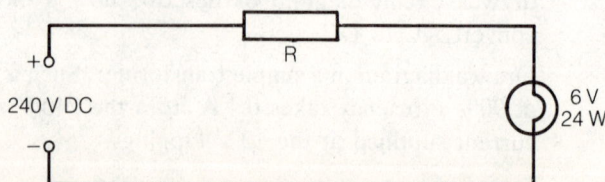

(i)   What is the resistance of the lamp? [2]
(ii) What is the p.d. across the resistor? [2]
(iii) What is the resistance of the resistor? [2]
(iv) How much energy is dissipated in the resistor in 1 s? [2]

c) Why may the method used to light the lamp described in a) be preferable to that described in b)? [3]

[London]

26. a) A circuit which is used to find out how the resistance of a coil of iron wire changes with the current through it consists of: a 6 V battery of unknown internal resistance, an ammeter, a rheostat and a coil of iron wire, all in series; and a voltmeter in parallel with the coil.

The corresponding readings of the current I through the coil and the potential difference V across the coil in the experiment are:

I in amperes	0.25	0.50	0.75	1.00	1.25	1.50
V in volts	0.50	1.00	1.70	2.50	3.60	5.00

(i)   Draw a labelled diagram of this circuit. [3]
(ii) Plot the graph for these readings. [3]
(iii) Explain why the graph is not a straight line. [3]
(iv) What is the value of the resistance of the coil of iron wire when the current through it is
        0.50 A;
        1.00 A;
        1.50 A? [4]
(v)   The readings $V = 5.00$ V, $I = 1.50$ A were taken when the rheostat was set at zero resistance. Assuming the ammeter has negligible resistance find:
        the 'lost' voltage in the battery; [2]
        the internal resistance of the battery. [2]
(vi) Find the resistance of the rheostat needed to obtain the readings $V = 1.00$ V, $I = 0.50$ A in the experiment. [4]

b) (i) Write down a formula for the heat produced per second in the coil of iron wire. [1]
   (ii) Calculate the power produced in the coil when the current through it is:
        0.50 A;
        1.50 A. [3]

[Oxford (part)]

27.   In an experiment, a 12 V battery was connected in series with a variable resistance (rheostat) and a car headlamp bulb. Draw a labelled circuit diagram, adding an **ammeter** to measure the current flowing through the bulb, and a **voltmeter** to measure the voltage across the bulb.   [4]

In this experiment, when the rheostat was varied the following results were obtained:

Current in AMPS (A)	Voltage in VOLTS (V)
1.0	2.0
1.5	6.0
1.8	9.0
2.0	12.0

Calculate the resistance of the bulb in **each** case, and explain why Ohm's Law is not obeyed.   [8]

Draw a graph of *voltage* against *current* and use it to estimate the current that would flow when the voltage was 4 volts.   [4]

[WJEC]

28.

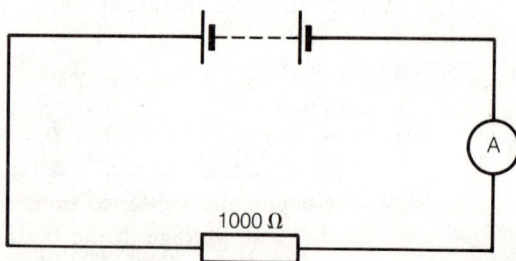

A large battery is connected as shown to a resistor of resistance 1000 Ω. The potential difference across the resistor is 50 V.

(i)   What is the reading on the ammeter in the circuit?   [2]
(ii)   How many coulombs of charge are supplied by the battery in 1 minute?   [2]
(iii) Calculate the energy dissipated by the resistor in this time. [2]
(iv)   What is the power dissipated by the resistor?   [2]

[London (part)]

29.

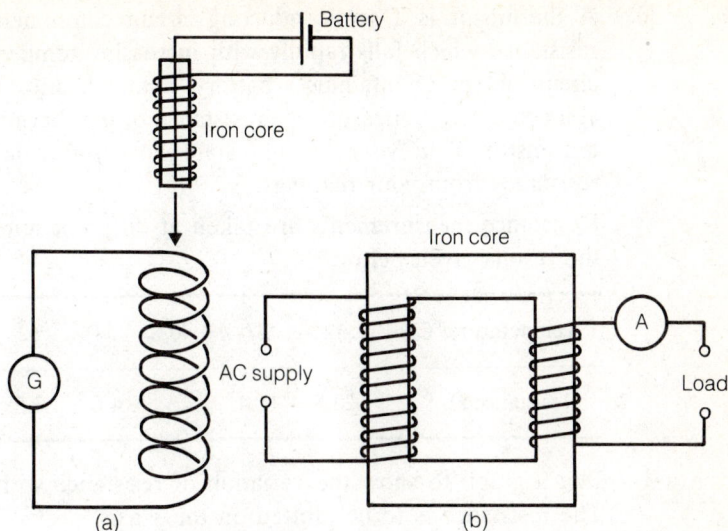

(a)   (b)

The diagrams illustrate two experiments (a) and (b).

In (a) a coil of wire wrapped around an iron core has a current passed through it from a battery. When this coil is moved into the larger coil the centre-zero galvanometer G deflects and then returns to zero.

In experiment (b) an AC supply is connected to the primary coil of a simple transformer. An AC ammeter A connected to the secondary coil of the transformer shows a steady deflection.

Explain in detail why the meters show a deflection in each case, and why the deflection is only for a short time in (a) but steady in (b).

[8]

The transformer used in (b) is ideal and has an input voltage of 24 V and an input power of 48 W. Its primary coil has 900 turns and its secondary 600 turns.

Calculate

(i)   the input current,

(ii) the output power,

(iii) the output voltage,

(iv) the output current.   [5]

Describe how a transformer can be designed to produce large increases in voltage.

State **two** advantages of using high voltage for long distance transmission.

[4]

[Cambridge]

30. A thermistor is a semiconducting circuit component which has a resistance which falls rapidly with increasing temperature. Draw a circuit diagram containing a battery, ammeter and voltmeter which you could use to measure the resistance of the thermistor. Label the thermistor T in your circuit. State how you would deduce the resistance from your readings.   [4]

Resistance measurements are taken at different temperatures with the results given below.

Temperature/°C	12	27	40	54	62	70	79
Resistance/Ω	20.5	11.4	7.3	4.6	3.5	2.6	2.0

Plot a graph to show the variation of resistance with temperature. The resistance is to be plotted on the y-axis.   [6]

Read from your graph the resistance at 15°C and record the value. Deduce the temperature at which the resistance will have fallen to half this value.   [2]

The thermistor is heated in a beaker of water which, in turn, is heated by a bunsen burner. What precautions would you take in order to ensure that your value for the temperature of the thermistor is as accurate as possible?   [3]

[Cambridge]

31. a) A battery of e.m.f. 12 V is connected to an ammeter of negligible resistance. If the battery has no internal resistance, calculate the ammeter readings when:

(i)   a 4 Ω resistor is added in series;   [2]

(ii) a second resistor of 4 Ω is placed in series with the first 4 Ω resistor;   [2]

(iii) this second 4 Ω resistor is placed in parallel with the first 4 Ω resistor.   [2]

If the battery had an internal resistance r:

(iv) what would be the value of r if the ammeter reading was 2.5 A when the battery of e.m.f. 12 V was in series with the 4 Ω resistor?   [3]

b) The voltage V across a filament lamp is increased in stages, and the current I through the lamp is measured in each case. The diagram shows a graph of V against I for the lamp.

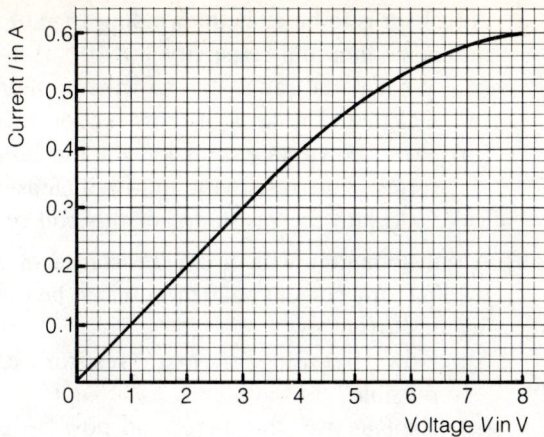

(i) Over what range of voltage values is the resistance of the lamp constant? Explain your answer. [2]

(ii) What is the resistance of the lamp over this range? [2]

(iii) Why is the resistance not constant beyond this? [2]

(iv) What is the resistance of the lamp at its working voltage of 8 V? [2]

(v) What is the working wattage of the lamp? [2]

c) A 12 volt battery is connected to three resistors as shown in the diagram. The battery has no internal resistance, and the current through it is 2 A. The current through resistor R is 0.8 A.

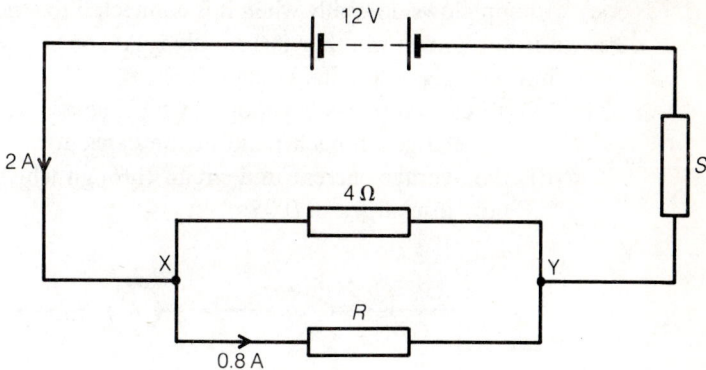

Calculate:

(i) the p.d. between X and Y; [2]

(ii) the value of resistor R; [2]

(iii) the value of resistor S. [2]

[Oxford (part)]

32. a) A resistor is to be made by winding 15 m of insulated iron wire of radius 0.5 mm and resistivity 2×10^{-7} Ω.m into a coil.
   (i)   What is the radius of the wire in metres? [1]
   (ii) Calculate the area of cross-section of the wire. [3]
   (iii) Write down an expression for the resistance of the wire in terms of its resistivity and its dimensions. [2]
   (iv) Calculate the resistance of this coil of iron wire. [3]

   b) A galvanometer with a coil resistance of 5 Ω gives a full-scale reading for a current of 20 mA. It is to be used to measure a much higher current.
   (i)   How, by using an extra resistor, could you make this possible? [1]
   (ii) Explain why the meter can now be used for measuring a higher current. [2]
   (iii) If a resistor of 0.2 Ω was used for this purpose, and the meter in its modified form showed a full-scale reading, calculate:
         the voltage across the meter; [2]
         the current through the 0.2 Ω resistor; [2]
         the current in the leads to the modified meter. [2]
   [Oxford (part)]

33. a) Describe the construction of a simple capacitor. State what must be done to make the value of its capacitance as large as possible. [6]
   b) What might be expected to happen if a capacitor designed for operation at 12 V was used at 100 V? Explain. [4]
   c) A lamp glows normally when it is connected to a power-pack, but it is not known whether this supply is AC or DC. Explain how to find out, given a suitable capacitor. [4]
   d) A 3 μF capacitor has a voltage of 50 V across it. Calculate:
   (i)   the charge on each plate of the capacitor; [3]
   (ii) the average current in a circuit through which the capacitor now discharges in 0.05 s. [3]
   [Oxford]

34.

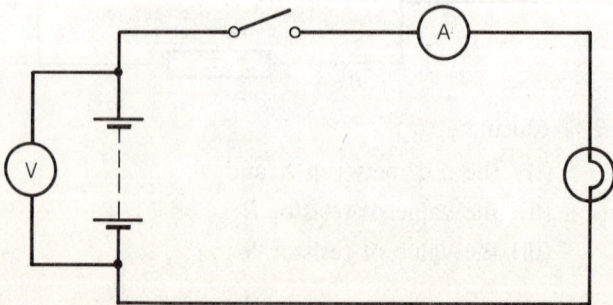

a) The diagram shows a light bulb connected to a battery, together with a voltmeter, ammeter and a switch. Two experiments are carried out using different batteries, and readings obtained as shown in the table.

Type of battery	Switch position	Voltmeter reading	Ammeter reading
Lead acid accumulator	Open (as shown) Closed	6.1 V 6.1 V	0.0 A 1.0 A
Torch battery	Open Closed	6.0 V 4.5 V	0.0 A 0.8 A

Explain
(i) which battery has the greater e.m.f. [5]
(ii) which battery has the greater internal resistance. [3]
Calculate the internal resistance of the battery consisting of torch cells.

b) A meter gives full-scale deflection for a current of 0.020 A. It has a resistance of 100 Ω. Explain, including a numerical answer, how it could be used as a voltmeter reading up to 10 V. [3]

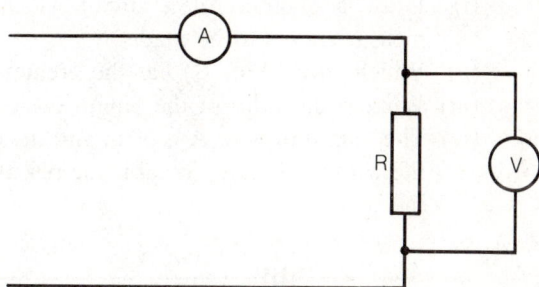

The diagram above shows this voltmeter connected across a resistor R in a circuit which also includes an ammeter. The reading on the ammeter is 0.030 A and the voltmeter is reading 5.0 V (half its full-scale deflection).
(i) What is the current through the voltmeter?
(ii) What is the current through the resistor R?
(iii) What is the p.d. across R?
(iv) What is the resistance of R? [6]
The resistor R consists of a wire 6.0 m long with a cross-sectional area of 0.012 mm². Find the resistivity of the material of which it is made. [3]

[Oxford and Cambridge]

35. a) A circuit was set up to enable a variable potential difference to be applied to a wire and for the current and potential difference to be measured.

   Two lengths of insulated wire, of the same cross-sectional area and made from the same material were connected into the circuit one at a time. Readings of the current through, and potential difference across, each wire were taken from which the graphs shown were plotted.

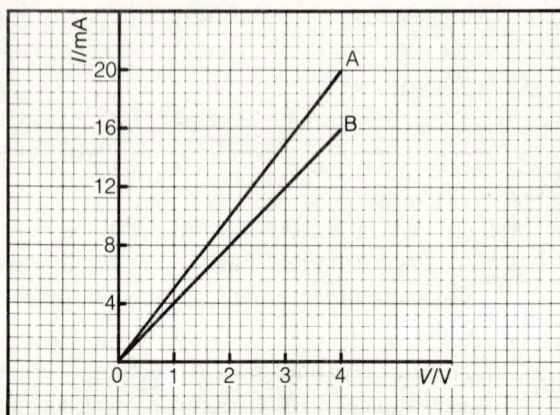

   (i) Draw a diagram of a circuit which would enable these measurements to be made. [4]
   (ii) Which wire (A or B) has the greater length? [2]
   (iii) What is the ratio of the length of A to that of B? [3]
   (iv) The length of wire A is 50 m and the cross-sectional area of the wire is $1.0 \, mm^2$. What is the resistivity of the material of the wire? [3]

   b)

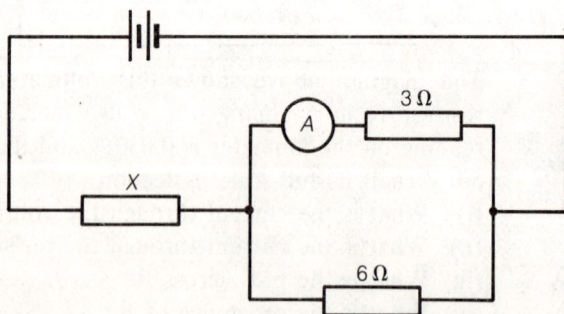

   The diagram shows a circuit in which a battery of e.m.f. 4 V and internal resistance $0.50 \, \Omega$ supplies current through a resistor X to resistors of $3 \, \Omega$ and $6 \, \Omega$ connected in parallel. An ammeter, of negligible resistance, connected in series with the $3 \, \Omega$ resistor indicates a current of 0.2 A.

Calculate

(i)   the current through the 6 Ω coil,   [1]

(ii) the charge which flows through X in 1 minute,   [3]

(iii) the potential difference across the terminals of the battery while it is delivering current to the circuit,   [2]

(iv) the power delivered by the battery to the external circuit.
                                                                                        [2]

[Oxford and Cambridge]

6. Radioactivity, Atomic and Nuclear Physics

Atomic number and mass number

An atom consists of a positively charged nucleus with one or more orbiting electrons. The nucleus, apart from in the most common form of hydrogen, is made up of protons and neutrons. The number of protons determines the actual element, and in an electrically neutral atom there are an equal number of protons and electrons.

A shorthand approach is often used to represent a particular nucleus:

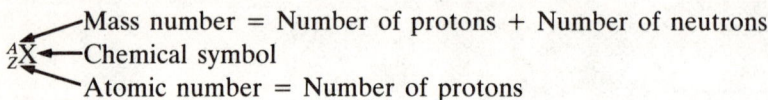

Mass number = Number of protons + Number of neutrons
$^A_Z X$ ← Chemical symbol
Atomic number = Number of protons

For example, $^{14}_6 C$ is a carbon atom with 6 protons and $(14-6) = 8$ neutrons
$^{238}_{92} U$ is a uranium atom with 92 protons and $(238-92) = 146$ neutrons.

Example Work out the number of protons and neutrons in the following elements:

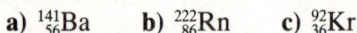

a) $^{141}_{56} Ba$ **b)** $^{222}_{86} Rn$ **c)** $^{92}_{36} Kr$

Method: The upper number gives the total number of protons and neutrons. The difference in the two numbers is equal to the number of neutrons.

Answers:

	Number of protons	Number of neutrons
a)	56	$(141 - 56) = 85$
b)	86	$(222 - 86) = 136$
c)	36	$(92 - 36) = 56$

Isotopes are atoms of a particular element which have the same number of protons but different numbers of neutrons.

Example The following are isotopes of lithium. Calculate the number of neutrons and protons in each atom:

a) $^5_3$Li   b) $^6_3$Li   c) $^7_3$Li

Method: The superscript (upper number) is the number of neutrons and protons and the subscript (lower number) is the number of protons. Notice that the number of protons is the same for each nucleus.

Answers:

	Number of protons	Number of neutrons
a)	3	$(5 - 3) = 2$
b)	3	$(6 - 3) = 3$
c)	3	$(7 - 3) = 4$

Radioactive decay

Many nuclei are unstable and will try to lose energy by emitting radiation or by disintegrating into smaller nuclei. A radioactive decay can be written using the ^A_ZX notation, e.g.

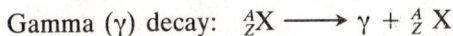

Alpha (α) decay: ^A_ZX $\longrightarrow$ $^4_2$He + $^{A-4}_{Z-2}$Y

Beta (β) decay: ^A_ZX $\longrightarrow$ $^0_{-1}$e + $^A_{z+1}$V

Gamma (γ) decay: ^A_ZX $\longrightarrow$ γ + ^A_ZX

Note: In these equations the superscripts and subscripts must balance, i.e. the total number of nucleons (protons plus neutrons) must be the same before and after the decay.

Example The following are radioactive decay equations for several different unstable nuclei. Work out the values of x and y in each of the equations:

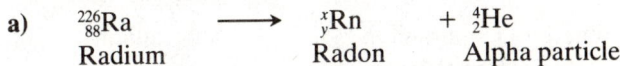

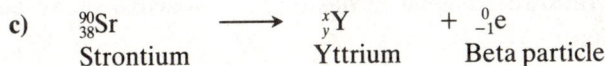

a) $^{226}_{88}$Ra $\longrightarrow$ ^x_yRn + $^4_2$He
   Radium   Radon   Alpha particle

b) $^{241}_{95}$Am $\longrightarrow$ ^x_yNp + $^4_2$He
   Americium   Neptunium   Alpha particle

c) $^{90}_{38}$Sr $\longrightarrow$ ^x_yY + $^0_{-1}$e
   Strontium   Yttrium   Beta particle

d) $^{14}_{6}C$ $\longrightarrow$ $^{x}_{y}N$ $+ \ ^{0}_{-1}e$

Carbon   Nitrogen   Beta particle

e) $^{60}_{27}Co$ $\longrightarrow$ $^{x}_{y}Co$ $+ \ \gamma$

Cobalt   Cobalt

f) $^{230}_{90}Th$ $\longrightarrow$ $^{x}_{y}Th$ $+ \ \gamma$

Thorium   Thorium

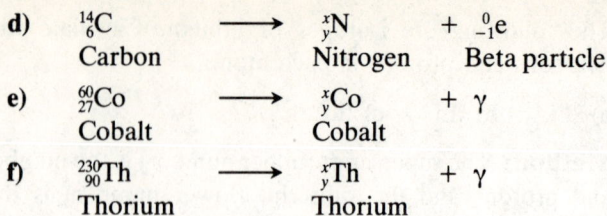

Method: In each of the radioactive decays the total number of nucleons (i.e. protons and neutrons) is the same before and after the decay. As a result the upper numbers (superscripts) must balance on both sides of the equation. This must also be true for the lower numbers (subscripts).

Answers:

	x	y
a)	222	86
b)	237	93
c)	90	39
d)	14	7
e)	60	27
f)	230	90

The following example refers to part of the uranium decay series.

Example What radioactive particles are emitted at each of the numbered stages in the following decay series?

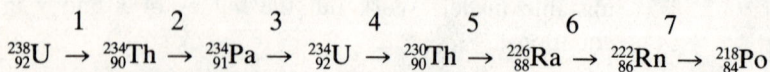

$$\overset{1}{} \qquad \overset{2}{} \qquad \overset{3}{} \qquad \overset{4}{} \qquad \overset{5}{} \qquad \overset{6}{} \qquad \overset{7}{}$$

$$^{238}_{92}U \rightarrow \ ^{234}_{90}Th \rightarrow \ ^{234}_{91}Pa \rightarrow \ ^{234}_{92}U \rightarrow \ ^{230}_{90}Th \rightarrow \ ^{226}_{88}Ra \rightarrow \ ^{222}_{86}Rn \rightarrow \ ^{218}_{84}Po$$

Where   U = uranium   Ra = radium

         Th = thorium   Rn = radon

         Pa = protactinium   Po = polonium

Method: Remember the three radioactive decay equations, and that:

a) during alpha (α) decay, the upper number decreases by 4 and the lower number by 2; and

b) during beta (β) decay, the upper number stays the same and the lower number increases by 1.

Unless you are told, there is no way of telling whether gamma (γ) radiation is emitted. Take each stage separately, e.g.

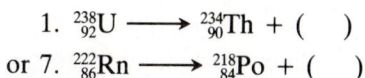

1. $^{238}_{92}U \longrightarrow \ ^{234}_{90}Th + (\quad)$

or 7. $^{222}_{86}Rn \longrightarrow \ ^{218}_{84}Po + (\quad)$

Answers: 1. $^{4}_{2}He$ (α)　　2. $^{0}_{-1}e$ (β)　　3. $^{0}_{-1}e$　　4. $^{4}_{2}He$

5. $^{4}_{2}He$　　6. $^{4}_{2}He$　　7. $^{4}_{2}He$

In a nuclear reactor a large atom is broken into two smaller atoms by bombarding the large atom with, typically, neutrons. (Neutrons are used because they have no electrical charge and so can penetrate the nucleus more easily.) A typical fission reaction might be:

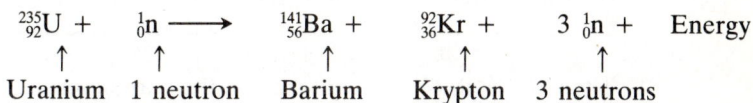

$$^{235}_{92}U + \ ^{1}_{0}n \longrightarrow \ ^{141}_{56}Ba + \ ^{92}_{36}Kr + 3\ ^{1}_{0}n + \text{Energy}$$

Uranium　1 neutron　Barium　Krypton　3 neutrons

The production of 3 neutrons means that fission may then be caused in up to 3 more uranium atoms — and is called a *chain reaction*.

The energy E released when a mass m is totally converted into energy can be calculated using Einstein's mass–energy equation

$$E = m \times c^2$$

where c is the speed of light ($= 3 \times 10^8$ m/s).

Half-life

Radioactive decay is a totally random process. If you were able to watch a group of radioactive atoms, it would be impossible to tell which, if any, atom would decay at any instant. However, if a given sample of a particular element is studied using, for example, a Geiger-Müller tube and a counter, an interesting result emerges. Regardless of the number of atoms in the sample, after a certain length of time exactly one half of the atoms will have decayed radioactively. This length of time is called the half-life. This would be observed on the counter by the fact that the count rate, corrected for background radiation, would have dropped by half.

Example   The half-life of a radioactive element is 2 minutes. The initial count rate, corrected for background radiation, is 256 counts per second (cps). What will the count rate be after:

a) 4 minutes   **b)** 8 minutes   **c)** 10 minutes?

Method: After one half-life, half of the radioactive atoms will have decayed. Therefore, after 2 minutes the count rate will be 256/2 = 128 cps etc.

Answers: a) 64 cps   **b)** 16 cps   **c)** 8 cps

You may, however, wish to know the count rate after, say, 5 minutes or 7.5 minutes. There is a formula which can be used but this is not easy and is best left until a more advanced level. The most straightforward method is to draw a graph, plotting the numbers that you do know. Using the information from the example the following table can be drawn up:

Time (min)	0	2	4	6	8	10	12
Count rate (cps)	256	128	64	32	16	8	4

Then plot a graph of count rate on the y-axis (vertical) against time in minutes on the x-axis (horizontal):

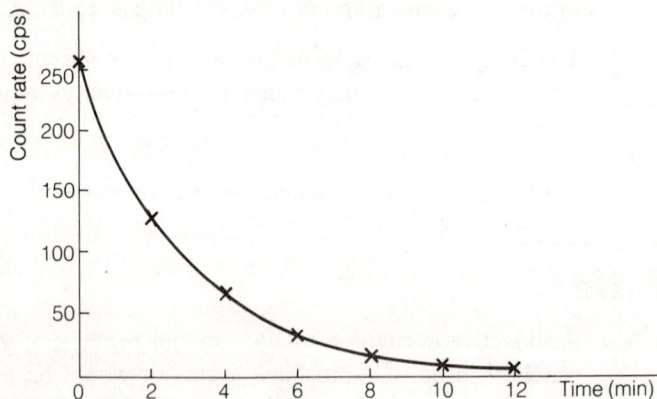

Alternatively, you may be given a set of results and asked to work out the half-life by drawing a graph.

Example   The following count rates were found at intervals of 1 day for a sample of radioactive material. The count rates are corrected for background radiation.

Count rate (cps)	128	80	51	32	20	12	8	5	3
Time (days)		0	1	2	3	4	5	6	7	8

Draw a graph of count rate on the y-axis against time in days on the x-axis, and from the graph calculate the half-life of the material.

Method: Using as large a scale as possible, plot the points on graph paper and draw the best *curve*. From the graph mark a particular value on the count rate axis, e.g. 128 cps, and find the time after which this value has dropped by half, i.e. the time when the count rate is 64 cps. The time taken to do this is the half-life. To get the best accuracy from the graph repeat this process to obtain three separate half-life values, e.g. the time for the count rate to drop from 100 to 50 and from 80 to 40. It is best to pick values which can be easily read on the time axis.

Answer: 1.5 days

Cathode ray oscilloscope (CRO)

Usually the cathode ray is swept horizontally across the screen at regular intervals. This is controlled by the time base. The signal in which the operator is interested is then connected across the Y plates.

The two examples given here are intended to give an understanding of how you might interpret the traces on the screen and by no means cover all the different uses of the oscilloscope.

Example   The diagram shows the trace obtained when a 5 V peak AC voltage supply is obtained to a CRO when the time base is switched off. What AC potential difference would give trace lengths of:

a) 4 cm   b) 2 cm   c) 1 cm?

Method: Remember that the trace is twice the peak voltage height, so that

$$8 \text{ cm} \equiv 10 \text{ V}$$
$$\therefore 1 \text{ cm} \equiv \frac{10}{8} = 1.25 \text{ V}$$

So, for example, a 4 cm trace corresponds to 5 V, but this is *twice* the peak voltage.

Answers: a) 2.5 V   **b)** 1.25 V   **c)** 0.625 V

If the time base is now switched on the trace will be spread out over time to give a trace looking like:

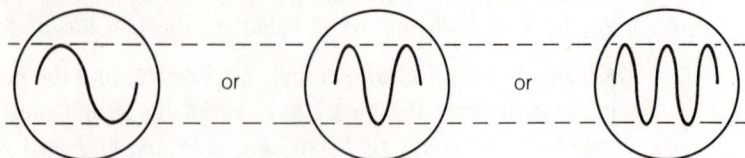

or   or

depending on the time base value.

Example   The time base of a CRO is set to 5 ms/cm. Calculate the wavelength of a wave of frequency:

a) 50 Hz   **b)** 80 Hz   **c)** 130 Hz

Method: A time base setting of 5 ms/cm means that each centimetre across the screen is equivalent to 5 ms or 0.005 s. A frequency of 50 Hz (from part **a)**) means that there are 50 oscillations every second, or that each oscillation lasts for $\frac{1}{50}$ s = 0.02 s. If each centimetre of the horizontal trace is equivalent to 0.005 s, then 0.02 s is equivalent to

$$\frac{0.02}{0.005} = 4 \text{ cm}.$$

Answers: a) 4 cm   **b)** 2.5 cm   **c)** 1.54 cm

Questions

1. The following results, corrected for background radiation, were obtained during a radioactivity experiment:

Time (hours)	0	2	4	6	8	10	12	14
Count rate (counts per minute)	100	61	40	25	16	10	6	3

Plot a graph of count rate against time. From the graph find the time taken for the count rate to drop from:

   a) 100 to 50   b) 80 to 40   c) 60 to 30   d) 40 to 20

What is the average of these four values? What is this average value called?

2. Write down two other possible isotopes of the element uranium if one isotope is $^{235}_{92}U$.

 a) How many protons are there in each of the nuclei?

 b) How many neutrons are there in each of the nuclei?

 c) How many electrons do you think there will be orbiting each of the nuclei if the atoms are electrically neutral?

3. Complete the following radioactive decay series by filling in the appropriate atomic number and the atomic mass number for each of the nuclei E, F, G, H:

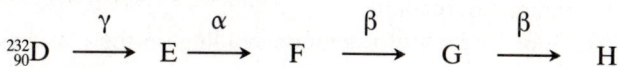

$$^{232}_{90}D \xrightarrow{\gamma} E \xrightarrow{\alpha} F \xrightarrow{\beta} G \xrightarrow{\beta} H$$

 Why is H an isotope of D?

4. Write out and complete the following table:

Radiation	Charge	Relative mass
α		
β	-1	1
γ		

5. a) A radioactive element has a half-life of 0.6 hours. If there are initially 4000 atoms of the element in a sample how many atoms of the element will there be after 2.4 hours?

 b) What is the minimum number of half-lives before the activity of a radioactive substance reduces to less than 10% of its initial value?

6. The following nuclear equation is one possible reaction within a nuclear reactor:

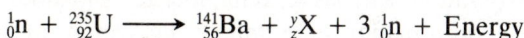

$$^{1}_{0}n + ^{235}_{92}U \longrightarrow ^{141}_{56}Ba + ^{y}_{z}X + 3\,^{1}_{0}n + \text{Energy}$$

 a) What are the values of y and z?

 b) By looking at a periodic table, what is the element X?

 c) Write out the reaction equation in words.

 d) Suggest why neutrons are preferable to alpha particles, beta particles or protons in the nuclear reaction.

7. The following results were obtained in an experiment to determine the half-life of a radioactive sample:

Time (days)	0	1	2	3	4	5	6
Corrected ratemeter readings (counts per minute)	505	350	255	175	130	90	70
	515	355	260	185	135	85	65
	510	360	250	180	125	95	60

a) Draw up a table showing the time in days and the average ratemeter reading.
b) Draw a graph of ratemeter reading on the y-axis against time on the x-axis.
c) From your graph find three separate half-life values and hence calculate an average value for the half-life of the radioactive sample.

Past examination questions

1. The table of readings shows how the radioactivity of a source changed with time

Time (min)	0	5	10	15	20	25	30	35	40	50	60	70
Count/sec	88	71	57	45	37	30	24		16	10	7	4

(i) Plot a graph of counts/sec on the vertical axis against time (min) on the horizontal axis.
(ii) Take care and draw a *smooth* curve to your readings.
(iii) Draw clear lines on your graph to show how it is used to:
    a) Find the count rate at the time 35 min.
    b) Find the time taken for the count rate to halve.

                                                               [SREB]

2. A nuclide of radon, Rn, has mass number 222 and atomic number 86.
a) Use this information to complete the symbol of this particular nuclide. [2]
b) Use this information to describe the composition of one *atom* of this nuclide. [3]
c) This radon nuclide decays by the emission of an alpha particle forming a nuclide of polonium, symbol Po.
Write an equation to represent this decay. [2]
d) In a given decay process, the total mass of the particles after the

decay is less than the original mass by 11×10^{-18} kg.
Calculate the corresponding quantity of energy released.   [3]
[The speed of light *in vacuo* is 3×10^8 m/s.]   [Cambridge]

3.

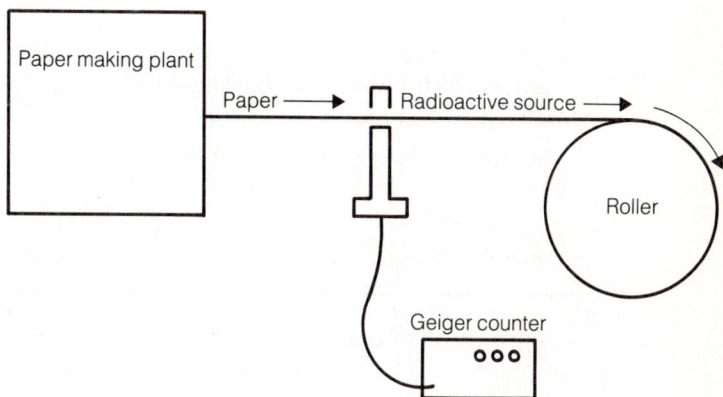

This question is about testing the thickness of paper using a
radioactive source which emits beta particles. The source is put on
one side of the paper and the Geiger counter on the other. The paper
rolls from the papermaking plant onto the roller.
a) What are beta particles?
b) Why are beta particles more suitable than alpha particles or
   gamma rays for this job?
c) Write down one precaution you would take when handling this
   radioactive source.

The table shows the reading on the counter during 70 seconds:

Table of results

Time in seconds	10	20	30	40	50	60	70
Total count since the start	50	100	150	195	235	275	315
Count in 10 seconds	50	50	50				

e) Write down the values which would complete the table to show
   the count in each 10 second time period.
f) Look at the table of results. What happened to the thickness of
   the paper?
   Why do you say this?
g) (i) At what time did the paper begin to change thickness?
   (ii) The paper was moving at 3 m/s. What length of paper passed
        the source before it changed thickness?

[SWEB (part)]

4.   Draw a diagram of a simple model of a helium atom, naming the three main components and indicating their charge and relative mass.
[8]

Explain what is meant by the terms *atomic mass* and *atomic number*.
[3]

A short half-life radioactive substance is monitored using a Geiger counter which gives the following data:

Time from beginning of experiment (in secs)	10	20	30	40	50	60	70	80
Count-rate (counts/sec)	91	67	51	38	29	22	15	10

Using a graph of **count-rate** against **time**, estimate the half-life of this substance.
[5]
[WJEC]

5.   a) A charged electroscope is used to check the activity of a radioactive source contained in a lead box.

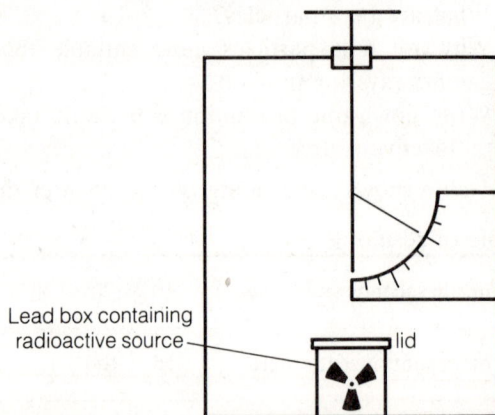

Lead box containing radioactive source
lid

After the lid is removed from the lead box the electroscope discharges. The leaf falls from a deflection of 60° to 0° in a time of 12.0 s.
(i)   Explain why the electroscope discharges after the lid is removed from the box.
(ii) Calculate the rate at which the leaf falls in degrees per second.
(iii) The half-life of the radioactive source used in the experiment is thought to be 120 minutes. Describe how the electroscope could be used to check this estimate for the half-life.   [4]

b) The apparatus used in the experiment that led to Rutherford's discovery of the atomic nucleus is represented below.

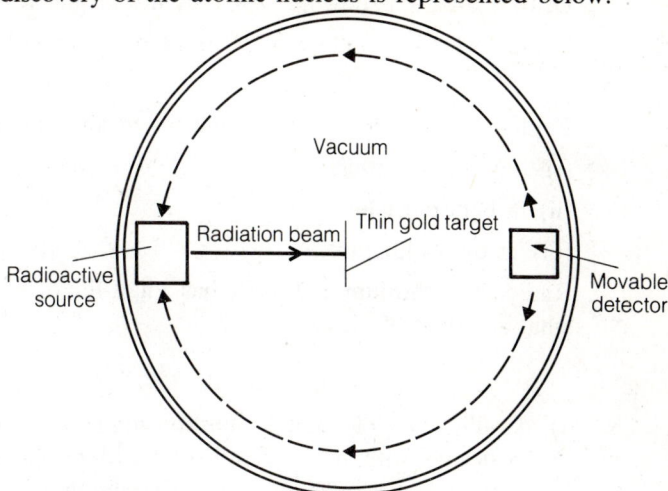

(i) What type of radiation was used?
(ii) The experiment was carried out in a vacuum. Suggest a reason for this.
(iii) What happened to the radiation beam on striking the target?
(iv) Explain how the results of the experiment led Rutherford to believe that the nucleus has a positive charge.   [6]

[Scottish]

6. a) Explain the terms mass number and atomic number and state how each changes when a nucleus emits
    (i) an alpha particle,
    (ii) a beta particle.   [4]
    b) Briefly describe an experiment which could be performed to distinguish between two radioactive samples, one of which gives out only α-particles, and the other which gives out only β-particles.   [4]
    c) The emission from a radioactive isotope of iodine was monitored for over 4 weeks and the following readings taken at the same time on certain days.

Time (days)	0	1	2	5	10	15	20	25	30
Counts/minute	1200	1120	1040	830	540	330	220	140	90

Draw a graph of count rate against time and, from the graph, estimate the half-life of the isotope of iodine.   [8]

[WJEC]

7.   Name the three kinds of particle present in the atom.

Draw a diagram showing how they are arranged in a $^{14}_{6}C$ atom. [6]

Explain what is meant by the terms **atomic number** and **mass number**.
[2]

Explain what happens to the nucleus of an atom when it emits

(i)   an alpha particle,

(ii) a beta particle,

(iii) gamma radiation. [6]

Radioactive thorium hydroxide has a half-life of 54 seconds. Explain what is meant by this. [2]

[WJEC]

8.   a) A radioactive element X of *mass number* 226 and *atomic number* 88 decays with the emission of an alpha particle. Explain the terms in italics. Write a suitable equation to illustrate the decay process, including the mass and atomic numbers for the new element Y formed. [7]

b) Describe simple experiments to show how beta particles are absorbed by certain materials and that they may be deflected by a magnetic field. State TWO precautions necessary in experimental work with radioactive materials. [7]

[SUJB]

9.   a) A Geiger-Müller tube attached to a scaler is placed on a bench in the laboratory. Over three consecutive minutes the scaler reads 11, 9 and 16 counts per minute.

When a radioactive source is placed near to the Geiger-Müller tube the counts over three consecutive minutes are 1310, 1270, and 1296 per minute.

When a piece of thick paper is placed between the source and the tube the counts are 1250, 1242, and 1236 per minute.

When the paper is replaced by a sheet of aluminium 2 mm thick the counts are 13, 12 and 11 per minute.

(i)   Why is there a reading when no source is present? [2]

(ii) Why do the three readings in any one group differ? [2]

(iii) What can be deduced about the nature of the emission? Give reasons for your answer. [5]

b) What do you understand by the *half-life* of a radioactive element? [2]

The graph is plotted from readings taken with a radioactive source at daily intervals.

Use the graph to deduce the half-life of the source. [2]

Hence give the count rate after 5 days, and the time when the count is 160 per minute. [4]

Would you expect the mass of the source to have changed significantly after 4 days? (Give a reason for your answer.) [3]

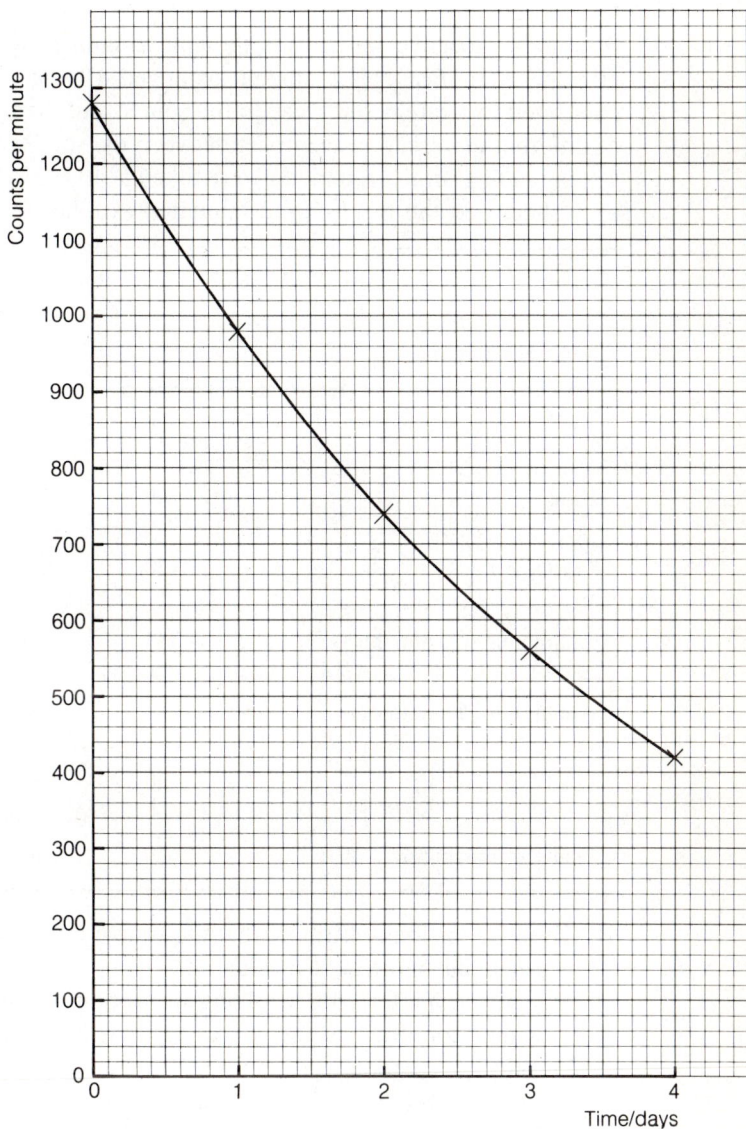

Time/days

[London]

10.

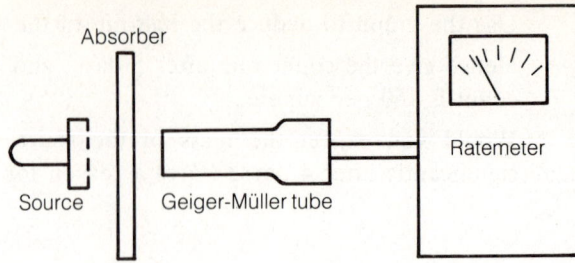

Absorber

Ratemeter

Source   Geiger-Müller tube

A weak radioactive source was thought to emit β-radiation. In an attempt to confirm this a student arranged a Geiger-Müller tube, connected to a ratemeter, close to the source and then placed sheets of different materials as absorbers between the source and the tube. Three readings of the ratemeter were taken at 10 second intervals for each sheet and the results were tabulated as follows:

Absorber material	Ratemeter reading Counts per minute		
	1	2	3
Air	120	110	130
Paper	100	120	110
Cardboard	130	130	100
Aluminium (0.5 mm thick)	110	120	110
Aluminium (5 mm thick)	50	60	40
Lead (5 mm thick)	40	50	50
Lead (50 mm thick)	50	40	50

a) Give reasons for confirming that the source does not emit α-rays or γ-rays but must emit β-radiation. [4]
b) Suggest another test, not involving absorption, you could perform to further confirm that the source emitted β-radiation. [4]
c) As only β-radiation was emitted, account for the ratemeter readings for the 50 mm thick lead absorber. [3]
d) Why were identical readings not obtained each time for the same absorber? [3]

[London (part)]

11. a) Draw and label a diagram to show the essential features of the tube of a cathode-ray oscilloscope. [8]

With reference to the diagram you have drawn, explain how the electron beam is produced and how the brightness of the spot is controlled. [6]

b)

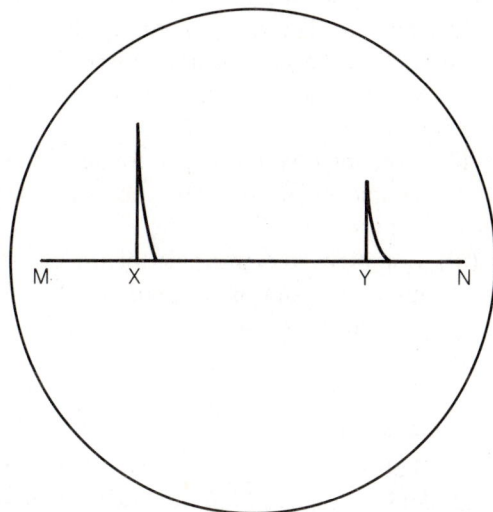

The diagram shows the screen of a cathode-ray oscilloscope. The time-base is set at 2.0 μs/mm (2.0 microsecond/millimetre) and the length of the time-base sweep MN is 100 mm.

(i) What time does the length MN represent? [1]

A radar signal sent from a radar station to a distant aircraft is displayed on the CRO at X and the signal received back from the aircraft, by reflection, is displayed at Y where the distance XY is 60 mm.

(ii) How far is the aircraft from the radar station? The speed of radar waves is 3.0×10^8 m/s. [5]

[Oxford and Cambridge]

12. A sample of a solid alpha-emitting nuclide has a mass of 20 g and a half-life of 140 days.

a) What is the composition of an alpha-particle? [2]
b) What is meant by *radioactive decay*? [2]
c) Explain the meaning of *half-life*. [2]
d) Could the half-life be confirmed by re-weighing the sample after 140 days? Explain. [2]
e) What fraction of the original sample would be undecayed after 420 days? [2]

[Oxford]

244 CALCULATIONS FOR EXAMINATION PHYSICS

13.   a) (i) Draw a diagram of the $^{12}_{6}C$ carbon atom, labelling the various particles from which it is made up. [3]

        (ii) In what way would an atom of carbon-13 differ from this? What name is given to such atoms? [2]

   b) Radium (Ra) has a half-life of 1620 years. A radium atom decays by emitting an α-particle to become emanation (Em), another α-particle to become polonium (Po), and may then emit a β-particle to become astatine (At).

        (i) What is meant by the half-life of radium being 1620 years? [2]

        (ii) How long would it take for the activity due to radium in a sample to fall from 800 counts per minute to 100 counts per minute? [2]

        (iii) Complete the symbols below to show how the proton number Z and the nucleon number A of an atom change as radium decays to astatine (At). [3]

$$^{226}_{88}Ra \longrightarrow \quad Em \longrightarrow \quad Po \longrightarrow \quad At$$

        Explain how you have determined these values. [2]

   c) The half-life of radon gas is 4 days. If some radon gas is accidentally released into a closed laboratory, how long would it take for the concentration of the gas to fall below 1 per cent of its initial value? [3]

[Oxford (part)]

7. Heat

Heat is a form of energy.

A thermometer is used to measure the temperature of something, or by how much the temperature of something has changed. Certain temperatures are taken to be *fixed*. For example, the boiling point of pure water is 100°C and the melting point of pure ice is 0°C, both when the external pressure is 760 mm of mercury.

When something gains heat energy, its temperature will usually increase. Alternatively, if the object is already at its boiling or melting point, it will change state from liquid to gas/vapour or solid to liquid respectively.

Liquid-in-glass thermometers

The general equation to find a temperature θ from a liquid-in-glass thermometer which has not been marked is

$$\theta = \frac{x}{y} \times 100$$

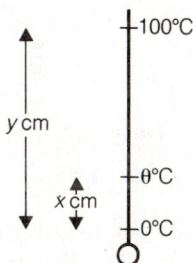

Example The diagram shows a mercury-in-glass thermometer. The upper and lower fixed points have been found and are 20 cm apart. The thermometer is then used to find a temperature θ°C and the mercury column stops at x cm above the 0°C mark.

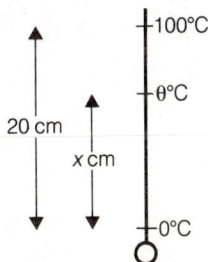

245

Find the value of θ if x is:

a) 4 cm   **b)** 5 cm   **c)** 6 cm

Method: You must assume that the mercury (or any other liquid in the thermometer) expands uniformly with temperature. This means that the distance between each of the degree marks is the same. For example, 50°C will be half-way between the 0°C and 100°C marks, i.e. 10 cm above 0°C. As a result, θ will be given by

$$\theta = \frac{x}{20} \times 100 = 5 \times x$$

Answers: a) 20°C   **b)** 25°C   **c)** 30°C

Example The situation outlined in the previous example is now made more difficult by measuring the height of the mercury column above the bulb of the thermometer.

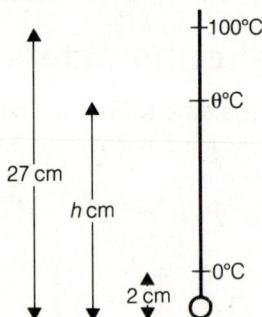

Find the value of θ if h is:

a) 17 cm   **b)** 20 cm   **c)** 22 cm

Method: Be careful not to use the method described in the last example straight away. The first thing to do is to find the distance between the two fixed points, which in this case is 25 cm (= 27 cm − 2 cm). Having done this, find the distance of θ above 0°C, i.e. $(y - 2)$ cm. The previous method can then be used, so that the slightly modified equation becomes

$$\theta = \frac{(y - 2)}{25} \times 100$$

Answers: a) 60°C   **b)** 72°C   **c)** 80°C

Specific heat capacity

If a substance remains in the same state when it is heated or cooled then there is a formula which you can use in calculations. It is

$$\underset{\substack{\text{or removed}}}{\text{Heat supplied}} = \text{Mass} \times \underset{\substack{\text{capacity}}}{\text{Specific heat}} \times \underset{\substack{\text{change}}}{\text{Temperature}}$$

or $\qquad H = m \times c \times \theta$

The specific heat capacity is a constant for any given substance and is different for different substances.

Example The specific heat capacity of water is 4200 J/kg K. Calculate the heat energy required to raise the temperature of 2 kg of water by

a) 10°C **b)** 40°C **c)** 100°C

Method: Use

$$H = m \times c \times \theta$$

and substitute the values given

$$H = 2 \times 4200 \times \theta$$

Then fill in the appropriate value of θ to give the heat energy supplied.

Answers: a) 84 000 J **b)** 336 000 J **c)** 840 000 J

Example Calculate the temperature gain of a 5 kg block of aluminium (specific heat capacity 900 J/kg K) when the following quantities of heat are given to it:

a) 9000 J **b)** 27 000 J **c)** 45 000 J

Method: The formula to use is

$$H = m \times c \times \theta$$

First rearrange the formula to make the temperature gain θ the subject of the equation. This gives

$$\theta = \frac{H}{m \times c}$$

The known quantities can then be substituted, i.e. mass $m = 5$ kg and specific heat capacity $c = 900$ J/kg K. This gives

$$\theta = \frac{H}{5 \times 900}$$

Finally substitute the different values for the heat energy supplied and calculate θ.

Answers: a) 2°C **b)** 6°C **c)** 10°C

Example   300000 J of heat energy are supplied to 3 kg of material. The following table gives the temperature rises of three different materials:

Material	Temperature rise (°C)
a) Aluminium	110
b) Copper	250
c) Methylated spirit	40

Calculate the specific heat capacity of each material.

Method: Again use

$$H = m \times c \times \theta$$

First rearrange the formula to make the specific heat capacity c the subject of the formula. This gives

$$c = \frac{H}{m \times \theta}$$

Now substitute the quantities you know — e.g. for aluminium, heat energy $H = 300000$ J,   mass $m = 3$ kg   and   temperature   rise $\theta = 110°C$.

This gives

$$c = \frac{300000}{3 \times 110}$$

(Although the temperature rise is given in °C, the units of specific heat capacity are in fact J/kg K, but some books may give J/kg °C. Both mean, in effect, the same thing, because a temperature change of 1°C is the same as a change of 1 K.)

Answers: a) 909 J/kg K   **b)** 400 J/kg K   **c)** 2500 J/kg K

In exam questions, the problems may be made harder than the preceding examples. This is because you may have to work out the heat supplied before you carry out calculations similar to the above. In most situations the heat supplied comes either from some substance cooling down or from an electrical supply.

Method of mixtures: Let us first consider a substance cooling down — the approach is often called the 'method of mixtures', but this is something of a misnomer because the separate substances often do not actually mix.

Example A piece of metal of mass 2 kg is heated to a temperature of 300°C. It is then dropped into a container holding 3 kg of water at 20°C. The specific heat capacity of water is 4200 J/kg K. The following table shows three different metals and the resulting (or 'mixture') temperature of the water in each case:

Metal	Resulting temperature of water (°C)
Lead	26
Iron	40
Brass	36

Calculate the specific heat capacity of each metal.

Method: If you adopt a step-by-step approach you will find that the problems can be made straightforward. In these three examples you are provided with enough information to work out the heat energy gained by the water. The following approach may be helpful.

Draw a longish starting line and mark on it the temperatures that you know. Here is an example for lead:

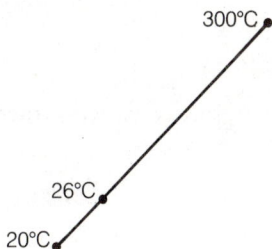

(*Note*: The lead cools down and the water warms up until they are *both* at the *same* temperature.)

Then work out the temperature change of the water warming up from 20°C to 26°C (a rise of 6°C) and the temperature fall of the lead from 300°C to 26°C (a drop of 274°C).

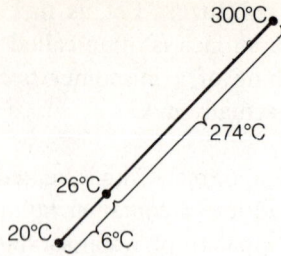

Add the other information given:

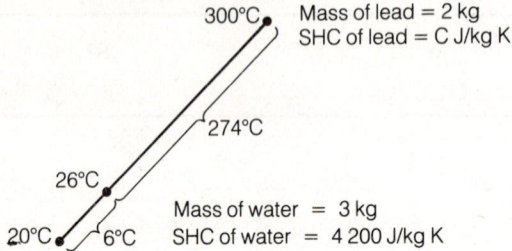

300°C Mass of lead = 2 kg
       SHC of lead = C J/kg K

Mass of water = 3 kg
SHC of water = 4 200 J/kg K

The heat gained by the water warming up can be calculated, and an expression can be written for the heat supplied by the lead to the water as it cools down.

Heat gained by the water
= Mass of water × Specific heat capacity of water
  × Temperature rise
= 3 × 4200 × 6
= 75 600 J

Heat supplied by the cooling lead
= Mass of lead × Specific heat capacity of lead
  × Temperature fall
= 2 × c × 274
= 548 × c J

Because energy is conserved, these two quantities are the same so that

$$75\,600 = 548 \times c$$

or
$$c = \frac{75\,600}{548} \text{ J/kg K}$$

Answers: a) 138 J/kg K **b)** 485 J/kg K **c)** 382 J/kg K

Electrical heating: Another way of providing the heat energy is to use a supply of electrical energy. This is easier than the previous problems. In an exam question, you will either be given, or will have to calculate, the power of the electrical heater. Since power is the rate at which one form of energy (e.g. electrical) is converted into another (e.g. heat) it is possible to work out the heat energy produced.

Example How much heat energy is produced by a 50 watt electrical heater in:

a) 60 seconds   **b)** 10 minutes   **c)** 25 minutes?

Method: A 50 watt heater produces heat energy at a rate of 50 joules per second. In order to work out the energy generated in a time t seconds the formula is

$$\text{Heat energy} = \text{Power} \times \text{Time in seconds.}$$

Answers: a) 3000 J   **b)** 30000 J   **c)** 75000 J

Alternatively, you may have to calculate the electrical power. To do this you can use one of three formulae:

$$\begin{aligned}\text{Power} &= I \times V \\ &= I^2 \times R \\ &= \frac{V^2}{R}\end{aligned}$$

where I is the current (in amperes) flowing through the heater; V is the potential difference (in volts) across the heater; and R is the resistance (in ohms) of the heater. Look at Chapter 5 on electricity if you do not remember the electrical terms.

Example If the potential difference across an electrical heater is 240 V, calculate how much heat energy is produced in 20 seconds when the current flowing through it is:

a) 0.25 A   **b)** 2 A   **c)** 12 A

Method: Given the potential difference V (in volts) and the current I (in amperes), the formula to calculate the power is

$$P = I \times V$$

To calculate the heat energy produced in 20 s, the power, which is the heat energy produced per second, must be multiplied by 20 s, i.e.

$$\text{Heat energy} = I \times V \times 20 \text{ Joules}$$

Answers: a) 1200 J   **b)** 9600 J   **c)** 57600 J

If either of the other two electrical power equations is used, be careful with the arithmetic, and square the correct quantities.

Example   If a current of 3 A flows through an electric heater calculate the power if the heater resistance is

a) 15 Ω   **b)** 50 Ω   **c)** 1000 Ω

Method: Use

$$\text{Power} = (\text{Current})^2 \times \text{Resistance}$$
$$= 3^2 \times \text{Resistance}$$
$$= 9 \times \text{Resistance W}$$

Answers: a) 135 W   **b)** 450 W   **c)** 9000 W

Example   The potential difference across a heater is 12 volts. If the heater is switched on for 20 minutes, calculate the heat energy produced if the resistance of the heater is

a) 5 Ω   **b)** 20 Ω   **c)** 300 Ω

Method: Use

$$\text{Power} = \frac{(\text{Potential difference})^2}{\text{Resistance}}$$

and

$$\text{Heat energy} = \text{Power} \times \text{Time in seconds}$$

The power of the heater is given by

$$\text{Power} = \frac{12^2}{\text{Resistance}}$$
$$= \frac{144}{\text{Resistance}} \text{ W}$$

The question asks for the heat energy produced in 20 minutes ($= 20 \times 60 = 1200$ seconds). You should use

$$\text{Heat energy} = \text{Power} \times \text{Time in seconds}$$
$$= \frac{144}{\text{Resistance}} \times 1200 \text{ J}$$

You could have written

$$\text{Heat energy} = \frac{(\text{Potential difference})^2}{\text{Resistance}} \times \text{Time in seconds}$$

straight away, but this is not necessary and tends to avoid the physics of the problem.

Answers: a) 34 500 J   **b)** 8640 J   **c)** 576 J

These methods can then be used in problems involving specific heat capacity.

Example   An electric kettle is rated at 2 kilowatts. The kettle contains 0.5 kg of water, of specific heat capacity 4000 J/kg K. By how much will the water temperature rise if it is heated for:

a) 0.5 minute   **b)** 1.0 minute   **c)** 1.5 minutes?

Method: 2 kilowatts, which is 2000 watts, means that 2000 J of electrical energy are changed into heat energy every second.

This heat energy warms up the water and so the equation to use is

$$\text{Heat energy} = m \times c \times \theta$$

The heat energy produced by the heating element in the kettle is given by

$$\text{Heat energy} = \text{Power} \times \text{Time (in seconds)}$$

Combining the two equations gives

$$\text{Power} \times \text{Time (in seconds)} = m \times c \times \theta$$

The problem asks you to find the temperature rise of the water and so you must make θ the subject of the equation, i.e.

$$\theta = \frac{\text{Power} \times \text{Time (in seconds)}}{m \times c}$$

Substituting the values stated gives

$$\theta = \frac{2000 \times \text{Time (in seconds)}}{0.5 \times 4000}$$

$$= 1.0 \times \text{Time in seconds } °C$$

Remember to change the minutes into seconds by multiplying by 60.

Answers: a) 30°C   **b)** 60°C   **c)** 90°C

Another, and slightly harder, way of asking this question is to ask you the new temperature of the liquid after it has been heated.

Example   A heater rated at 50 watts is placed in 0.25 kg of methylated spirit, whose specific heat capacity is 2500 J/kg K. If the initial temperature of the methylated spirit is 20°C, what will be its new temperature after:

a) 2 minutes   **b)** 5 minutes   **c)** 7 minutes?

Method: As in the previous example, use

$$\text{Power} \times \text{Time (in seconds)} = m \times c \times \theta$$

You must make θ the subject of the equation, giving

$$\theta = \frac{\text{Power} \times \text{Time (in seconds)}}{m \times c}$$

$$= \frac{50 \times \text{Time (in seconds)}}{0.25 \times 2500}$$

$$= 0.08 \times \text{Time (in seconds)} \ °C.$$

Convert the minutes into seconds. Having worked out the temperature rise then work out the new temperature of the methylated spirit. To do this, remember that the initial temperature of the methylated spirit was 20°C and so the temperature rise must be added to this to give the new temperature.

Answers: a) 29.6°C   **b)** 44.0°C   **c)** 53.6°C

You should now feel confident to tackle the hardest of this type of problem. This includes not only the heat gained by the substance on one side of the equation, but also calculating the heat energy supplied by the electrical heater on the other side of the equation.

Example

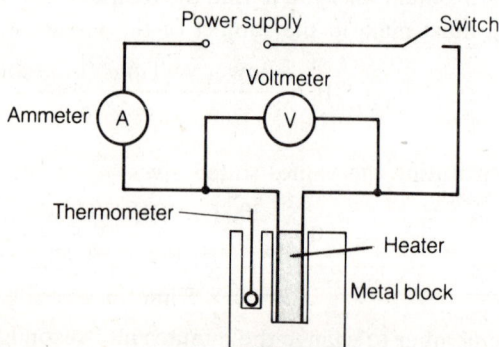

In the diagram shown, the metal block has a mass of 1 kg. The starting temperature is 20°C and the highest temperature reached after heating is 60°C. The ammeter reading is 4 A, the voltmeter reading is 12 V and the heater is switched on for 12 minutes. What is the specific heat capacity of the metal?

Method: You will appreciate that:

Heat energy supplied by heater = Heat gained by metal block

or

$$\text{Power} \times \text{Time (in seconds)} = m \times c \times \theta$$

Remember that you have a choice of three equations when working out electrical power. You are given the current (I) and potential difference (V), so the equation to use is

$$\text{Power} = \text{Current} \times \text{Potential difference.}$$

The whole equation now becomes

$$I \times V \times t = m \times c \times \theta$$

or

$$c = \frac{I \times V \times t}{m \times \theta}$$

When you substitute the given values into this equation you will be able to calculate the specific heat capacity of the metal.

Answer: 864 J/kg K.

Example This example will help you to practise your arithmetic on problems involving electrical heating and specific heat capacity. In each row of the table you must work out the missing quantities.

	Resistance $R(\Omega)$	Current $I(A)$	Potential difference $V(V)$	Time t(s)	Mass m(kg)	Specific heat capacity c(J/kg K)	Temperature rise (°C)
a)	—	5	10	1200	2.0	560	—
b)	20	2	—	2500	3.0	—	16
c)	25	—	240	600	—	900	100
d)	—	—	12	900	0.5	400	108
e)	—	13	—	120	1.2	4000	80
f)	6.5	—	—	1900	4.5	130	200

Method: In each of the questions you should use

Heat energy provided = Mass × Specific heat × Temperature
electrically   capacity   rise

or

Power × Time in seconds = $m \times c \times \theta$

Remember that

$$\text{Electrical power} = I \times V = I^2 \times R = \frac{V^2}{R}$$

Answers: a) $2\,\Omega$, $53.6°C$ **b)** 40 V, 4170 J/kg K
c) 9.6 A, 15.4 kg   **d)** $6\,\Omega$, 2 A   **e)** $18.9\,\Omega$, 246 V
f) 3.08 A, 20 V

Note: In all the questions looked at so far we have assumed that *all* of the heat energy available either from a substance cooling down or from the electrical heater is used to heat the material which is to be heated. This made our calculations more straightforward. In practice, however, not all of the heat will be used to raise the temperature of the material to be heated. Some of it may escape from the system by conduction, convection and/or radiation. If the material is a liquid some of the heat will heat the container in which the liquid is held.

Specific latent heat

In the last section we looked at how heat energy raised the temperature of different substances. However, the temperature of a material does not always change when heat energy is applied to it. Such a situation occurs when the substance changes state, for example a solid turning into a liquid, or a liquid changing into a gas at the boiling point of the liquid. The heat energy is used to change the molecular structure of either the solid or the liquid. The equation used in problems on change of state is

$$\text{Heat energy} = \text{Mass} \times \text{Specific latent heat}$$

or

$$H = m \times L$$

If the substance is changing from solid to liquid, L may be written as L_F, which is the *specific latent heat of fusion*. If the substance is changing from liquid to gas, L becomes L_V, which is the *specific latent heat of vaporization*.

Example   The specific latent heat of fusion of ice is 340000 J/kg. Calculate the mass of ice melted by a 1000 watt heater, if the heater operates for:

a) 680 s   **b)** 1700 s   **c)** 3400 s

Method: Use

$$\text{Heat energy supplied} = \text{Mass} \times \text{Specific latent heat of fusion}$$

or

$$H = m \times L_F$$

You are asked to work out the mass melted and so m must be made the subject of the equation. Rearranging gives

$$m = \frac{H}{L_F}$$

$$= \frac{\text{Power} \times \text{Time (in seconds)}}{L_F}$$

$$= \frac{1000 \times t}{340\,000}\text{kg}$$

Answers: a) 2.0 kg   **b)** 5.0 kg   **c)** 10.0 kg

The other use of the equation is for liquids changing into gases at the liquid's boiling point.

Example   An electric kettle heats water until it is boiling. Calculate the latent heat of vaporization of the water if the heating element is rated at 1.5 kW and 0.5 kg of water is changed into steam in 12.5 minutes.

Method: Use

Heat energy supplied = Mass × Latent heat of vaporization

or $H = m \times L_V$

or   Power × Time in seconds = $m \times L_V$

Substituting the values given and remembering that minutes must be converted into seconds and that the power must be changed from kW into watts gives

$$1500 \times 750 = 0.5 \times L_V$$

$$L_V = \frac{1500 \times 750}{0.5}\text{J/kg}$$

Answer: 2 250 000 J/kg

Example   How long would it take to convert 2 kg of ice at −20°C into steam at 100°C using an electrical heater rated at 2000 W? (Specific heat capacity of ice = 2100 J/kg K, L_F = 330 000 J/kg; Specific heat capacity of water = 4200 J/kg K, L_V = 2 300 000 J/kg.)

Method: You are most unlikely to meet a question as involved as this in your exam but you could easily meet certain parts of the problem. The easiest way to answer the problem is to draw a mathematical picture:

Water to steam
100°C ——————————— 100°C
$m = 2$ kg
$L_V = 2300000$ J/kg K

Water
100°C
$m = 2$ kg
SHC = 4200 J/kg K

Ice to water
0°C   0°C
$m = 2$ kg
$L_F = 330000$ J/kg
Ice
20°C
−20°C
$m = 2$ kg
SHC = 2100 J/kg K

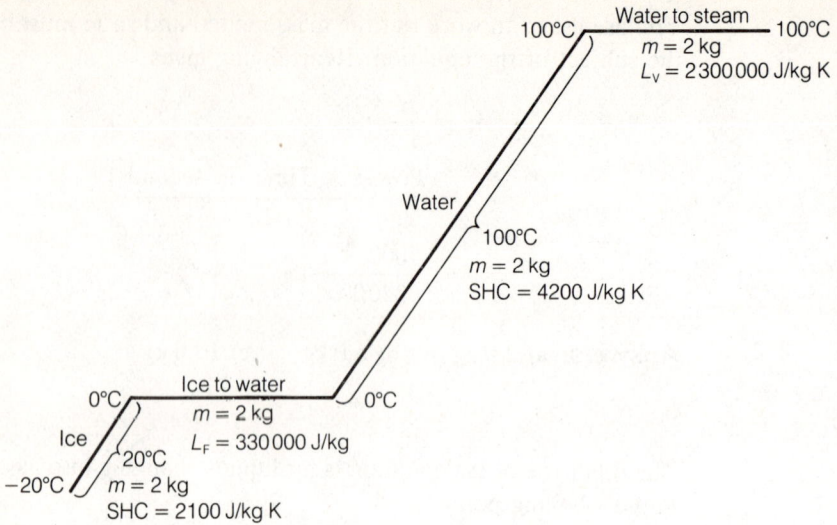

The diagram helps to divide the heating process into four separate stages, each represented by a line. The full heating equation becomes

Heat energy supplied = Heat to raise temperature of ice
from −20°C to 0°C
+ Heat to melt ice
+ Heat to raise temperature of water
from 0°C to 100°C
+ Heat to vaporize water

which becomes

Power × Time in seconds =
$m \times C_I \times \theta_I$ I subscript refers to ice
$+ m \times L_F$
$+ m \times C_W \times \theta_W$ W subscript refers to water
$+ m \times L_V$ Note: Mass is 2 kg throughout

Substitute the given values:

$2000 \times t$
$= 2 \times 2100 \times 20 + 2 \times 330\,000 + 2 \times 4200 \times 100 + 2 \times 2\,300\,000$

You can then work out a value for t.

Answer: 3092 s or 51.5 minutes.

It is quite interesting in this type of problem to work out the time taken for each stage of the problem. Ask yourself in advance which stage of the process will take longest.

Expansion

The previous two sections on the methods of mixtures and electrical heating have looked at how a supply of heat energy may increase the temperature of a substance. During such a process the substance may try to take up more space — a process called *expansion*. The mathematical problems met in your exams usually only involve the expansion of solids — although you may be required to describe the expansion of liquids.

You need to know only one formula for the expansion of solids. This is

$$\text{Linear expansivity} = \frac{\text{Change of length}}{\text{Original length} \times \text{Temperature rise}}$$

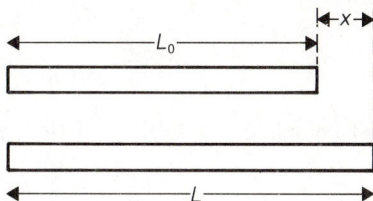

L_0 = original length
L = final length
x = change of length

Note that the expansion is considered in one direction only — in your exam the object expanding may be a rod of metal.

Substituting the letters into the equation gives:

$$\text{Linear expansivity} = \frac{x}{L_0 \times \text{Temperature rise}}$$

$$= \frac{L - L_0}{L_0 \times \text{Temperature rise}}$$

Finally, this becomes:

$$\alpha = \frac{L - L_0}{L_0 \times \theta}$$

where α is the linear expansivity and θ is the temperature rise.

This formula can also be written as

$$L = L_0(1 + \alpha\theta)$$

(You may care to practise your algebra and show that the two equations are the same.)

The major difficulty with problems on linear expansivity is the fact that linear expansivity has a small value for metals; e.g. aluminium has a linear expansivity of 0.000 026 per K, also written 2.6×10^{-5} per K.

Example   The linear expansivity of steel is 0.000 011 per K. Calculate the change in length of a 200 m length of railway track (measured at 0°C) if the temperature of the surrounds is:

a) 5°C   **b)** 20°C   **c)** 30°C

Method: Use

$$\text{Linear expansivity} = \frac{\text{Change in length}}{\text{Original length} \times \text{Temperature change}}$$

or

$$\alpha = \frac{x}{L_0 \times \theta}$$

x must be made the subject of the formula, i.e.

$$\begin{aligned} x &= \alpha \times L_0 \times \theta \\ &= 0.000011 \times 200 \times \theta \\ &= 0.0022 \times \theta \end{aligned}$$

or using the 'power of ten' notation

$$\begin{aligned} x &= 1.1 \times 10^{-5} \times 200 \times \theta \\ &= 2.2 \times 10^{-3} \times \theta \end{aligned}$$

Answers: a) 0.011 m   **b)** 0.044 m   **c)** 0.066 m

The last of these three answers means a 6.6 cm expansion between a winter's night when the temperature is at freezing and a hot summer's day.

The other way in which this type of problem can be put is to ask what the new length of the rod will be after it has expanded.

Example   A yacht's mast is made of aluminium, the linear expansivity of which is 0.000 026 per K. The mast is 12 m long at 10°C. What is its new length at:

a) 20°C   **b)** 24°C   **c)** 30°C?

Method: The most straightforward way to solve this problem is to find the change of length and add it to the original length.

$$\text{Linear expansivity} = \frac{\text{Change in length}}{\text{Original length} \times \text{Temperature rise}}$$

or, on rearranging

Change   = Linear   × Original   × Temperature
in length   expansivity   length   rise

$$= 0.000026 \times 12 \times \theta$$
$$= 0.000312 \times \theta$$
$$= 3.12 \times 10^{-4} \times \theta$$

Having substituted the value for θ and obtained the change in length, you then add this to the original length of 12 m.

Answers: a) 12.003 12 m   **b)** 12.004 37 m   **c)** 12.006 24 m

In all the answers you will see that the expansion is only a few millimetres. In practice this would not be important and expansion only becomes significant for fairly long lengths of material.

The gas laws

So far we have looked at the effect of heat on solids and liquids. Because the molecules of a gas are not held together in the same way as those in solids and liquids there are two quantities which may vary with temperature. They are the pressure and the volume of the gas.

In the pressure law experiment, it is found that a straight line is obtained, which, when produced backwards, passes through the point −273°C. This is also the case in the Charles' (volume) law experiment.

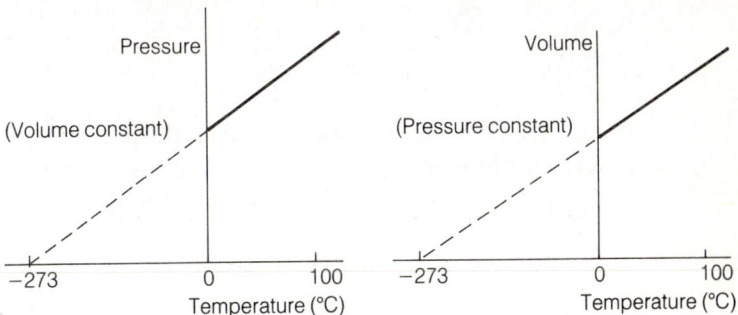

The vertical axes can be moved from 0°C to −273°C so that both the straight lines pass through the origin.

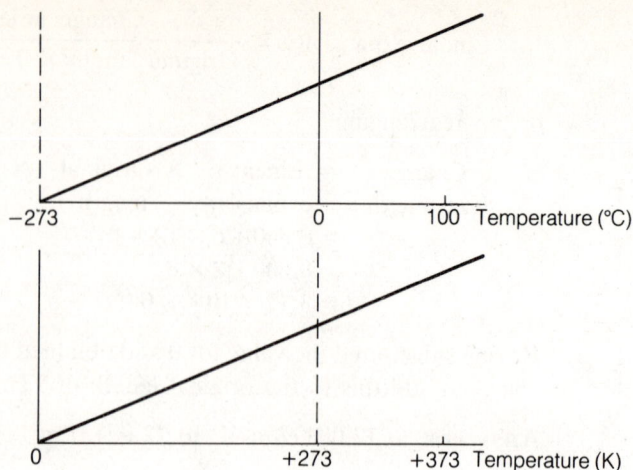

The temperature axis is now redefined so that $-273°C$ becomes 0 Kelvin. This temperature is called *absolute zero,* and the scale starting at this temperature is called the absolute temperature scale. °C can be converted to K by adding 273.

The pressure law is written as

$$\text{Pressure} \propto \text{Absolute temperature}$$

or
$$\frac{P}{T} = \text{constant}$$

This can also be written as

$$\frac{P_1}{T_1} = \frac{P_2}{T_2}$$

and Charles' law as

$$\text{Volume} \propto \text{Absolute temperature}$$

or
$$\frac{V_1}{T_1} = \frac{V_2}{T_2}$$

The third of the gas laws is called Boyle's law and involves the variation of pressure and volume when the temperature is constant.

The law states that:

$$\text{Pressure} \times \text{Volume} = \text{Constant}$$

or
$$P_1 \times V_1 = P_2 \times V_2$$

The ideal gas equation: The pressure law, Charles' law and Boyle's law equations can all be combined into a single equation.

This is called the ideal gas equation:

$$\frac{P_1V_1}{T_1} = \frac{P_2V_2}{T_2} \quad \text{or} \quad \frac{PV}{T} = \text{Constant}$$

Example   At 27°C, the pressure of the gas in a steel cylinder is 1.2×10^6 Pa. What will the pressure be at:

a) 127°C   **b)** 277°C   **c)** 327°C?

Method: In order that you are consistent in problems involving gases you should always write down the full gas equation, although you will soon realize that this is not always necessary.

$$\frac{P_1V_1}{T_1} = \frac{P_2V_2}{T_2}$$

Write down the values that you are given:

$P_1 = 1.2 \times 10^6$ Pa $P_2 =$ to be calculated
$V_1 =$ not given $V_2 =$ not given
$T_1 = 273 + 27 = 300$ K $T_2 = 127 + 273 = 400$ K
                                                   $277 + 273 = 550$ K
                                                   $327 + 273 = 600$ K

Note: Temperatures must *always* be converted to Kelvin. This is done by adding 273 to the Celsius temperature.

Because the cylinder is made of steel, and because you are not told of any change of volume, you can assume that the volume is constant, i.e. $V_1 = V_2 (= V$, say). If we take the temperature to be 127°C i.e. from calculation **a)**, substituting the quantities given leads to

$$\frac{1.2 \times 10^6 \times V}{300} = \frac{P_2 \times V}{400}$$

Making P_2 the subject of the equation gives

$$P_2 = \frac{1.2 \times 10^6 \times V \times 400}{300 \times V}$$

$$= \frac{1.2 \times 10^6 \times 400}{300} \text{ Pa} \quad \text{(because } V \text{ cancels)}$$

Answers: a) 1.6×10^6 Pa   **b)** 2.2×10^6 Pa   **c)** 2.4×10^6 Pa

Alternatively, you may see a problem in which the pressure does not change. This is in effect an application of Charles' law, but again it is worth writing out the equation in full.

Example $2 \, m^3$ of oxygen are stored at $-23°C$. Assuming that the pressure does not change, what volume will the oxygen occupy at:

a) 77°C   **b)** 127°C   **c)** 227°C?

Method: The full gas equation is

$$\frac{P_1 V_1}{T_1} = \frac{P_2 V_2}{T_2}$$

and P_1 = not given P_2 = not given
     V_1 = 2 m^3 V_2 = to be calculated
     T_1 = 273 − 23 = 250 K T_2 = (value given + 273) K

Let $P_1 = P_2 = P$, say, and substitute the values:

$$\frac{P \times 2}{250} = \frac{P \times V_2}{T_2}$$

Making V_2 the subject gives

$$V_2 = \frac{P \times 2 \times T_2}{P \times 250}$$

$$= \frac{2 \times T_2}{250} \, m^3$$

Answers: a) 2.8 m^3 **b)** 3.2 m^3 **c)** 4.0 m^3

As stated, the third of the three separate gas laws is Boyle's law, and although this is not really to do with heat, because the temperature remains constant, it is appropriate to include an example of it at this stage.

Example   A gas has a volume of 4 m^3 and exerts a pressure of 2.0×10^5 Pa. If the temperature does not change, calculate its new pressure when the volume is:

a) 8 m^3 **b)** 2 m^3 **c)** 1 m^3

Method: The temperature remains constant throughout, i.e. $T_1 = T_2 = T$, say.

The gas equation is

$$\frac{P_1 V_1}{T_1} = \frac{P_2 V_2}{T_2}$$

and P_1 = 2.0×10^5 Pa P_2 = to be calculated
     V_1 = 4 m^3 V_2 = volume given
     T_1 = T T_2 = T

Substituting in the equation gives

$$\frac{2.0 \times 10^5 \times 4}{T} = \frac{P_2 V_2}{T}$$

or
$$P_2 = \frac{2.0 \times 10^5 \times 4 \times T}{T \times V_2}$$

$$= \frac{8 \times 10^5}{V_2} \text{ Pa}$$

Answers: a) 1.0×10^5 Pa   **b)** 4.0×10^5 Pa   **c)** 8.0×10^5 Pa

You should note that as the volume decreases the pressure increases.

Where all three quantities (i.e. pressure, volume and temperature) vary you will need to use the gas equation and substitute for all the quantities.

Example   Complete the blanks in the following table:

	P_1	V_1	T_1	P_2	V_2	T_2
a)	1.3×10^5 Pa	3 m³	0°C	2.6×10^5 Pa	6 m³	—
b)	76 cm Hg	1.5 m³	27°C	—	4.5 m³	227°C
c)	2.0 atmospheres	22 cm³	127°C	1.0 atmospheres	—	27°C

Notice that the units for the pressures are different, but because they will be the same on both sides of the equation you need not convert them into pascals. However, remember to convert all temperatures into kelvins.

Method: Write out the gas equation:

$$\frac{P_1 V_1}{T_1} = \frac{P_2 V_2}{T_2}$$

and then list each of the quantities:

$P_1 =$ $P_2 =$
$V_1 =$ $V_2 =$
$T_1 =$ $T_2 =$

Substitute these values into the equation and rearrange the equation to make the unknown quantity the subject of the equation. As long as the units are the same on both sides of the equations your final answer will have the units of its counterpart. For example, if P_1 is given in centimetres of mercury, then P_2 will also have these units.

Answers: a) 819°C   **b)** 42.2 cm Hg   **c)** 33 cm³.

Questions

1. Calculate the unknown quantity in the following:
    a) Temperature is kept constant:

    $P_1 = 8$ atmospheres $P_2 = 4$ atmospheres
    $V_1 = 30$ cm³ $V_2 =$

    b) Volume is kept constant:

    $P_1 = 6 \times 10^5$ Pa $P_2 =$
    $T_1 = 27°C = \qquad$ K $T_2 = 327°C = \qquad$ K

    c) Pressure is kept constant:

    $V_1 = 20$ cm³ $V_2 =$
    $T_1 = 27°C$ $T_2 = 227°C$

    d) $P_1 = 1.5 \times 10^5$ Pa $P_2 =$
        $V_1 = 40$ cm³ $V_2 = 80$ cm³
        $T_1 = 0°C$ $T_2 = 273°C$

    e) $P_1 = 3$ atmospheres $P_2 = 6$ atmospheres
        $V_1 = 50$ cm³ $V_2 = 75$ cm³
        $T_1 = 17°C$ $T_2 =$

2. A 100 watt heater operates for 10 minutes ($= 10 \times 60$ s)
    a) Calculate the heat energy given out in 10 minutes.
    b) It is then used to heat 2 kg of water, of specific heat capacity 4000 J/kg K. Calculate the temperature rise.
    c) If the initial temperature was 20°C, what is the final temperature?
    d) In practice the final temperature is less than that calculated in c). Suggest two reasons for this.

3. A 1 kW ($= 1000$ watt) heater is used to heat 3 kg of copper, specific heat capacity 400 J/kg K. If the temperature rise is 40°C, for how long was the heater working?

4. The average bath requires 250 kg of water. This water is heated by an immersion heater rated at 5000 watts and the water temperature rises from 20°C to 50°C.
    a) Calculate the heat energy gained by the water (specific heat capacity $= 4200$ J/kg K).

b) Calculate the time taken to heat the water.

c) In practice, how can one ensure that as much heat energy as possible is kept inside the immersion tank?

d) State two other ways in which the water might be heated.

5. A blacksmith has been making a horseshoe and wishes to cool it quickly and so drops it into a trough of water. If the horseshoe is made of iron (specific heat capacity = 400 J/kg K) and has a mass of 1.25 kg, and the trough contains 10 kg of water (specific heat capacity = 4000 J/kg K) initially at 20°C:

a) Calculate the heat energy gained by the water if the mixture temperature is 25°C.

b) Assuming the answer to a) is equal to the heat lost by the horseshoe, calculate the initial temperature of the hot horseshoe.

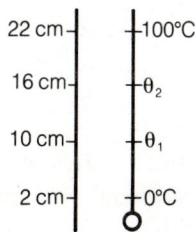

6.

22 cm	100°C
16 cm	θ_2
10 cm	θ_1
2 cm	0°C

a) Calculate θ_1 and θ_2.

b) What would be the height of the column for a temperature of 80°C?

c) What would be the height of the column for a temperature of 25°C?

7. A gas with properties P_1, V_1, T_1 changes to have properties P_2, V_2, T_2. Complete the following table of values for pressure, volume and temperature (remember that temperature must be worked out in K).

P_1	V_1	T_1	P_2	V_2	T_2
2 atm	3 m³	27°C	4 atm	6 m³	—
76 cm Hg	50 cm³	127°C	114 cm Hg	—	127°C
2 × 10⁵ Pa	4 m³	250 K	—	2 m³	500 K

8. a) Calculate the amount of heat energy required to:
    (i) convert 1 kg of ice into water at 0°C
    (ii) raise the temperature of 1 kg of water from 0°C to 100°C
    (iii) convert 1 kg of water into steam at 100°C.
  b) If the heat energy required in (i), (ii) and (iii) is provided by a 2 kW (= 2000 W) heater, calculate how long it will take to convert 1 kg of ice into steam. (Specific latent heat of fusion of water = 330000 J/kg, specific latent heat of vaporization of water = 2300000 J/kg, specific heat capacity of water = 4200 J/kg K.)

9.

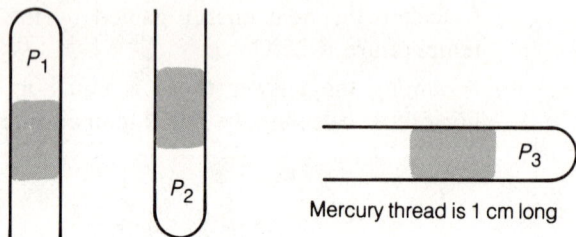

Mercury thread is 1 cm long

If the atmospheric pressure is 76 cm of mercury, calculate the values of P_1, P_2 and P_3.

10. The following results were obtained by a student carrying out a Charles' law experiment (variation of volume with temperature, pressure kept constant):

Volume (cm³)	17.0	17.6	18.3	18.8	19.6	20.1	20.8	21.4	22.0	22.6	23.3
Temperature (°C)	0	10	20	30	40	50	60	70	80	90	100

  a) Plot a graph of y = volume against x = temperature (start the temperature axis at −350°C). Produce your graph back and determine the temperature at which the volume is zero.
  b) At what temperature is the volume 12 cm³?
  c) Determine the volume at 55°C.

11. The following results were obtained by a student carrying out a pressure law experiment (variation of pressure with temperature, volume kept constant):

Pressure (10^5 Pa)	0.95	0.98	1.02	1.05	1.09	1.12	1.16	1.20	1.22	1.26	1.30
Temperature (°C)	0	10	20	30	40	50	60	70	80	90	100

a) Draw a large, well-labelled diagram of the apparatus which might have been used.
b) Plot a graph of y = pressure against x = temperature, starting the temperature axis at $-350°C$.
c) From your graph estimate a value for absolute zero.
d) In theory, what are the gas molecules doing at absolute zero?
e) Use your graph to estimate the temperature at which the pressure was $0.5 \times 10^5 \, N/m^2$.
f) What was the pressure at $-200°C$?
g) Suggest how you might use this graph to measure a temperature of $+300°C$ (you may require a larger piece of graph paper).

12. The following results were obtained by a student carrying out a Boyle's law experiment (variation of volume with pressure, temperature kept constant):

Pressure (10^4 Pa)	2.0	3.0	4.0	5.0	6.0	8.0
Volume ($10^{-4} \, m^3$)	4.0	2.7	2.0	1.6	1.3	1.0
1/Volume ($10^4/m^3$)	0.25					

a) Copy out the table and complete the other values for 1/volume.
b) Plot a graph of y = pressure against x = 1/volume, starting both axes at zero.
c) What is the volume when the pressure is 7.0×10^4 Pa?
d) What is the pressure when the volume is $3.0 \times 10^{-4} \, m^3$?

13. The linear expansivities of several metals are:

Aluminium	0.000026 or 2.6×10^{-5} per K
Brass	0.000019 or 1.9×10^{-5} per K
Steel	0.000011 or 1.1×10^{-5} per K

a) Calculate the expansion of a 2 m aluminium rod if its temperature rises by $80°C$.
b) By what temperature would a brass rod of the same length have to rise in order to achieve the same expansion?
c) What would be the expansion of a $0.5 \, m$ rod of steel if the temperature increased by $250°C$?

14. The following results were obtained from a Boyle's law experiment:

Pressure/10^5 Pa	1.0	1.1	1.2	1.3	1.4	1.5	1.6	1.7	1.8	1.9	2.0
Volume/cm³	50.0	45.8	40.8	38.2	36.0	33.5	31.2	29.4	27.6	26.2	25.0
Pressure × Volume											
1/Pressure											
1/Volume											

a) Copy and complete the table, completing the units in the headings to the columns.

b) Plot the following graphs; starting all at (0,8), (0,0)
   (i) y = pressure against x = volume
   (ii) y = pressure against x = 1/volume
   (iii) y = 1/pressure against x = volume
   (iv) y = pressure × volume against x = pressure

c) What are your conclusions from the four graphs that you have drawn in part b)?

15.

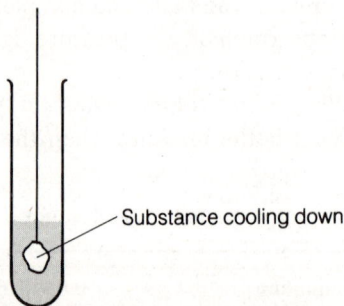

Substance cooling down

The substance in the test tube was allowed to cool and its temperature taken at $\frac{1}{2}$ minute (i.e. 30-second) intervals for about 10 minutes. The following results were obtained:

Temperature (°C)	Time (min)
95.0	0
85.5	$\frac{1}{2}$

80.5	1
80.0	$1\frac{1}{2}$
80.5	2
80.0	$2\frac{1}{2}$
79.5	3
80.0	$3\frac{1}{2}$
80.5	4
80.0	$4\frac{1}{2}$
79.5	5
79.5	$5\frac{1}{2}$
78.5	6
77.5	$6\frac{1}{2}$
76.5	7
76.0	$7\frac{1}{2}$
74.5	8
74.0	$8\frac{1}{2}$
73.5	9
72.5	$9\frac{1}{2}$
72.0	10

Plot a graph of temperature against time and use it to find the freezing point of the substance.

Past examination questions

1. The apparatus below was used to measure the energy supplied to the liquid by the immersion heater. (The joule meter has dials similar to those on a domestic electricity meter.)

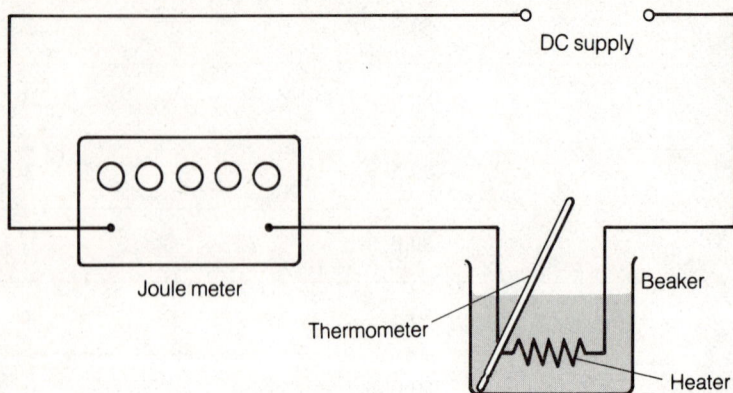

Set A below shows the positions of the dial needles before the experiment.

Set A

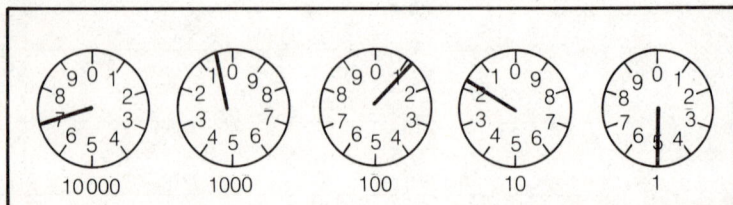

| 10 000 | 1000 | 100 | 10 | 1 |

Set B below shows the positions of the dial needles after the experiment.

Set B

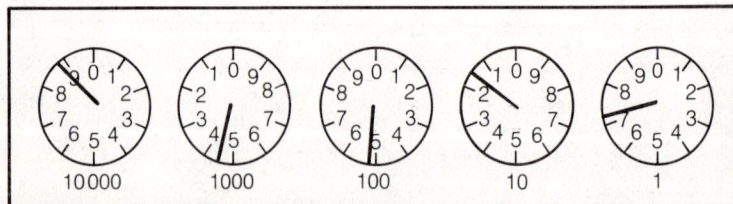

| 10 000 | 1000 | 100 | 10 | 1 |

a) (i) What are the readings shown by set A and set B?

   (ii) How many joules of energy were supplied to the heater?

b) In a second similar experiment it was found that 15 750 J of energy were supplied to the liquid. The liquid had a mass of 0.5 kg and its temperature rose by 7.5°C. How much energy is needed to raise the temperature of 1 kg of the liquid by 1°C?

c) State briefly how you could use the apparatus in (a) to compare the rate of heat loss from two metal cans which are identical except that one is highly polished and the other is painted dull black. [LREB]

2. a) In an experiment to measure the specific heat capacity of copper a pupil transferred a hot piece of copper at a known temperature to a beaker of cold water. Some of the results which the pupil obtained are shown below.

    Starting temperature of the copper = 100°C
    Starting temperature of the water = 20°C

    (i) In order to calculate the specific heat capacity of the copper, what other measurements would the pupil have to take?
    (ii) If the water and the copper have the same mass will the final temperature of the water and copper be nearer to 100°C or 20°C?
    Explain your answer carefully.
    (Specific heat capacity of copper = 380 J/kg °C. Specific heat capacity of water = 4200 J/kg °C.)

    b) (i) Name two ways in which heat energy could be lost from a beaker of hot water.
    (ii) Suggest simple methods of reducing these heat losses and name any materials which you would use. [LREB]

3. A 180-watt heater and a thermometer were immersed in 0.5 kg of water in a copper calorimeter. The following readings were obtained:

Temperature/°C	30	36	40	45	49	54	57
Time/minutes	3	4	5	6	7	8	9

On graph paper plot a graph of temperature against time. Start the axes from the origin and draw the best straight line through your points. [8]

Using your graph, or otherwise, find
a) room temperature (the temperature at which heating started), and [2]
b) the specific heat capacity of water. [6]

Give two reasons why the value obtained for the specific heat capacity is more than the accepted value. [2]

State two precautions you would take in carrying out this experiment to ensure a more accurate value for the specific heat capacity. [2]

[London]

4.   The apparatus shows a simple arrangement for finding out how the volume of a fixed mass of dry air changes with its pressure.

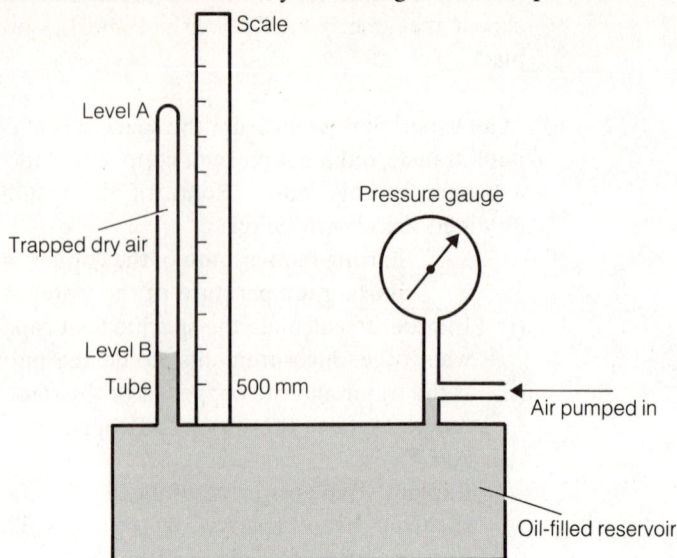

The pressure is altered by pumping air into the reservoir which forces oil up the tube and compresses the trapped air in the tube.

The levels A and B are recorded and the pressure measured on the gauge. As the tube is of uniform cross-sectional area, different *volumes* can be represented by different *lengths* of air from A to B.

The readings recorded are as follows:

Level A (mm)	Level B (mm)	Length of air in tube (B − A)	Pressure of air ($\times 10^5$ N/m^2)
100	500		1
100	380		1.4
100	321		1.8
100	282		2.2
100	260		2.5
100	242		2.8
100	225		3.2

(i) Complete the third column in your exercise book by working out the length of the air column in the tube.

(ii) Plot a graph of 'length of air' (y-axis) against 'pressure of air' (x-axis).

(iii) Copy the following table into your exercise book and record in the spaces the lengths of the air columns corresponding to the pressures shown:

Pressure of air ($\times 10^5$ N/m²)	Length of the air column (mm)
1	
2	
3	

(iv) Study these results and write what you conclude about the way in which the length of the air column changes with the pressure of the air. [SREB]

5. Describe what is meant by *latent heat*.

Explain its involvement in the following cases:
(i) cooling a drink with lumps of ice;
(ii) the severity of a steam scald;
(iii) petrol spilt on the hand makes the hand feel cold. [9]

An electric kettle which takes 12.5 A from a 240 V mains supply is left boiling for 20 seconds. Calculate how much water will be turned to steam, ignoring heat absorbed by the kettle and lost to the atmosphere. [7]
[*Specific latent heat of vaporization of water* = 2 400 000 J/kg]
[WJEC]

6. A beaker contains 200 g of water at 15°C. 25 g of ice at 0°C is added to the water which is stirred until the ice is completely melted.
a) How much heat is needed to melt all the ice?
b) What is the mass of water produced by melting all the ice?
c) Calculate the lowest temperature of the mixture, assuming that all the heat to melt the ice is taken from the water and that no heat enters or leaves the system. [10]
(Assume Specific heat capacity of water = 4200 J/kg K.
   Specific latent heat of fusion of ice = 336 000 J/kg.)
[JMB]

7. Define *specific heat capacity* and show how you would determine its value for water by an electrical method. [10]

Calculate the minimum mass of ice at 0°C that would have to be added to 160 g of water at 15°C to bring its temperature down to 0°C.
[Latent heat of fusion of ice = 336000 J/kg.] [6]
[Specific heat capacity of water = 4200 J/kg °C.] [WJEC]

8. A thin open metal can contains a little water at room temperature of 283 K. It is heated at a uniform rate on an electric hot plate. The water is observed to reach boiling point in 2.1 minutes and after a further 12.0 minutes it has just completely boiled away. Draw a sketch graph to show how the water temperature changes with time over the whole period. How does the average kinetic energy of the water molecules change over this period? [6]

Use the data to estimate a value for the specific latent heat of vaporization of water and say why the estimate is only approximate. (Specific heat capacity for water = $4.2 \, \text{kJ kg}^{-1} \text{K}^{-1}$.) [7]

How and why would you expect the observations to differ if atmospheric pressure was much lower than normal? [2]
[SUJB]

9. a) A bicycle pump, with its exit hole closed, contains $80 \, \text{cm}^3$ of air at atmospheric pressure of 760 mm of mercury and a temperature of 280 K. When the air has been compressed to $38 \, \text{cm}^3$ and the temperature has risen to 301 K, what is the pressure of the enclosed air? [4]

b) Describe, with the aid of a clear diagram, how you would use a manometer to measure the pressure of the laboratory gas supply. Show clearly the required observations and how the result is obtained. [6]

c) Explain the essential principle of operation of a Bourdon gauge and refer briefly to a typical use. [5]
[SUJB]

10. a) A gas cylinder has volume 20 litres and contains gas at a pressure 25 times that of the atmosphere. A leak occurs and the pressure drops to 0.8 of the initial value. What volume of gas, at atmospheric pressure, has escaped? State what assumption must be made in your calculation. [5]

b) Draw a diagram of a Bourdon gauge and explain its action. [5]

c) By means of a labelled sketch graph, show how the pressure exerted by a gas changes with temperature, when its volume

remains constant. Comment on how the speed of the gas
molecules alters during such changes, with particular reference to
low temperatures. [5]

[SUJB]

11. a) Describe an experiment to find the relationship between the
volume and temperature of a fixed mass of gas.
Your answer should include
(i)   a carefully labelled diagram of the apparatus;
(ii) a description of how you would use the apparatus;
(iii) a list of any measurements made.
State one factor, other than the mass of the gas, that should be
constant throughout the experiment. [$4\frac{1}{2}$]

b) The results from such an experiment are shown on the graph.

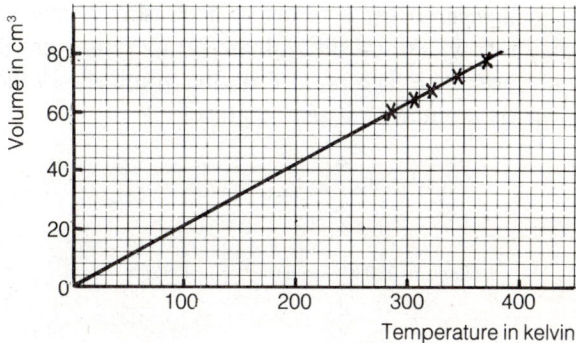

(i) What is the relationship between volume, V, and Kelvin
temperature, T?
(ii) Use the graph to find the volume of this mass of gas at 22°C.
[2]

c) A gas cylinder contains oxygen at a high pressure. The valve on
the cylinder is faulty so that the oxygen escapes slowly into the
atmosphere.
(i) What will happen to the pressure of the oxygen in the
cylinder as the gas escapes? You may assume temperature
stays constant.
Explain your answer in terms of the behaviour of the gas
particles left in the cylinder.
(ii) Eventually no more oxygen leaks from the cylinder. A pupil
says this is because the cylinder is empty.
Explain why the pupil's statement is wrong. [$3\frac{1}{2}$]

[Scottish]

12.

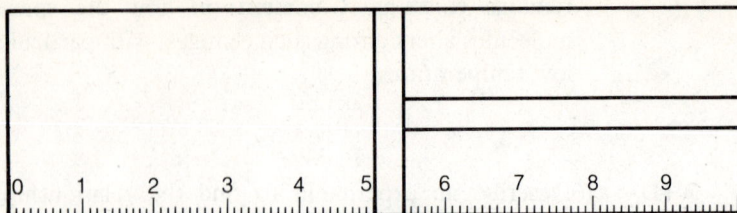

The diagram shows a syringe, calibrated in centimetres, with a gas-tight piston which is free to move. The cross-sectional area of the syringe is 12.0 cm^2. The syringe contains a mass of gas at 300 K and 100 kPa (atmospheric pressure) and the reading on the scale is then 5.00.

a) Find the volume of the gas in the syringe at 300 K.　　　　[2]

b) All the gas in the syringe is to be heated to a higher *uniform* temperature. Describe how you would attempt to do this.　[2]

c) The volume and temperature of the gas in the syringe were measured for a series of increasing temperatures. On the axes below, sketch the volume–temperature graph which should be obtained. The point P on the graph shows the original values of the volume and temperature.　　　　[3]

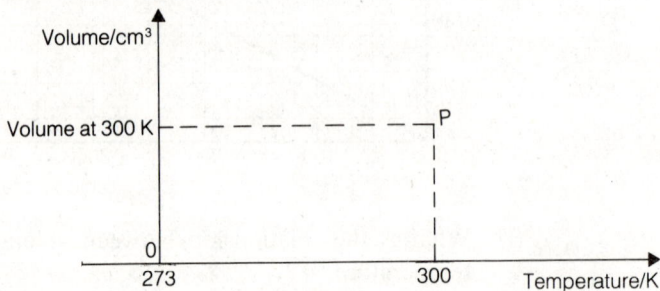

d) Calculate the volume of the gas in the syringe when the temperature becomes 400 K and the pressure exerted by the piston on the gas is increased to 500 kPa.　　　　[3]

[Cambridge]

13.　Describe an experiment you would perform to find the specific heat capacity of a liquid. State the precautions you would take to obtain an accurate result and show how you would calculate the result. [10]

A saucepan of mass 0.75 kg containing 0.50 kg of water is placed on a gas burner. The initial temperature of the water is 20°C. It takes 5 minutes before the water starts to boil. Find the rate at which heat is supplied to the water by the burner.　　　　[7]

(Specific heat capacity of water = 4000 J/kg K.

Specific heat capacity of the material of the saucepan = 600 J/kg K.)

It is found to take less time to boil water and cook vegetables in a saucepan with a lid than in a similar saucepan without a lid. Explain why this is so. [3]

[London]

14. a) Describe differences in the behaviour of the molecules of a substance in its solid, liquid and gaseous states. [3]
Using these differences as a basis, explain why
(i) energy must be removed from a liquid at its freezing point for it to solidify, [2]
(ii) evaporation of a liquid may produce a cooling of the liquid. [5]
Explain why the pressure of an enclosed gas at a constant temperature increases when the volume is reduced. [2]

b) It is required to convert 0.5 kg of water at 20°C into ice using a refrigerator which can extract heat at an average rate of 20 J/s. Determine whether this is possible within a period of 2 h.
(Specific heat capacity of water = 4200 J/kg K.
Specific latent heat of fusion of ice = 336000 J/kg.) [8]

[London]

15. a) Describe an experiment you could perform to determine the *specific latent heat of steam*. [9]

b) A highly polished copper can contains 0.20 kg of water at room temperature. The water is heated by a small immersion heater rated at 50 W.
(i) How much energy is supplied by the heater in 3 minutes? [2]
(ii) During the heating the temperature of the water rises by 9°C. Calculate the heat energy absorbed by the water. The specific heat capacity of water is 4200 J/(kg K). [2]
(iii) Why do your answers to (i) and (ii) differ? [2]
(iv) Had the water been heated for 6 minutes would the increase in temperature have been 18°C, or more than 18°C, or less than 18°C? [2]
(v) The outer surface of a similar copper can is painted matt black and contains 0.20 kg of water at room temperature. The water is heated by the same immersion heater for 3 minutes. Would you expect the rise in temperature of the water to be 9°C, or more than 9°C, or less than 9°C? [3]

[Oxford and Cambridge]

16. a) The apparatus shown in the diagram is used to find the specific heat capacity of iron.

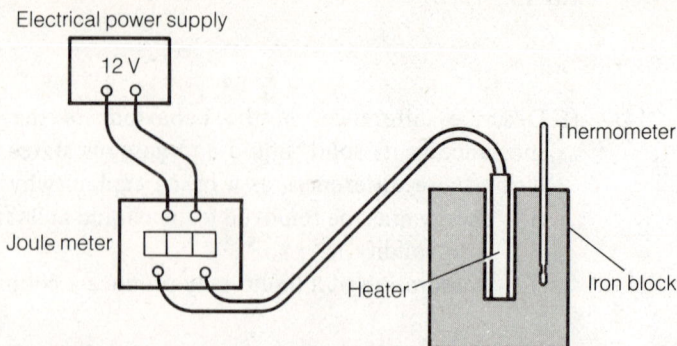

Electrical power supply

12 V

Joule meter

Thermometer

Heater   Iron block

(i)   Write down a list of the measurements you would require to make to find the specific heat capacity of iron.

(ii) If the experiment is run for the same time with insulation round the iron block, explain the effect on the temperature rise.   [3]

b) A heating engineer has to design a heating system for a room. The system has to be capable of raising the temperature of the room from $-3°C$ to $25°C$ in a time of 20 minutes. She estimates that the mass of air in the room is 78 kg.

Calculate

(i)   the energy required to produce this rise in temperature;

(ii) the power of the heating system.

(Take the specific heat capacity of air as $1000 \, J \, kg^{-1} \, K^{-1}$.)

A number of important factors have not been considered in the above calculation.

(iii) State **one** of these factors and explain whether taking it into account would lead the engineer to increase or decrease the proposed power of the heating system.   [7]

[Scottish]

17. A sample of ice at $-10°C$ is heated until it becomes steam at $100°C$. State the effect that the heat has on the sample at each stage of the heating.   [4]

Describe an experiment used to determine the specific latent heat of steam. Include in your answer a labelled diagram of the apparatus used and details of how to work out the result.   [8]

So that payment may be made for the use of an immersion heater, the heater is wired to a switch which is controlled by a slot-meter. The meter is set so that 1 kW h of energy costs 3.33p. The immersion heater can be considered to heat 60 kg of water to a uniform temperature. A 10p coin is inserted in the slot-meter. Find the temperature rise which has occurred when the current switches off. Assume no heat is lost from the water.

(Specific heat capacity of water is 4.2 kJ/kg K; 1 kW h is equivalent to 3600 kJ.) [5]

[Cambridge]

18. A simple gas thermometer consists of a cylinder of gas enclosed in an extendable bellows, as shown in the diagram. The volume of the gas is kept constant for different oven temperatures by changing the length of the spring S by movement of the screw T.

At 300 K the pressure of the gas is atmospheric, and the spring is uncompressed.

In a separate experiment it is found that a force of 12.5 N will compress the spring by 10 mm. The cross-sectional area of the bellows is 0.001 m².

[Take the atmospheric pressure to be 100000 N/m².]

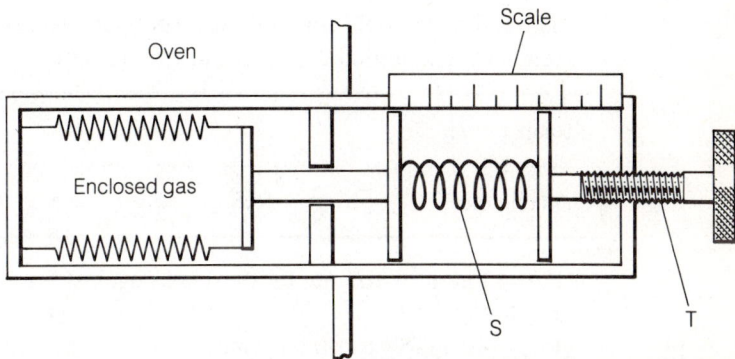

When the oven has reached a steady temperature, it is found that the spring is compressed by 40 mm to keep the gas volume constant.

(i) Calculate the force due to the spring on the bellows. [2]

(ii) Calculate the pressure on the enclosed gas due to this spring compression. [2]

(iii) What is the total pressure on the enclosed gas at this steady temperature? [2]

(iv) Calculate the temperature of the oven. [3]

[Oxford (part)]

19.

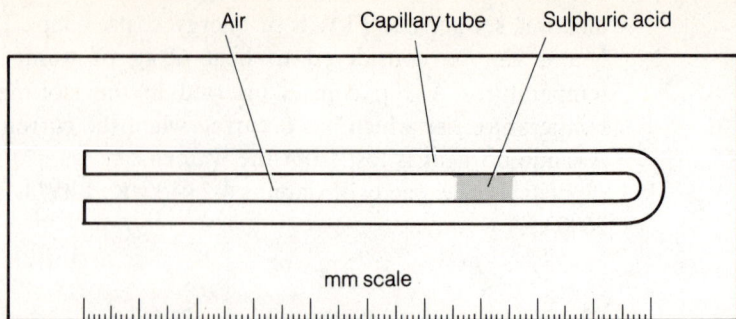

The diagram shows an apparatus which can be used to investigate how the volume of air changes with its temperature while its pressure remains constant.

a) What measurement would you make which would represent the volume of the trapped air? Explain your answer, stating the assumption you are making. [3]

b) Describe briefly how you would measure the temperature of the air in the capillary tube. State **two** precautions you would take to ensure that your temperature measurement was as accurate as possible. [5]

c) Why is the air enclosed by a plug of concentrated sulphuric acid? [2]

d) The following table contains corresponding values of volume and temperature obtained in such an experiment.

Temperature/°C	20	40	60	80	100
Volume/mm^3	58.5	63.0	66.5	71.0	75.0

Plot a graph of volume on the y-axis against temperature on the x-axis.
Use your graph to obtain values for
(i)   the volume of trapped air at 0°C,
(ii) the temperature at which the volume of the trapped air would become zero. [7]

e) What is the significance of the temperature in d)(ii)? What assumption about the behaviour of the gas did you make when you calculated the temperature in d)(ii)? [4]

f) What conclusion might be drawn from the results of this experiment? [4]

[JMB]

20.   A saucepan containing boiling water and potatoes is standing on a hotplate set at 400 W, and left for 20 minutes. The rate of energy loss

is 250 W, and the rest is used in the production of steam.
[Take the specific latent heat of vaporization of water to be
2.2×10^6 J/kg.]
(i)   What is the power used in producing steam?   [1]
(ii) Calculate the energy used in producing steam for 20 minutes.
                                                          [2]
(iii) Calculate the mass of water lost from the saucepan in
      20 minutes.   [3]
(iv) If the setting of the hotplate was reduced to 200 W, what would
      the effect be? Explain.   [2]
(v)   What setting of the hotplate power would keep the water boiling
      with the least waste of electricity? Explain your answer.   [3]
                                          [Oxford (part)]

21. A constant-volume air thermometer contains air. The air pressure is
    measured, with the volume kept constant, at three different
    temperatures, and the results given in the table are observed.

Temperature	Pressure (N/m^2)
Steam point	3.2×10^5
Ice point	2.3×10^5
Freezing point of mercury ($-39°C$)	2.0×10^5

a) Draw a simple constant-volume air thermometer and describe
   how it could be used to give a pressure reading corresponding to
   the boiling point of brine.   [6]
b) Assuming a linear relationship between pressure and temperature, use the results above to plot the graph of pressure against
   temperature over the range $-300°C$ to $200°C$.   [4]
   Estimate:
   (i) the temperature at which the pressure would be 3.0×10^5
        N/m^2;   [2]
   (ii) the pressure when the temperature is $150°C$.   [2]
c) Explain why, in practice, air would not behave like this for the
   whole of the temperature range $-300°C$ to $200°C$.   [3]
d) Use the graph to introduce the concept of absolute zero of
   temperature. State the relationship between the pressure of an
   ideal gas and its absolute temperature.   [3]
                                                    [Oxford]

22.   An insulated metal block of mass 2 kg has a 50 W heater embedded in it. After switching on the heater, the temperature of the block is measured every minute, with the following results:

Time in minutes	0	1	2	3	4	5	6	7	8
Temperature in °C	20.0	22.1	24.1	26.0	28.1	29.3	31.5	33.0	34.3

(i)   Plot a graph of temperature against time, choosing suitable scales.   [4]

(ii)   From the graph, state the period of time for which the loss of heat through the insulation is negligible.   [1]

(iii)   What is the increase in temperature of the metal block during this time?   [1]

(iv)   How much heat is supplied by the heater during this time?
                                                                         [2]

(v)   Calculate the specific heat capacity of the metal from these values.   [2]

[Oxford (part)]

23.   a)   Complete the statements:

When boiling water is converted to steam, it has changed its .... For this to happen, ... has to supplied to the water. At standard atmospheric pressure, this change takes place at a precise .... If sufficient heat is .... from water, the water can be turned into ....   [5]

b)   A small flame is used to heat an aluminium block of mass 2 kg from 20°C to 40°C in exactly 90 seconds. [Take the specific heat capacity of aluminium to be 900 J/kg K.]

(i)   What is meant by the *specific heat capacity* of a substance?
                                                                         [3]

(ii)   How much heat is gained by the aluminium block?   [3]

(iii)   Calculate the heat output of the flame in watts, assuming that all the heat is gained by the block.   [2]

c)   A large lump of ice taken from a freezer at −20°C is placed in a metal pan of low heat capacity and heated by a flame of constant heat output. The graph shows how the temperature of the contents of the pan changes with the time, until the pan is empty. [Specific heat capacity of ice = 2000 J/kg K; specific heat capacity of water = 4200 J/kg K. Specific latent heat of fusion of ice = 3.3×10^5 J/kg. Specific latent heat of vaporization of water = 2.2×10^6 J/kg.]

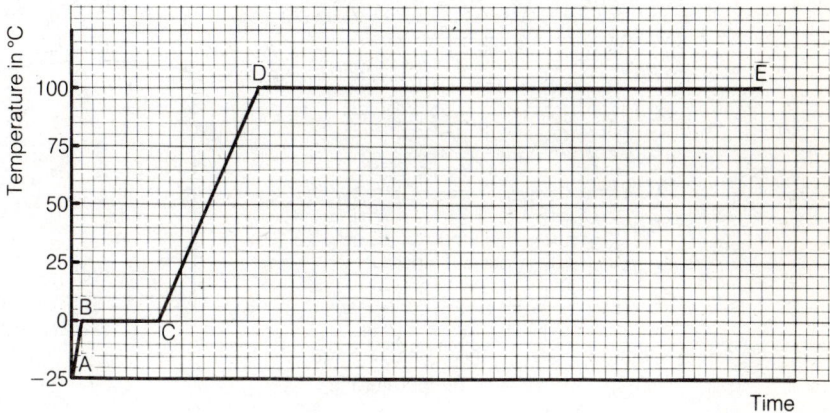

With the help of these values but without calculation, explain why:

(i) the temperature is constant between B and C; [2]

(ii) the temperature is constant between D and E; [2]

(iii) the slope of the line is steeper between A and B than between C and D; [2]

(iv) the line DE is longer than the line BC. [2]

d) The temperatures of pure melting ice and steam at standard atmospheric pressure are used for the fixed points 0°C and 100°C respectively.

(i) Why is this so? [2]

(ii) Some mercury thermometers can measure over the range of temperature 0–300°C. Explain how the thermometer can be calibrated for this range. [3]

(iii) What assumption is made for this calibration method? [2]

(iv) Why cannot mercury-in-glass thermometers be made to measure very much higher temperatures? [2]

[Oxford]

24. Diagram (a) shows a graph of the saturated vapour pressure p of water against temperature. Diagram (b) illustrates a pressure cooker. [Take the atmospheric pressure to be 0.10 N/mm².]

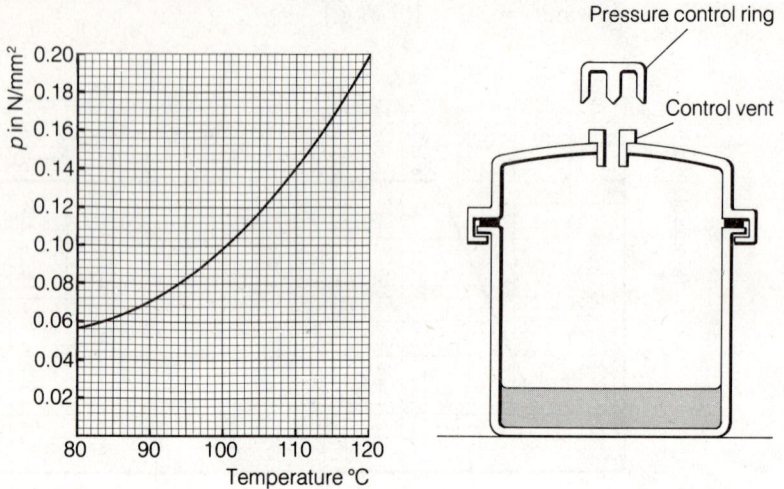

a) Find from the graph, the saturated vapour pressure of water at:
   (i)   100°C;
   (ii) 110°C.   [2]

b) In order to increase the pressure within the cooker (containing water and water vapour only), a pressure control ring of mass 0.12 kg is used. What is the upwards force in newtons needed to lift the control ring?   [1]

c) The control ring is lifted by the pressure due to the water vapour acting on it through a control vent of cross-sectional area 15 mm². What is the pressure (above atmospheric) in N/mm² of the water vapour needed to lift the control ring?   [3]

d) What is then the total pressure of the water vapour within the cooker?   [1]

e) Hence, what is the temperature within the cooker?   [1]

f) Explain the advantages gained by the use of a pressure cooker.
                                                                      [2]
                                                                 [Oxford]

8. Waves

Waves are one way of transferring energy from one place to another. There are a large number of different types — such as sound waves, radio waves, water waves and light waves. All are made up of a vibration or oscillation which progresses from a source to receiver or detector. Such waves are called progressive waves. We look later at stationary or standing waves.

Progressive waves

There are two types of progressive wave — transverse and longitudinal. The velocity of any wave is given by the formula

$$\text{Velocity} = \text{Frequency} \times \text{Wavelength}$$

or

$$v = f \times \lambda$$

Example The speed of sound in air is 330 m/s. Calculate the wavelength of a sound, the frequency of which is:

a) 256 Hz **b)** 512 Hz **c)** 1000 Hz

Method: Using

$$v = f \times \lambda$$

and rearranging to make the wavelength λ the subject of the equation gives:

$$\lambda = \frac{v}{f}$$

Then substitute the values given for velocity v and frequency f.

Answers: a) 1.29 m **b)** 0.64 m **c)** 0.33 m

Electromagnetic waves

Radio waves and light waves are both types of electromagnetic wave. Other examples of electromagnetic waves are X-rays, ultraviolet, infra-red and television broadcast signals. All electromagnetic waves are transverse waves and they all travel with the same speed in air or in a vacuum — this is 300 000 000 m/s or 3×10^8 m/s. The frequencies and wavelengths of electromagnetic waves are typically either very large or very small numbers, and so are often written in powers of ten.

Example   Work out the frequency of the following electromagnetic waves, given that the speed of electromagnetic waves is 3×10^8 m/s.

Wave type	Wavelength (m)
a) Radio wave	275
b) Red light	7.0×10^{-7}
c) X-ray	2.0×10^{-10}

Method: Using

$$v = f \times \lambda$$

and rearranging it to make the frequency f the subject of the equation gives

$$f = \frac{v}{\lambda}$$

Substitute the values given to calculate f.

Answers: a) 1.09×10^6 Hz or 1.09 MHz   **b)** 4.3×10^{14} Hz
c) 1.5×10^{18} Hz

All types of wave have four basic properties — reflection, refraction, diffraction and interference. Only refraction and interference involve calculations of any importance.

Refraction: Refraction takes place when the velocity and wavelength of a wave change. This usually results in a change in the wave's direction (see fig. a)). However there is one situation in which the wave's direction does not change, and this is shown in fig. b). Refraction was discussed at length in the section on light (see p.34), but here we shall concentrate on the wave properties involved in refraction.

a)

b)

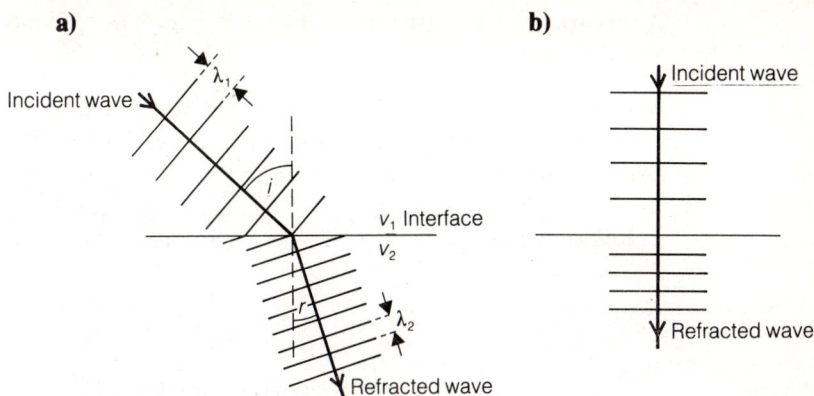

You will remember that

$$\text{Refractive index} = \frac{\text{sine (angle of incidence)}}{\text{sine (angle of refraction)}}$$

$$= \frac{\text{sine } i}{\text{sine } r}$$

but the refractive index is also given by

$$\text{Refractive index} = \frac{\text{Velocity in medium 1}}{\text{Velocity in medium 2}}$$

Example Complete the following table

Refractive index	Velocity in medium 1 (m/s)	Velocity in medium 2 (m/s)
1.5	3.0×10^8	—
—	3.0×10^8	1.8×10^8
2.0	—	1.4×10^8

Method: Rearrange

$$\text{Refractive index} = \frac{v_1}{v_2}$$

to make the term you wish to calculate the subject of the equation. Substitute the values given.

Answers: a) 2.0×10^8 m/s   **b)** 1.67   **c)** 2.8×10^8 m/s

Another important point to remember is that the frequency of the wave does *not* change when the wave is refracted. The previous formula can then be developed to give

$$\text{Refractive index} = \frac{f \times \lambda_1}{f \times \lambda_2} \text{ where } \lambda \text{ refers to the wavelength}$$

or

$$\text{Refractive index} = \frac{\text{Wavelength in medium 1}}{\text{Wavelength in medium 2}}$$

Example   The velocity of light in air is 3×10^8 m/s. When white light enters a glass prism it may be split up into the colours of the spectrum. If the wavelength of red light in air is 7×10^{-7} m and the wavelength of blue light is 4×10^{-7} m, and the refractive index of the glass is 1.50 for red light and 1.52 for blue light, calculate:

a) the velocity of red light and blue light in the glass

b) the wavelength of red light and blue light in the glass

c) the frequency of the red and blue light.

Method: In part **a)** use

$$\text{Refractive index} = \frac{\text{Velocity in air}}{\text{Velocity in glass}}$$

In part **b)** use

$$\text{Refractive index} = \frac{\text{Wavelength in air}}{\text{Wavelength in glass}}$$

Part **c)** can be worked out using

$$\text{Velocity} = \text{Frequency} \times \text{Wavelength}$$

It does not matter whether you choose the velocity and wavelength in air or in glass, as long as you are consistent. Why not try both and so confirm that the frequency does not change on refraction?

Answers:

	Red	Blue
a)	2.00×10^8 m/s	1.97×10^8 m/s
b)	4.67×10^{-7} m	2.63×10^{-7} m
c)	4.29×10^{14} Hz	7.50×10^{14} Hz

Interference

This will take place when two or more waves of comparable amplitude and similar frequency (and therefore wavelength) come together. The questions which you will meet will be about waves of the same amplitude and frequency. When the waves meet and are in phase, i.e. doing exactly the same thing at the same time, constructive interference takes place:

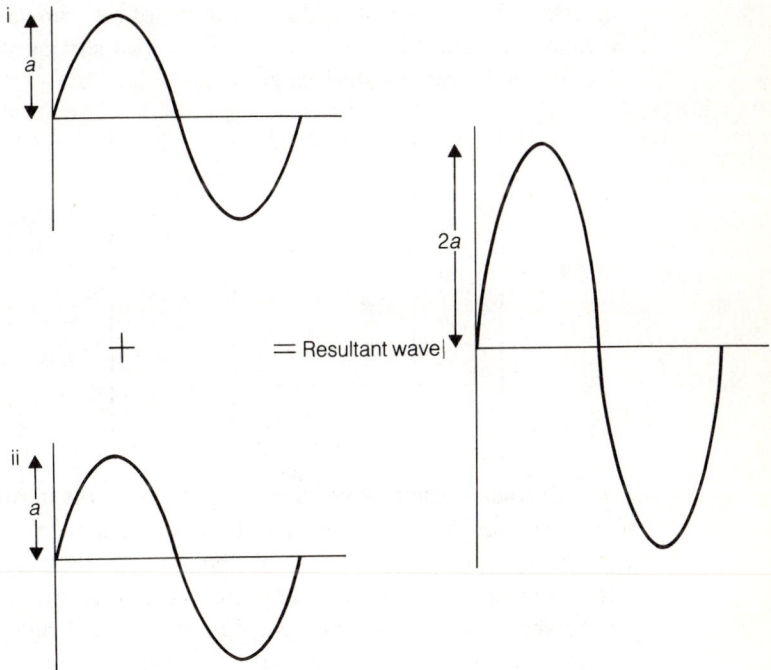

If the two waves are exactly out of phase, then destructive interference takes place:

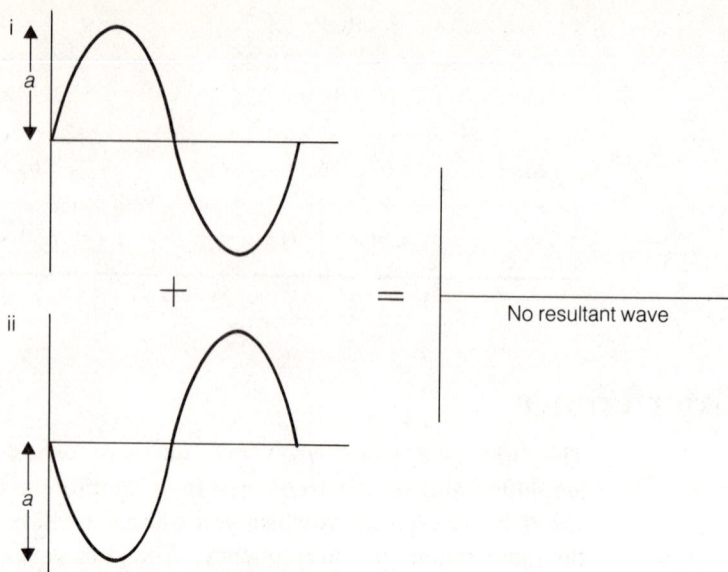

Interference of light waves

Interference between light waves can be produced by having two narrow slits close together. Light of a single wavelength (monochromatic light) is directed at the two slits as shown. This is often called Young's slits experiment.

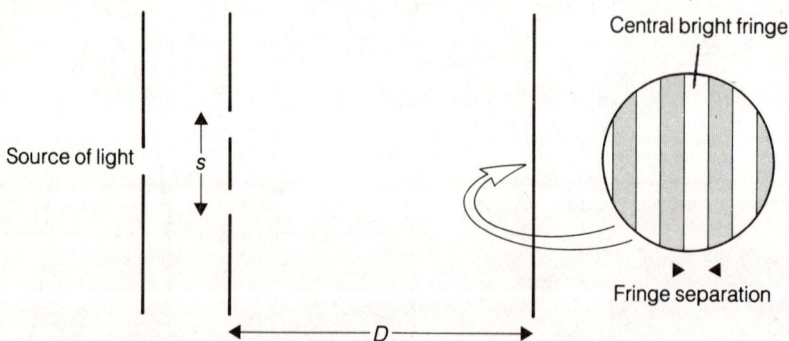

The diffracted waves emerging from the two slits interfere with one another. At points where the two waves are in phase there is constructive interference, and at points where they are out of phase the interference is destructive. This pattern of interference can be observed on a screen, and the separation of the bright (constructive interference) fringes and the dark (destructive interference) fringes is given by the formula

$$\text{Fringe separation} = \frac{\lambda \times D}{s}$$

where λ = wavelength of light.

Example A laser beam is used as the source of light with two slits of slit separation 1.5 mm. When the slits are 5 m from the screen, calculate the fringe separation for light of wavelength

a) 4.5×10^{-7} m **b)** 5.8×10^{-7} m **c)** 6.3×10^{-7} m

Method: Using

$$\text{Fringe separation} = \frac{\lambda \times D}{a}$$

and converting all the quantities to metres, substitute the values into the equation. This gives

$$\text{Fringe separation} = \frac{\lambda \times 5}{1.5 \times 10^{-3}}$$
$$= \frac{\lambda \times 5}{1.5} \times 10^3 \, \text{m}$$

The values for the wavelength λ can then be substituted in this equation.

Answers: a) 1.50×10^{-3} m or 1.50 mm **b)** 1.93×10^{-3} m or 1.93 mm **c)** 2.10×10^{-3} m or 2.10 mm

Standing waves and the resonance tube

If a wave is reflected from a boundary then, under certain conditions, an interesting interference effect takes place. The interference is produced between the incident wave and the reflected wave (same amplitude and frequency) and a standing, or stationary, wave is produced.

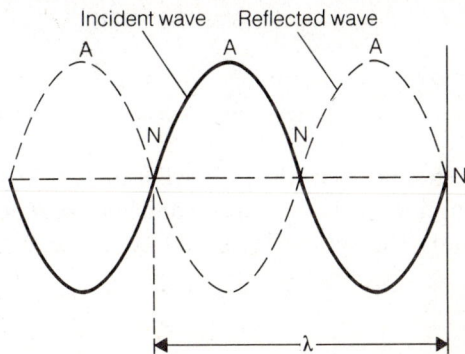

The points labelled N are called nodes and are points where there is no disturbance in the resulting wave. The points labelled A are called antinodes and are points of maximum disturbance in the resulting wave. The distance between successive nodes is half a wavelength. This is also the distance between successive antinodes.

An experiment using a glass tube of variable length, called a resonance tube, can be used to calculate the velocity of sound. In this experiment a standing wave may be set up in the air column by an external frequency source such as a loudspeaker or a tuning fork. Because the air column is open to the air at the top there is an antinode at this end. Where the air column ends at the bottom there is a node because the wave strikes the water surface. The wave which is set up has the same frequency as the external frequency (this is called resonance).

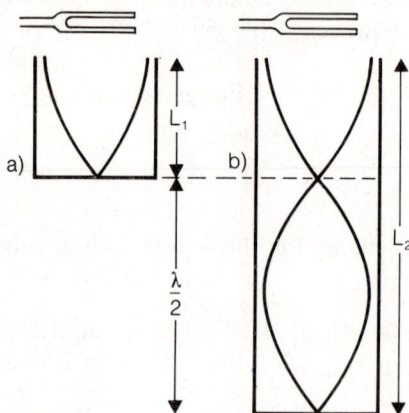

Diagram a) shows the wave pattern for the first position of resonance, where a loud sound is heard. The loud sound is repeated at the second position of resonance shown in b). The distance between the first and second positions of resonance can be found by subtracting L_1 from L_2. You will see from the diagrams that

$$L_2 - L_1 = \frac{\lambda}{2}$$

and so

$$\lambda = 2 \times (L_2 - L_1)$$

The frequency of the fork will usually be marked on it (or if you are using a frequency generator and loudspeaker you can read it from the scale). The velocity of sound in air can be worked out, using

$$v = f \times \lambda$$
$$= f \times 2 \times (L_2 - L_1)$$

Example The following results were obtained from a resonance tube experiment using a frequency generator and loudspeaker. Complete the table of values for wavelength and velocity of sound.

Frequency (Hz)	1st position of resonance L_1 (m)	2nd position of resonance L_2 (m)	Wavelength λ (m)	$v = f \times \lambda$ (m/s)
200	0.41	1.24		
250	0.34	1.01		
300	0.27	0.82		
350	0.23	0.69		
400	0.21	0.62		
450	0.19	0.57		
500	0.16	0.48		

Method: The distance between the first and second positions of resonance gives λ/2, and so you can calculate a value for the wavelength. Using $v = f \times \lambda$ you can then work out the velocity of the sound wave.

Answers:

Wavelength (m)	1.66	1.34	1.10	0.92	0.82	0.76	0.64
Velocity (m/s)	332	335	330	322	328	342	320

From these answers what is your estimate for the speed of the sound wave? Can you reach any conclusions about the speed of sound and the frequency of the wave?

Standing waves are set up in strings or wires that are under tension. The standing wave may be set up by plucking or by placing a tuning fork vibrating at the natural frequency of the string on the string. The fundamental standing wave is shown in the diagram.

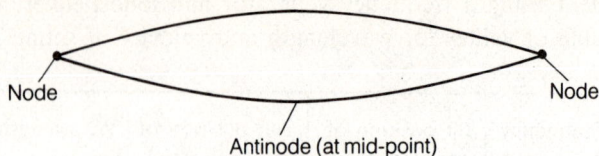

Node   Node
Antinode (at mid-point)

The frequency of the wire is given by the formula

$$f = \frac{1}{2L}\sqrt{\frac{T}{\mu}}$$

where L = Length of wire
T = Tension in wire
μ = Mass per unit length of wire

It is unlikely that you will be asked to use the formula, but you should be aware of the factors which affect the frequency of a wire.

Questions

1. Water waves are produced by a vibrating dipper. The speed of the water waves is 5 cm/s. Calculate the frequency of the dipper vibration if the waves have a wavelength of

   a) 1 cm   b) 2 cm   c) 2.5 cm.

2. The speed of electromagnetic waves in air is 3×10^8 m/s. With this knowledge, complete the following table.

	Type of wave	Frequency (Hz)	Wavelength (m)
a)	Long radio waves	—	1500
b)	Microwaves	3×10^{10}	—
c)	Infra-red	4.5×10^{13}	—
d)	Blue light	—	4×10^{-7}
e)	X-rays	—	6×10^{-10}
f)	γ-rays	10^{21}	—

3. A man stands at different distances from a cliff and fires a gun. If the speed of sound in air is 330 m/s, calculate how far the man is standing from the cliff if he hears the echo after:

   a) 2 s   b) 5 s   c) 7 s

4. A wire has a fundamental frequency of 256 Hz.
   a) Sketch the vibrating pattern of the wire in its fundamental mode.
   b) Sketch the 1st, 2nd and 3rd overtones and calculate the frequency of each of these.

5. Draw full-scale diagrams showing two complete wavelengths of transverse waves with the following properties:

	Amplitude (cm)	Wavelength (cm)
a)	2.0	5.0
b)	2.5	8.0
c)	3.0	2.5

6. A sound wave of constant frequency from a loudspeaker is reflected from a reflecting surface. Interference between the reflected wave and incident wave produces a standing wave. Calculate the frequency of the wave if the separation of 7 successive minima (nodes) is:

   a) 0.6 m   b) 1.8 m   c) 3.0 m

   (The speed of sound is 330 m/s.)

7. a) The wavelengths in air of red and blue light respectively are 7×10^{-7} m and 4×10^{-7} m. Calculate their wavelengths in water, if the refractive index of the water is 1.32 for red light and 1.34 for blue light.

   b) If the speed of both colours in air is 3×10^8 m/s, calculate the speed of both colours in water.

8. A sonometer wire was kept under constant tension and different tuning forks were placed on the end of the wire. The length of the wire was varied until a small piece of paper placed at the centre of the wire jumped off, i.e. the fork and the wire have the same frequency. The following results were obtained:

Frequency of fork (Hz)	Length of wire (cm)
512	30.0
480	32.0
456	33.7
427	36.0
384	40.0
362	42.4
341	45.0
320	48.0
304	50.5
288	53.3
256	60.1

a) Plot a graph of y = frequency against x = length of wire. What are your conclusions from the graph?

b) What would the length of wire be if the frequency of the fork is 400 Hz?

c) Calculate values for 1/length and plot a graph of y = frequency against x = 1/length. What are your conclusions from this graph?

9. Using a resonance tube, a student found that the wavelengths of the waves emitted by tuning forks of known frequency were as follows:

Frequency (Hz)	Wavelength (m)
512	0.64
480	0.72
456	0.74
427	0.76
384	0.86
362	0.94
341	0.98
320	1.10
304	1.12
288	1.20

a) Calculate the velocity of the sound wave at each frequency. What is the average velocity?
b) Plot a graph of y = frequency against x = wavelength. Can you draw any conclusions from this graph?
c) Work out values for 1/wavelength, and plot a graph of y = frequency against x = 1/wavelength. Can you draw any conclusions from this graph?
d) Calculate a value for the gradient of the graph drawn in c). How does this compare with the value you obtained in a)?

10. The diagram shows a water wave which experiences a change of depth.

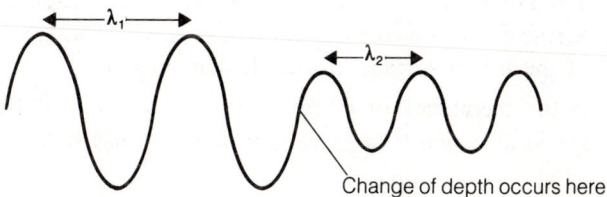

Change of depth occurs here

Calculate the refractive index caused by this change of depth for the following values of λ_1 and λ_2:

	λ_1 (cm)	λ_2 (cm)
a)	1.5	1.1
b)	1.3	0.8
c)	1.1	0.6

11. In a Young's slits experiment, the fringe separation is given by the formula:

$$\text{Fringe separation} = \frac{\lambda \times D}{s}$$

where λ = wavelength of light
         D = separation of viewing screen from slits
         s = separation of slits

If $D = 1.0\,\text{m}$, and $s = 0.20\,\text{mm}\ (= 2 \times 10^{-4}\,\text{m})$, calculate the fringe separation if the source of light is:

a) red light of wavelength $7 \times 10^{-7}\,\text{m}$
b) yellow light of wavelength $6 \times 10^{-7}\,\text{m}$
c) green light of wavelength $5 \times 10^{-7}\,\text{m}$
d) blue light of wavelength $4 \times 10^{-7}\,\text{m}$.

What would you expect to see if the source were a white light source?

Past examination questions

1. Transverse waves of wavelength 40 mm and amplitude 15 mm travel across a liquid surface. Draw a full scale diagram showing a side view of the liquid surface at a particular instant.

   If the frequency of vibration of the waves is 12 Hz, calculate the speed at which they travel across the liquid surface.   [Cambridge]

2. Amanda measures the speed of sound using the echo from a high wall. She claps and her friend measures the time between the clap and the echo.

Wall

Results

Distance from wall (m)	0	60	80	100	120	140
Time between clap and echo (sec)	0	0.35	0.45	0.60	0.75	0.85

a) Plot a graph of time on the vertical axis against distance from the wall on the horizontal axis.

b) (i) How far must they stand from the wall for the echo to take 0.5 seconds? (Use your graph.)
   (ii) How far does the sound travel during this 0.5 seconds?
   (iii) Calculate the speed of sound in air.

c) (i) Why is the echo time difficult to measure accurately?
   (ii) Explain how Amanda and her friend could have measured the echo times more accurately.

d) (i) Find from your graph the time between clap and echo when they stand 30 metres from the wall.
   (ii) Why do you think the results are less accurate for shorter distances?

e) Explain how echoes are used to find the depth of the sea.

[SWEB]

3. a) In an experiment to measure the wavelength (*L*) of a source of light using Young's slits to form an interference pattern on a screen, the band separation (*y*) is given by the formula:

$$y = \frac{L \times D}{s};$$

where s is the distance between slits and D is the distance from the slits to the screen. Calculate y for yellow light ($L = 5.9 \times 10^{-7}$ m) if $s = 0.25$ mm and $D = 50$ cm.

Name a possible source of yellow light and indicate how it is situated for this experiment. What changes would you expect in the observed pattern if (i) red, (ii) white light had been used? Give reasons.

b) Consider the following types of wave: infra red, ultra violet, sound, X-rays, radio.
(i)   Which of these is NOT part of the electro-magnetic spectrum.
Of those that are electro-magnetic,
(ii) which has the shortest wavelengths,
(iii) which has the lowest frequencies,
(iv) which is unlikely to be detected by a photographic method,
(v)   what is significant about their speed?   [SUJB]

4.   a) Sketch a displacement–distance graph for a transverse wave, showing two complete cycles. Mark on your graph distances to show what is meant by
(i)   wavelength,
(ii) amplitude.
Label a point A anywhere in your graph and then label
(iii) a point B which is vibrating in-phase with A,
(iv) a point C which is vibrating in anti-phase (180° out of phase) with A.   [5]
b) If a wave has a velocity of 330 m/s and a wavelength of 0.5 m, calculate the frequency of the vibrator producing the wave.   [3]
c) Name **one** example of a transverse wave and **one** example of a longitudinal wave.   [2]
[JMB]

5.   Describe an experiment which may be performed to determine the unknown frequency of a tuning fork.   [8]

An observer stands 700 m away from a tall cliff-face. Half way between the observer and that cliff a second person fires a gun.
Explain why the observer hears two reports. If the time interval between the two reports is 2 seconds calculate the velocity of sound in air. How long after seeing the gun-flash would the first sound have been heard?   [8]
[WJEC]

6. a) What is the essential difference between a *longitudinal* wave and a *transverse* wave? Why is the sound wave in air produced by a vibrating tuning fork longitudinal? [4]

b)

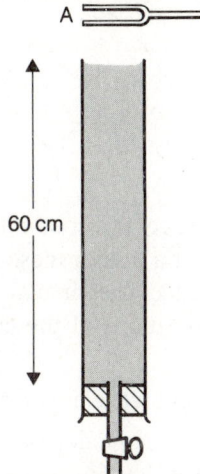

A student holds a vibrating tuning fork A, which has the number 256 engraved on it, just above a glass tube of length 60 cm containing water. The tube is allowed to slowly empty of water and the student hears a loud sound when there is 25.0 cm of water left in the tube. On repeating the experiment with tuning fork B, which has the number 512 engraved on it, he hears a loud sound on two occasions as the tube empties of water.

(i) What is the meaning of the number 256 on tuning fork A? [2]

(ii) Explain why the student hears a loud sound when using fork A and state the name of this effect. [4]

(iii) Use the figures given for tuning fork A to calculate a value for the speed of sound in air. Suggest a reason why this value is only approximately correct. [5]

(iv) Explain why, when using tuning fork B, there were two occasions as the tube was emptying of water when a loud sound was heard, whereas with tuning fork A there was only one. [5]

[London]

7. Explain the meaning of the terms *superposition*, *destructive interference* and *reinforcement* by reference to waves on the surface of water. Illustrate your answer by labelled diagrams. [6]

With the aid of a labelled diagram, describe how a ripple tank could be set up and used to show the interference of water waves.

Make clear
a) how the waves are generated,
b) how the interference is viewed. [7]

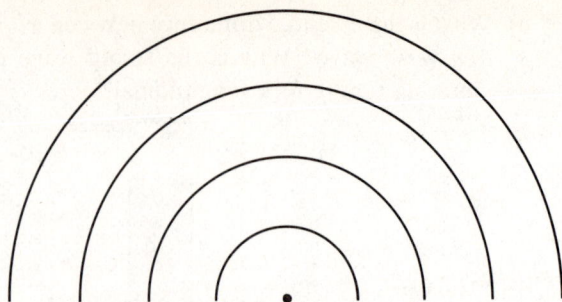

A vibrator at the central spot in the diagram produces circular ripples on the surface of a liquid; these ripples travel across the surface at a speed of 420 mm/s. The circular arcs in the diagram, drawn full size, represent the positions of the crests of these ripples at a particular instant.

c) Determine the wavelength of the ripples from the diagram.

d) Calculate the frequency of the vibrator. [4]

[Cambridge]

8. a) A long vertical tube open at the top and with a tap at the bottom is full of water. A vibrating tuning fork of frequency 512 Hz is held over the open end of the tube and water is run out through the tap. Loud sounds are heard first when the level of the water is 15 cm from the top of the tube and again when the level is 48 cm from the top. Explain why two loud sounds are heard and calculate the speed of sound in air. [7]

The experiment is repeated
(i) with the tube filled with brine instead of water, and
(ii) with water, but on a day when the air temperature is considerably higher than when the original experiment was carried out.

State what differences, if any, you would expect for the readings of the liquid level in each case, compared with the original experiment. (Give reasons for your answers.) [5]

b) Describe how you would set up a practical demonstration to show the diffraction of waves using any *one* type of wave. [8]

[London]

9. a) Describe and explain how you would determine, using Young's slits, the wavelength of a source of light. (If the double slits are distance s apart and at a distance D from the screen, then for light of wavelength L, the fringe separation = DL/s.) [9]

b) The speed of light in air $= 3 \times 10^8 \, ms^{-1}$. Calculate the speed of light in glass of refractive index 1.5. Rays of light, in air, are incident on a plane air/glass boundary. Show on clear diagrams the directions the rays would take in glass when the angles of incidence are

(i) 0°,
(ii) 60°. [6]

[SUJB]

10. a) What is (i) a transverse wave, (ii) a longitudinal wave? [4]
    b) State how you would produce transverse waves using a stretched string and make a sketch of the appearance of the string at any one instant. On your sketch mark and label the amplitude by a and the wavelength by λ. [4]
    c) A student tuning into a radio station noted that its wavelength was 1500 m. He deduced that the frequency of its transmission was 200 kHz. Show that the student was correct. (Speed of radio waves $= 3 \times 10^8$ m/s.) [4]
    d)

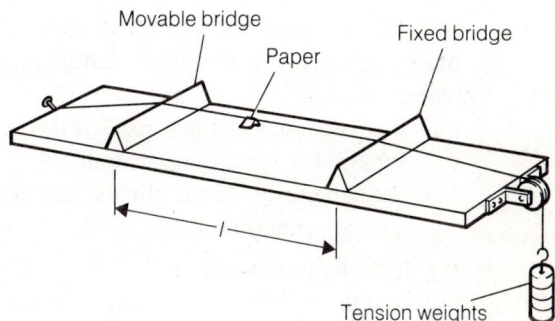

Movable bridge
Paper
Fixed bridge
l
Tension weights

The diagram shows a length of wire on a sonometer. A vibrating tuning fork of frequency 256 Hz was placed on the wooden base of the sonometer and the length l was adjusted until the small piece of paper jumped off the wire.
(i) Explain why this happened.
(ii) What is the name for this phenomenon? [5]

    e) When the wire of the same sonometer is plucked it vibrates, emitting a note. State the effect on the fundamental frequency of the note, if
    (i) the length of the wire were halved with no change in the tension;
    (ii) the tension were made four times as large, with the original length unchanged;
    (iii) the wire in the diagram were replaced by one of mass per unit length four times as large, the length and tension being the same as in the first experiment. [6]

f) A student, standing between two vertical cliffs and 480 m from the nearest cliff, shouted. She heard the first echo after 3 s, and the second echo 2 s later. Use this information to calculate
   (i) the velocity of sound in air,
   (ii) the distance between the cliffs. [8]

   [AEB]

11. a) Describe an experiment to show constructive and destructive interference of water waves passing through a double slit arrangement.
   Your answer should include
   (i) a labelled sketch of the apparatus,
   (ii) a description of your procedure,
   (iii) a plan diagram of the ripple tank showing the wave pattern which your experiment would produce, indicating clearly where constructive and destructive interference has taken place. [10]

   b) With the aid of **two** clearly labelled diagrams (one for each), explain how constructive interference and destructive interference was produced in the experiment described in part a). [7]

   c) **State** the effect on the wave pattern you have drawn in a) (iii) when
   (i) the frequency of the source of the waves is increased, the slit separation remaining unchanged,
   (ii) the separation of the slits is increased, the frequency of the source remaining unchanged. [3]

   d) When red light of wavelength 7×10^{-7} m was used in a double slit experiment it was found that ten bright fringes occupied a distance of 0.18 m.
   Calculate
   (i) the distance between one bright fringe and the next using red light,
   (ii) the distance between one bright fringe and the next if light of wavelength 5×10^{-7} m was used instead of red light, the arrangement of the apparatus remaining unchanged. [5]

   [JMB]

12. a) Explain what you understand by resonance. Describe briefly how this phenomenon may be demonstrated by TWO methods involving different aspects of physics. [10]

   b) A thin wire under tension is 60 cm long and fixed at both ends. The wire emits a note of frequency 255 Hz when plucked at its mid-point. What would you expect to observe if a sound generator of frequency 256 Hz is set up near the vibrating wire? If

the vibrating length is reduced to 50 cm what frequency note
would you then expect from the wire?   [5]
[SUJB]

13.   a) The table below shows the results of an experiment in which the
         length of a stretched wire (a sonometer) was varied until it
         vibrated in unison with each of several tuning forks taken in turn.
         The tension of the wire was kept constant throughout the
         experiment.

Frequency of tuning fork/Hz	256	288	341	384	512
Length of wire/mm	942	837	707	628	471

   (i)   What do you understand by the frequency of a tuning fork?
                                                               [2]
   (ii) Plot a graph of the frequency of the tuning fork against the
         length of the wire.   [6]
   (iii) Use the graph to determine the frequency of the tuning fork
         which will vibrate in unison with a wire of length 754 mm at
         the same tension as in the experiment.   [2]

   b)

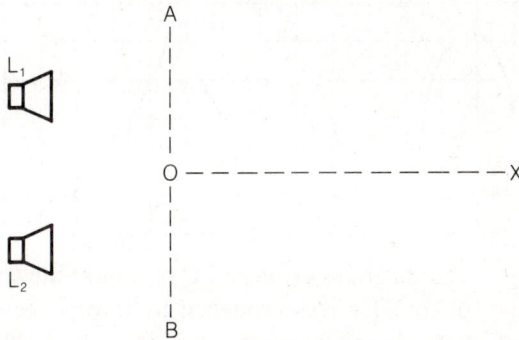

The diagram shows two small loudspeakers L_1 and L_2. They are
connected to the same oscillator and emit notes of the same
loudness. A microphone connected to a loudness meter, whose
pointer gives a deflection dependent upon the loudness of the
sound reaching it, is placed at O.
Describe and account for the reading of the meter when the
microphone
   (i)   remains stationary at O,
   (ii) is moved along the line OX, and
   (iii) is moved along the line AOB.   [10]
[London]

14. a)

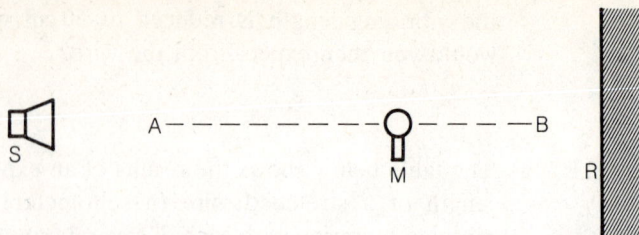

A source of sound S is placed in front of a large plane reflector R.

(i)   A microphone M which is connected to a cathode ray oscilloscope, is moved along the line AB perpendicular to the reflector. The oscilloscope shows maxima and minima of sound intensity. Explain this and name the maxima and minima.   [5]

(ii) The distance between 11 successive minima is 2.5 m. Assuming the speed of sound to be 340 m/s find the frequency of the source.   [4]

Why is it better to use 11 successive minima instead of two to determine the frequency of the source?   [1]

(iii) State, giving your reason, what you would expect to happen to the distance between the minima as the frequency of the source is increased.   [2]

b)

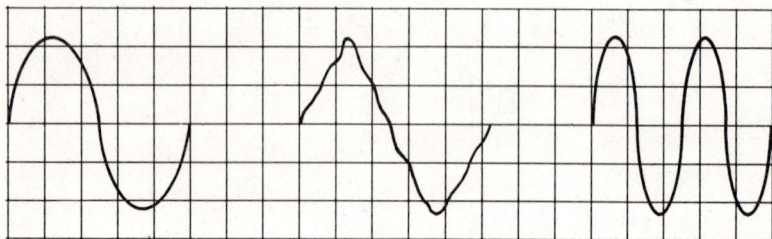

The diagrams A, B and C represent the traces on an oscilloscope of sound waves produced by three different instruments. Compare the pitch, quality and intensity of the three sounds. (Give your reasons.)   [8]

[London]

15. In a laboratory there is a long tank in which the behaviour of water waves is observed.

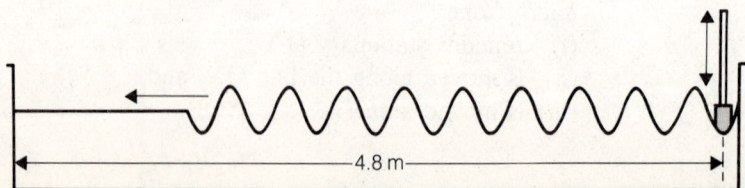

Waves are created by a paddle moving up and down at one end of the tank.

a) The paddle makes 2 'up and down' movements every second. The distance from one crest to the next is 0.4 m
   (i)   At what speed do the waves travel?
   (ii) How long does it take a crest to travel from the paddle to the far end of the tank, 4.8 m away?   [4]

b) A shallow region is created by placing a shaped block in the tank as shown. The diagram shows the tank viewed from above. The crests are shown as dark lines.

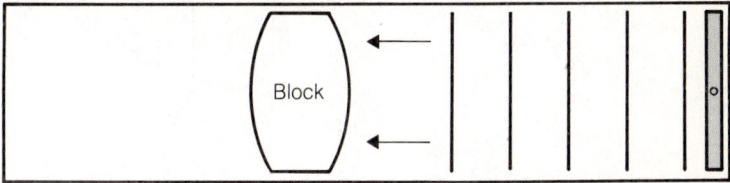

The waves travel more slowly in the shallow region above the block.
Copy the diagram and carefully draw the pattern of wave crests on both sides of the shallow region.   [3]

c) The action of a 'breakwater' is studied by placing a barrier part way across the tank. The sketch shows the view from above.

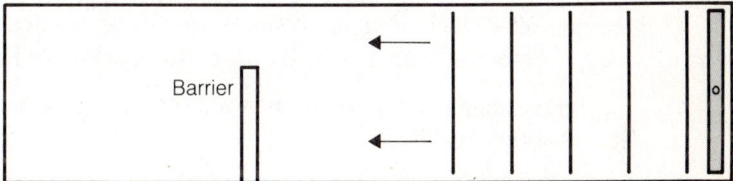

It is observed that the water behind the barrier does not remain calm.
   (i)   Draw a sketch showing the wave pattern behind the barrier.
   (ii) What name is given to this effect?
   (iii) What difference would you observe in this effect if waves of shorter wavelength are used?   [3]

[Scottish]

16. Two boys, determining the speed of sound, stand together 100 m from a high flat wall. One boy claps his hands at regular intervals so that he hears the echo of each clap half way between the clap and the next clap. The second boy measures the time for 20 claps to be 25 s.
   (i)   What is the time interval between one clap and the next? [2]
   (ii) What is the time interval between one clap and its echo? [2]
   (iii) How far does the sound travel before the boys hear its echo?
                                                                      [2]
   (iv) Calculate the speed of sound from these results.   [2]

[Oxford (part)]

17.   A tuning fork of frequency 256 Hz is sounded over a measuring cylinder which is slowly filled with water. When the length of air column remaining in the cylinder is 300 mm, as shown, there is a louder response than at any other length.

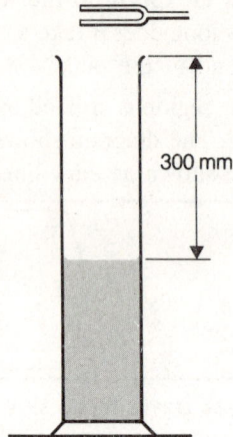

a) Explain in detail why there is a louder response at this one particular length than at any other. [4]

b) Explain how the experiment can be used to find the speed of sound in air. Calculate the value that it gives. [7]

c) What length of air column would be needed to give a loud response with a tuning fork of frequency 320 Hz? [4]

d) Explain what is meant by *resonance*, and give two examples from everyday life. [3,2]

[Oxford]

18.   a) Explain with the help of diagrams what is meant by *longitudinal* waves and *transverse* waves. Show on each diagram the wavelength. [6]

b) A stretched wire vibrates on a sounding board to give the same note as a tuning fork of frequency 256 Hz. The wire is 0.4 m long and is vibrating in its fundamental mode. Calculate the speed of the wave along the wire. Explain your reasoning. [6]

c) How could the same wire, with no change in tension, be made to give a fundamental note of three times the frequency? What would be the speed of the wave along the wire? [4]

d) If the tuning fork note has a wavelength in air of 1.3 m, with what speed does the sound travel in air? [4]

[Oxford]

19. a) Ripples are produced on the surface of the water in a ripple tank by a straight vibrator which dips regularly into the surface of the water at a frequency of approximately 20 Hz.

   (i) How would you determine the frequency of the ripples? [6]

   (ii) What additional apparatus would you require in order that you could demonstrate the diffraction of the ripples? Sketch the pattern of ripples you would expect to see. [4]

b)

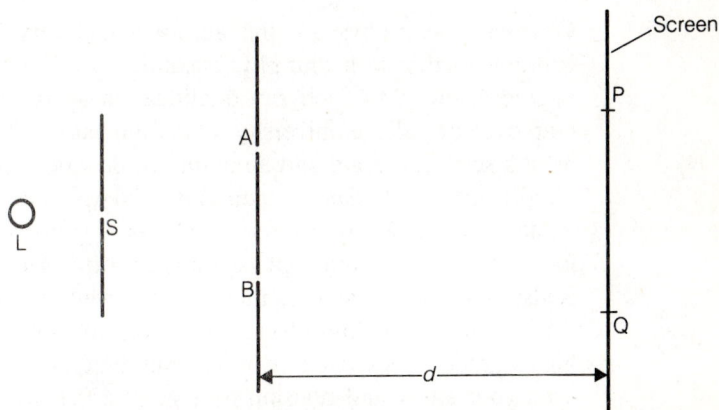

The diagram which is not drawn to scale shows the arrangement of a monochromatic light source L, a single slit S and two narrow parallel slits A and B set up to produce interference fringes on the screen. The distance between the screen and the plane of the slits A and B is d. The pattern on the screen directly opposite the slits A and B consists of a few equidistant bright and dark bands in the region PQ.

   (i) How is the presence of bright and dark bands explained by the wave theory of light? [8]

   (ii) The separation of two adjacent bright (or dark) bands x is given by the equation

$$x = \frac{\lambda d}{AB}$$

   where λ is the wavelength of the light used and AB is the separation of the slits A and B. When AB is 0.5 mm and d is 2000 mm the separation of the bands x is 1.6 mm. Calculate the wavelength of the light used. [2]

[Oxford and Cambridge]

Revision and Examination Techniques

Obviously, as a physicist, this author would very much like you to continue further with your physics studies, possibly to A-level or even degree level. With a physics qualification at any level, a potential employer or college/university admission tutor will realize that you have a scientific brain and an ability to do calculations and to carry out practical work. Employment potential with a physics qualification is also good. Many careers such as engineering, architecture, medicine etc all require a physics qualification. However, this author is also realistic and realizes that you may well have entirely different career aspirations. In both cases however you will want to achieve as high a grade as possible in your examination, and in so doing to have used your study and revision time most efficiently.

There are a variety of different ways of learning physics so that you can do as well as possible in examinations. You can learn all of the material in your notebooks and textbooks off by heart, a task which will probably involve you in many hours of hard slog. However, such an approach does not necessarily ensure understanding or most effective use of your revision time.

This author has found a more effective approach to be:

1. Obtain a copy of the syllabus, either from your teacher or write to the examination board direct.
2. As you cover a topic in class read through your notes soon after you have written them (this may also help you to get more out of later lessons).
3. In parallel with 2 read through the same topic in your main theory textbook.
4. At the end of each topic make your own set of *brief* notes on the topic, taking points from both your class and homework notes and your textbook. These notes should include any definitions, formulae and units; and may involve some labelled sketch diagrams.
5. At the end of each topic learn by heart the notes you have made.
6. If possible, read through some past examination questions on the topic. Your teacher may provide these, or again you can order

them through a bookshop or direct from the examination board. Indeed you may use certain questions from this book. The language of examination papers is often difficult and you must learn to translate from the language of physics into English. Many students understand physics and can discuss it knowledgeably — but they then proceed to do less well in exams than they should. Examination practice is therefore essential and should form a major part of your revision. By looking at questions you will get a feel for the way examiners set questions.

7. At the end of your course you should have a complete set of notes built up from class and homework notes as well as additional information from textbooks. Your run-up revision to the examination will then involve you in learning these notes off by heart. You may, in fact, be able to condense these into shorter notes as you go along.

The major benefit to be obtained from this approach is that you build up your knowledge and understanding of physics as you go along, rather than leaving it all to a mad dash in the few weeks before the examination. If you follow the same approach in other subjects, you will find that you will probably get more out of lessons as those courses proceed. It will possibly involve you in about an extra five hours homework per week for all courses, but you will appreciate the benefit that you receive in return.

A revision sheet is a useful memory aid. This will involve you in writing all formulae, definitions and units on a large sheet of paper. Pin this sheet somewhere so that you will look at it regularly — the back of a wardrobe door or the inside of your bedroom door. Every time that you pass it read through a small section of it. You will be surprised to discover how quickly you learn the information on it. You can also ask someone else to test you on the formulae.

You may be one of those people who can revise for long periods at a time. However, you will probably find that the most effective revision is short and sharp. Perhaps 30–45 minutes reading a topic, and then spending the next 30–45 minutes going over it. As you progress you will find that you can spend longer studying, but the limit is probably $2\frac{1}{2}$–3 hours at any one time.

One of the most important parts in revision is to plan a revision programme in advance. Divide your work into sections and allocate definite lengths of time to each section. Then try to keep to your programme as closely as possible. The final two weeks before the examination should be used to consolidate your revision. For example, a possible physics revision programme could be:

Month	Week	Topic
January	1	Expansion of solids, liquids and gases
	2	Specific heat capacity and latent heat
	3	Methods of heat transfer and kinetic theory
	4	Electrostatics
February	1	Current electricity
	2	Speed, velocity and acceleration
	3	Work, energy and power
	4	Forces — resolution etc, and moments
March	1	Pressure and density
	2	Archimedes' Principle and law of flotation
	3	Wave properties and sound
	4	Light — reflection and refraction
May	1	Magnetism and electromagnetism
	2	Electron beams and radioactivity
	3	Electromagnetic induction
June	–	Physics examinations

If your examinations are not in June, then you should organize a similar programme to include the appropriate months.

There are, of course, Christmas, Easter and half-term holidays. During these holidays you should be able to plan 10×3-hour sessions of revision per week. But remember, if you organize your time well, then your success in the examination will improve.

In the examination hall:

1. Read the front page of the question paper carefully.
2. You should know the style of the paper from your preparation and revision work and so you should know how long to spend on each question.
3. Read through the examination paper itself.
4. Attempt to answer the required number of questions. Remember that it is easier to gain the first 50 per cent of the marks for any question than it is to gain the second 50 per cent, and so you should not spend longer than the allotted time on any one question. You may have time over at the end and can come back to complete unfinished answers.
5. Many examination boards give an approximate mark allocation at the side of each question. If part of a question is worth two marks you need not write two sides of notes. Similarly an eight-mark question is unlikely to be complete if you manage to write it in eight words. The mark allocation is only approximate and so you

should always attempt to give three 'marks worth' of answer to a two-mark question, six 'marks worth' to a five-mark question etc.

6. When writing your answer, answer the question that you are asked and do *not* rewrite the question to suit yourself.
7. When writing out calculations follow a style similar to that used in this book. Write down the formula or formulae and explain what each letter or symbol represents. Show all stages of your working and remember to include the units, if there are any, with your answer. When you get really competent, you may even write down that an answer has 'no units' if it has none.

Good luck and best wishes in your examinations!

Quantities, Symbols and Units

Quantity	Symbol	S.I. unit	Some other possible units
Distance or displacement	s	m	cm, km
Speed or velocity	v or u	m/s	cm/s, km/h
Acceleration	a	m/s^2 or m/s/s	cm/s^2, km/h/s
Time	t	s	min, h, day
Temperature	θ	K	°C
Current	I	ampere	milliamp, microamp
Potential difference	V	volt	millivolt, kilovolt
Charge	Q	coulomb	microcoulomb
Resistance	R	Ω	megohm, kilohm
Power	P	watt	kilowatt
Area	A	m^2	cm^2, mm^2
Volume	V	m^3	cm^3, mm^3
Mass	m	kg	g
Density	d	kg/m^3	g/cm^3
Pressure	p	Pa	N/m^2, cm of Hg
Wavelength	λ	m	cm, nm
Frequency	f	Hz	kHz, MHz
Force	F	N	kN
Energy	E or H	J	kJ, MJ
Capacitance	C	F	μF, pF
Specific latent heat	L	J/kg	J/g
Specific heat capacity	c	J/kg K	J/kg°C, J/g K
Linear expansivity	α	K^{-1}	—
Resistivity	ρ	Ω m	Ω cm

S.I. prefixes

Multiplication factor	Prefix	Symbol
$1\,000\,000\,000\,000 = 10^{12}$	tera	T
$1\,000\,000\,000 = 10^{9}$	giga	G
$1\,000\,000 = 10^{6}$	mega	M
$1\,000 = 10^{3}$	kilo	k
$0.01 = 10^{-2}$	centi	c
$0.001 = 10^{-3}$	milli	m
$0.000\,001 = 10^{-6}$	micro	μ
$0.000\,000\,001 = 10^{-9}$	nano	n
$0.000\,000\,000\,001 = 10^{-12}$	pico	p

Answers

Chapter 1   Some useful mathematics

1. 2.5, 10, 4500
2. 0.1, 7, 90
3. 0.08, 2, 61250
4. 3, 10, 13
5. 0.4, 8, 20
6. 0.05, 0.6, 2
7. 0.45, 80, 500
8. 1.25, 5, 7.2
9. $v = a \times t, t = \dfrac{v}{a}$;

   $m = \dfrac{H}{L}, L = \dfrac{H}{m}$;

   $Q = C \times V, V = \dfrac{Q}{C}$

10. $\rho = \dfrac{R \times A}{L}, L = \dfrac{R \times A}{\rho}$,

    $A = \dfrac{\rho \times L}{R}$

11. $\lambda = \dfrac{a \times s}{D}, D = \dfrac{a \times S}{\lambda}$,

    $s = \dfrac{\lambda \times D}{a}$

12. $6 \times 10^7, 2 \times 10^{12}, 4.2 \times 10^{15}$
13. $2 \times 10^5, 2.5 \times 10^2, 3$
14. $6 \times 10^{-6}, 2 \times 10^{-7}, 3 \times 10^{-8}$
15. $50, 0.2, 2 \times 10^{-9}$
16. $0.12, 6 \times 10^{-5}, 4 \times 10^{-2}, 3 \times 10^4$
17. 0.3420, 0.5736, 0.8480, 0.9903
18. 30°, 45°, 60°, 80°
19. 0.9063, 0.7660, 0.5736, 0.3420
20. 30°, 50°, 60°, 80°
21. 0.1763, 0.5774, 1.0000, 1.7321
22. 15°, 25°, 50°, 70°
23.

x (cm)	y (cm)
2.50	4.33
3.54	3.54
4.33	2.50
4.83	1.29

24.

Gradient	y intercept
2	5
0.5	3
2	1.5
0.33	2.33

Chapter 2   Light

Questions

1. a) 1.5 m   b) 3.0 m
2. 7 m
3. 25 cm (perpendicular)
4. 0.50, 0.34, 1.47
   58°, 0.85, 0.64
   0.93, 40°, 0.64
5. a) 0.050, 0.033, 0.083, 12 cm
   30 cm, 0.033, 0.017, 0.050
   0.022, 22 cm, 0.045, 0.067
   b) 12 cm, 30 cm, 22.5 cm

6. a) −30 cm; virtual; on same side
of lens as object; upright;
magnified.
   b) −6.7 cm, −6.0 cm, −3.3 cm;
virtual, same side as
object, upright, diminished
7. a) 1.50   b) 1.50
8, 9. a) 60 cm, 30 cm tall
   b) 30 cm, 10 cm tall
   c) 24 cm, 12 cm tall
   d) 21.4 cm, 8.6 cm tall
   e) 20 cm, 10 cm tall
   f) 60 cm, 20 cm tall
   g) 40 cm, 10 cm tall
   h) 33.3 cm, 13.3 cm tall
   i) 30 cm, 10 cm tall
   k) −30 cm, 30 cm tall
      (negative indicates
      virtual image)
   m) −60 cm, 80 cm tall
      (negative indicates
      virtual image)

10. a) 30 cm, magnification ×2
    b) 30 cm, magnification ×2
11, 12. a) 12 cm b) 10 cm
    c) 8.4 cm
13, 14. a) 22.5 cm b) 20 cm
    c) 15 cm
15. 0.013, 0.043, 0.056, 17.9
    0.017, 0.038, 0.055, 18.2
    0.025, 0.030, 0.055, 18.2
    0.033, 0.022, 0.055, 18.2
    0.050, 0.006, 0.056, 17.9
    $f_{av} = 18.1$ cm
16. 4.45, 4.44
    3.00, 3.00
    1.65, 1.67
    1.00, 1.00
    0.35, 0.33
17. 0.040, 0.010
    0.033, 0.017 $f = 20$ cm
    0.029, 0.021
    0.025, 0.025
    0.022, 0.028
    0.020, 0.030
    0.017, 0.033

Past examination questions

1. a) 0.156 0.105 1.4
      0.342 0.259
      0.500 0.358
      0.719 0.500
      0.883 0.643
   b) 48.8°
      TIR 40°
      0.60 m
2. 0.80 m from object
   0.64 cm
3. 20 cm, 15 cm
4. (see Chapter 8 on Waves)
   2×10^8 m/s, 41.8°
5. (virtual) 10 cm behind mirror,
   4 cm

6. 48.8°, total angle 97.6°
7. c) (virtual) 100 mm on same side
   as object; 86 mm on same side
   (virtual), 8.6 mm tall
8. 22.0 cm, 66.0 cm, 3
   63.0 cm, 21.0 cm, 0.33
   16.5 cm
9. 1 m from lens, 0.91 m
10. d) 333 mm
11. b) 100 mm; c) 0.05 m
12. 1.45
13. Virtual, 12 cm on same side
    as object, 1.5 cm high
14. 150 mm, 300 mm
15. 48.6°, 27.1°, TIR, 1.34

Chapter 3 Machines and Mechanics

Questions

1. 200 000 N; 200 000 N; 20 m³;
   0.04 m
2. 2250 cm³; 2.25 kg, 22.5 N;
   2.25 N, 22.5 kg; 0.67 g/cm³
3. 12 g, 0.12 N; 12 cm³; 12 cm³
4. 60 cm³; 60 g, 0.6 N;
   0.6 N; 0.4 N; 1.67 g/cm³

5. 400 kg, 4000 N; 9000 N;
   26 000 N; 17 000 N
7. 48.5%
8. 1.75 N/cm², 3.5 N/cm²
9. 1.5 N/cm², 1.0 N/cm², 2.0 N/cm²
10. 31 kg, 116 kg, 310 kg
11. 4 N/cm², 240 N

12. 2.5 cm, 47 N, 7.5 N
13. 17 N, 3 N
    (direction of 10 N force)
    12.2 N, 55° (to 7 N);
    14.8 N, 36° (to 7 N);
    7.7 N, 84° (to 7 N)
14. 14.1 N, 156°; 15.0 N, 127°;
    19.3 N, 156°; 32.9 N, 162°
15. 6 cm, 6 cm, 6 cm, 6 cm
16. 106 N, 115 N, 131 N
17. 2.75 g/cm^3, 8.0 g/cm^3,
    8.6 g/cm^3, 1 g/cm^3

18. 19.2 g/cm^3, 28.6 g, 1.74 g/cm^3,
    2380 kg/m^3, 0.91 g/cm^3, 23.4 kg,
    0.79 g/cm^3, 217.5 g, 142 kg,
    1.25 kg/m^3
19. 2.05 × 10^4 N/m^2,
    3.08 × 10^5 N/m^2,
    4.10 × 10^6 N/m^2
20. 4, 4, 100%; 30 N, 4, 75%;
    25 N, 5, 80%; 6, 5 m, 10;
    250 N, 2.5, 80%

Past examination questions

1. a) 20 cm^2, 50 cm^2, 10 cm^2
   b) 0.1 N/cm^2
2. a) 1.67
   b) 1.5, 66.7%
3. a) 5 N point   e) 3.0 cm
4. 40 J, 50 J, 5
5. 2.5, 1.67, 4.2 m
6. d) 900 J
7. a) 1000 N   b) 5000 J
8. a) 0.5 m 300 J b) 75 W c) 0.2 m
10. 4 × 10^6 J, 10%
11. 1800 J
12. 5.0, 4, 80%
13. 17.2 N, 21.5° to 7.0 N, 12.5 m/s^2
14. b) 0.07, 0.18, 0.29, 0.36
15. a) 24000 N   b) 6000 N
    c) 3.33 m/s^2; 667 kg/m^3
16. 80 cm, 75%
17. i) A: 800 N downwards;
       B: 1200 N upwards
    ii) A: 900 N downwards;
       B: 1500 N upwards

18. 4.0–4.4 N
19. 4, 320 J, 200 J, 62.5%
20. 141.7 N, 408.3 N
21. 2600 kg/m^3, 800 kg/m^3
22. 900 N, 100 N, 0.4 m
23. 0.76 N
24. 0.05 kg, 52 cm mark
    (32 cm from glued on piece)
25. 15.0 cm, 5 cm^2
26. a) 2.5 × 10^3 N, 5 × 10^4 J,
       2 × 10^3 W, 5 × 10^3 W
    b) 0.8 m, 400 N cm, 200 N, 175 N
27. 4 × 10^{-4} g, 0.5 × 10^{-3} cm^3,
    314 cm^2, 1.59 × 10^{-6} cm
28. 5 N at 37° to 4 N force, 2.5 m/s^2
29. 280 J, 9.3 W; Jack (Jill 8.8 W);
    6.25 N
30. 48 mm, 120 g, 80 mm, 20 mm
31. 0.8 N, 0.32 N m, 0.6F N m,
    0.53 N

Chapter 4   Moving Objects
Questions

1. 0.6 m/s^2, 36 m/s, 360 m/s
2. 1200 m/s
3. 7 s, 12 m/s
4. 0.75 km/min, 0.0125 km/s,
   12.5 m/s
5. 108000 m/hour, 108 km/hour
6. 10 m/s
7. 46.9 s
8. 50 s
9. 15 m/s, 11.3 m; 4.5 × 10^4 N,
   5.1 × 10^5 J; 1.02 × 10^5 W
12. 25 m/s
13. 60 J; 60 J, 7.7 m/s, 15.4 kg m/s

15. a) 5 m/s^2, 22.5 m
    b) −4 m/s^2, 72 m
    c) 5 m/s^2, 0 m/s^2, −3 m/s^2, 510 m
    d) 0.33 m/s^2, 0 m/s^2, 0.17 m/s^2,
       6600 m
16. a) 20 kg m/s, 40 J
    b) 60 kg m/s, 600 J
    c) 10 m/s, 100 J
    d) 5.5 m/s, 33 kg m/s
    e) 4 kg, 72 J
    f) 40 kg, 120 kg m/s
    g) 25 kg, 4 m/s

17. 12 kg m/s, 30 kg m/s, 18 kg m/s,
    24 J, 150 J, 126 J
18. 5000 N, 500 N
19. a) 6 m/s^2, 18 N
    b) 16 m/s, 4 m/s^2
    c) 4 kg, 4 s
    d) 6 m/s, 30 N
    e) 5 m/s^2, 30 N
    f) 20 kg, 24 m/s
    g) 8 kg, 10 m/s
20. a) 21 m, 3.3 m/s^2
    b) 84 m, 6 s
    c) 20 s, 0.3 m/s^2
    d) 40 m/s, 4 m/s^2
    e) 7 m/s, 2 s
    f) 152 m, 3 m/s

21. a) 5 m
    b) 20 m
    c) 180 m
    d) 500 m
22. a) 200 J
    b) 6.3 m/s
    c) 50 J
23. 1 m/s, 0.1 J
24. 3 m/s, 9 J, 0.45 m
25. 0.6 m/s, 0.9 m/s, 1.2 m/s
26. 14.1 s, 3525 m
27. a) 7.1 m/s, 10 m/s^2
    b) 2 kg, 1 m
    c) 54 N, 18 m/s^2
    d) 0.21 m, 30 m/s^2

Past examination questions

1. 60 cm/s
2. 30 m/s^2, 400 s
3. 20 m/s, 4 s
4. 2000 N, 8 m/s, 6 s
5. a) 18 kg m/s, 3 m/s, 2 m/s
   b) 6 m/s
6. 6 N, 2 N, 9 m/s, 18 kg m/s
8. e) 40 m/s^2, 10 m/s f) 10 m
   g) 3.0 s h) 35 m
9. 0.125 m/s^2, 112 500 J,
   15 000 kg m/s
10. 0.300 kg m/s, 0.275 kg m/s,
    0.025 kg m/s, 0.05 N (into truck),
    0.05 N (into buffers)
11. 5 m/s, 20 m/s, 0 m/s, 900 m
12. 0.4 m/s, 0.6 m, 0 m/s^2, 0.2 m/s^2,
    0.008 m
13. 2 s/$\sqrt{m}$, 10 m/s^2
14. a) 160 J, 80 m, 8 s
15. 24 m/s, 0.2 m/s^2, 7–10 min,
    10 800 m, 18 m/s
16. a) s = area = 105 m
    b) 6 m/s^2, 9000 N
    d) 6.75 × 10^5 J

17. b) 36 m, 6 m/s^2
18. a) 4 m/s b) 0.33 J c) 0.48 J
19. A 1.2 m/s^2 B 0.6 m/s^2
20. 9 × 10^5 J, 6 × 10^4 kg m/s,
    4 × 10^5 J, 4.5 × 10^4 kg m/s,
    1.5 × 10^4 kg m/s
21. 50 cm/s^2
22. 13 cm/s, 32.5 cm/s^2, 24 cm/s^2,
    33 cm/s^2, 65 cm/s^2
23. 1.00 kg m/s, 200 m/s, 1.00 J, 100 J
24. 0.05 s, 6.5 cm, 19.0 cm, 130 cm/s,
    380 cm/s, 0.25 s, 1000 cm/s^2
25. a) 12 cm, 0.2 s, 60 cm/s
    b) 0.08 s, 4 cm, 24 cm, 50 cm/s,
       300 cm/s, 250 cm/s, 625 cm/s^2
26. 200 m
27. 5 cm/s
28. 500 N, 1000 J, 1200 J,
    100 N, 20 N;
    250 kg m/s, 100 kg m/s,
    150 kg m/s, 150 kg m/s,
    3.75 m/s, 525 J, 281 J
29. −4.05 s^2/m, 0.05 m

Chapter 5   Electricity

Questions

1. 5 A, 2 A, 0.5 A
2. i) 9 Ω, 2 Ω
   ii) 15 Ω, 2.4 Ω
   iii) 25 Ω, 4 Ω
3. 100 A, 5 A, 2.2 A

4. a) 200 V, 40 Ω
   b) 0.17 A, 1410 Ω
   c) 14.1 A, 213 V
   d) 2880 W, 20 Ω
   e) 72 W, 6 A
   f) 1600 W, 160 V

5. 3×10^4 J, 9×10^4 J, 2.7×10^6 J
6. 0.9p, 0.03p, 0.5p, 30p
7. 0.56 A, 12.6 V
9. 9 Ω, 2 A, 12 V, 6 V
10. 2.5 A, 10 V
11. 2 Ω, 2 A, 4 V, 0.67 A, 1.33 A
12. 6 Ω, 2 A, 8 V, 4 V, 0.67 A, 1.33 A
13. 0.082 Ω
14. 2.4 m

15. 0.0021 g/C
16. 41 Ω, 4.1×10^{-3} W
17. 0.5:1
18. 3.6 Ω
19. 0.02 cm
20. 4 Ω, 5.7 Ω, 10 Ω, 12 Ω
21. 50 cm, 40 cm, 33.3 cm, 37.5 cm, 60 cm, 33.3 cm
22. 1.36, 2.0 V, 0.6 V, 1.35

Past Examination Questions

1. 2 A, 30 mV, 0.008 Ω
2. 60, 0.1 A
3. 15p, 12.5p
4. 800 J, 40000 J, 5 °C
5. 2 Ω, 3 Ω, 0.5 W, 27.0 W
6. 3.6 Ω, 2.4 Ω, 24 W
7. 0.25 A, 4.5 V, 18 Ω, 1.13 W, by 2 if V reads the same or by 4 if V doubles
8. b) 2 A, 10 V   d) 4.5 V
9. 3.33 Ω, 0.3 W; 4.0 Ω, 1.0 W; 5.0 Ω, 1.8 W
10. 0.8 A, B to D
11. 4 A, 5 A fuse
12. 6.25 V, 80.0 A
13. 5 Ω, 1.2 A, 0.2 A (meter), 1.0 A (6 Ω resistor)
14. 8 Ω, 0 A
15. 3050 W, 12.2 A, 4.39×10^7 J
16. 0.20 Ω, 0.33 Ω, 0.52 Ω, 0.95 Ω, 1.80 Ω, 2.80 Ω; 0.16 Ω
17. 24 W, 18 W, 75%
18. 0 A, 2 A, 3 A, 5 A
19. 1 Ω, 150 J
20. 2.0 A (3.6 Ω), 1.2 A (4 Ω), 0.8 A (6 Ω), 24 W

21. 0.075 V, 0.025 Ω in parallel, 995 Ω in series
22. 5 kW h, 30p, 40 A
23. 1.8 A
24. 10 Ω
25. a) 4 A, 40:1, 0.1 A
b) 1.5 Ω, 234 V, 58.5 Ω, 936 J
26. 2.0 Ω, 2.5 Ω, 3.3 Ω, 1.0 V, 0.7 Ω, 4.4 Ω; 0.5 W, 7.5 W
27. 2.0 Ω, 4.0 Ω, 5.0 Ω, 6.0 Ω; 1.3 A
28. 0.05 A, 3 C, 150 J, 2.5 W
29. 2 A, 48 W, 16 V, 3 A
30. 17.5 Ω, 36 °C
31. 3 A, 1.5 A, 6 A, 0.8 A; 0–3.4 V, 10 Ω, 13.3 Ω, 4.8 W; 4.8 V, 6 Ω, 3.6 Ω
32. 0.5×10^{-3} m, 0.79×10^{-6} m^2, 3.8 Ω; 0.1 V, 0.5 A, 0.52 A
33. 1.5×10^{-4} C, 3×10^{-3} A
34. a) 1.88 Ω
b) 400 Ω in series; 0.01 A, 0.02 A, 5 V, 250 Ω, 5×10^{-7} Ω m
35. a) B, 1.25:1, 4×10^{-6} Ω m
b) 0.1 A, 18 C, 3.85 V, 1.16 W

Chapter 6   Radioactivity

Questions

1. 2.9 days, 3.0 days, 3.2 days, 3.0 days
2. Must have atomic number of 92, neutron number = (Mass number − 92), 92 electrons.

3. $^{232}_{90}$E, $^{228}_{88}$F, $^{228}_{89}$G, $^{228}_{90}$H; same atomic number
4. +2, 8000; 0, 0
5. 250, 4
6. $^{92}_{36}$X, Krypton
7. 510, 355, 255, 180, 130, 90, 65; 2 days

Past examination questions

1. 20, 16 s
2. 86 protons, 136 neutrons,
   $^{218}_{84}$Po, 0.99 J
3. 45, 40, 40, 40; at 40 s, 120 m
4. 25 s
5. 5°/s
6. 8.0 days

8. $^{222}_{86}Y$
9. b) 2.5 days, 320, 7.5 days
11. 200 μs, 1.8×10^4 m
12. $^4_2$He, 2.5 g
13. 4860 years, $^{222}_{86}$Em, $^{218}_{84}$Po, $^{218}_{85}$At, 28 days

Chapter 7   Heat

Questions

1. 60 cm^3, 1.2×10^6 Pa, 33.3 cm^3, 1.5×10^5 Pa, 597 °C
2. 6×10^4 J, 7.5 °C, 27.5 °C
3. 48 s
4. 3.15×10^7 J, 1 hour 45 min
5. 2×10^5 J, 425 °C
6. 40 °C, 70 °C, 18 cm, 7 cm

7. 927 °C, 33.3 cm^3, 8×10^5 Pa
8. 3.3×10^5 J, 4.2×10^5 J, 2.3×10^6 J, 25 min 25 s
9. 75 cm Hg, 77 cm Hg, 76 cm Hg
10. −275 °C, −80 °C, 20.5 cm^3
11. −275 °C, −130 °C, 0.26×10^5 Pa
12. 1.14×10^{-4} m^3, 2.67×10^4 Pa
13. 0.0042 m, 111 °C, 0.0014 m

14.

$P \times V$/cm$^3 \times 10^5$ Pa	50.0	50.4	49.0	49.7	50.4	50.3	49.9	50.0	49.7	49.8	50.0
$1/P$/1/Pa $\times 10^5$	1.00	0.91	0.83	0.77	0.71	0.67	0.63	0.59	0.56	0.53	0.50
$1/V$/1/cm$^3 \times 10^{-2}$	2.00	2.18	2.45	2.62	2.78	2.99	3.21	3.40	3.62	3.82	4.00

15. 80 °C

Past examination questions

1. a) 70 115 J, 84 517 J, 14 402 J
   b) 4200 J/kg °C
2. 26.6 °C
3. 18 °C, 4890 J/kg °C
4. 400 mm, 280 mm, 221 mm, 182 mm, 160 mm, 142 mm, 125 mm; 400 mm, 200 mm, 130 mm
5. 0.025 kg
6. 8400 J, 25 g, 4.44 °C
7. 0.03 kg
8. 2.16×10^6 J/kg
9. 1720 mm Hg
10. 100 litres
11. 62 cm^3
12. 60.0 cm^3, 16.0 cm^3
13. 653 W

14. No
15. 9000 J, 7560 J, less, less
16. 2.18×10^6 J, 1.82×10^3 W
17. 42.9 °C
18. 50 N, 5×10^4 N/m^2, 1.5×10^5 N/m^2, 450 K
19. 54.0 cm^3, −260 °C
20. 150 W, 1.8×10^5 J, 0.082 kg, 150 W
21. 80 °C, 3.6×10^5 N/m^2, −270 °C
22. 4 min, 8.1 °C, 1.2×10^4 J, 741 J/kg °C
23. 3.6×10^4 J, 400 W
24. 0.10 N/mm^2, 0.14 N/mm^2, 1.2 N, 0.08 N/mm^2, 0.18 N/mm^2, 117 °C
26. 202 s, 0.33 kg

Chapter 8   Waves

Questions

1. 5 Hz, 2.5 Hz, 2 Hz
2. 2×10^5 Hz, 0.01 m,
   6.7×10^{-6} m, 7.5×10^{14} Hz,
   5×10^{17} Hz, 3×10^{-13} m
3. 330 m, 825 m, 1155 m
4. 512 Hz, 768 Hz, 1024 Hz
6. 1650 Hz, 550 Hz, 330 Hz

7. 338 m/s
8. 38.3 cm
9. 5.3×10^{-7} m, 2.9×10^{-7} m;
   2.27×10^8 m/s, 2.24×10^8 m/s
10. 6, 1.63, 1.83
11. 3.5 mm, 3.0 mm, 2.5 mm, 2.0 mm

Past examination questions

1. 0.48 m/s
2. 84 m, 168 m, 336 m/s, 0.18 s
3. 1.18 mm
4. 660 Hz
5. 350 m/s, 1 s
6. 358 m/s
7. 0.9 cm, 47 Hz
8. 338 m/s
9. 2×10^8 m/s, 0°, 35.3°
10. 320 m/s, 1280 m

11. 0.020 m, 0.014 m
12. Beats at 1 Hz, 306 Hz
13. 320 Hz
14. 680 Hz
15. 0.8 m/s, 6 s
16. 1.25 s, 0.625 s, 200 m, 320 m/s
17. 307.2 m/s, 240 mm
18. 4.0×10^{-7} m
19. 205 m/s, 205 m/s, 333 m/s